3-

THE GAME OF WORDS

*To the Reader**

> I'll never **** as ***'* own kissing kin,
> As none who **** this puzzle book can doubt.
> Still, I am pleased you worked my **** in,
> And hope you work it out.

*The missing words: *Pose; Poe's; opes; epos.*

THE **GAME** OF **WORDS**

THE REMARKABLE EXUBERANCE OF THE ENGLISH LANGUAGE

WILLARD R. ESPY

BLACK DOG
& LEVENTHAL
PUBLISHERS
NEW YORK

Published by
Black Dog & Leventhal Publishers
151 West 19th Street
New York, NY 10011

Distributed by
Workman Publishing Company
708 Broadway
New York, NY 10003

Manufactured in the United States of America.

ISBN: 1-57912-324-4

g f e d c b a

ACKNOWLEDGMENTS

The author's estate would like to thank publishers, agents and authors for permission to reprint the following material:

The Daily Telegraph for *Intercom in Nasakom* by Towyn Mason (from *The Daily Telegraph* 24 Dec. 1967).

Cleveland Amory, David M. Glixon and the *Saturday Review* for extracts from "Our Gray Nashnul Pastime" and "Your Literary I.Q.". Copyright 1970 Saturday Review, Inc.

A. D. Peters and Company for *Hush, Hush* from *The Best of Beachcomber* by J. B. Morton (published by William Heinemann Ltd. and reprinted by permission of A. D. Peters and Company).

Methuen Publishing Ltd. for *How I Brought The Good News From Aix To Ghent* from *Horse Nonsense* by W. C. Sellar and R. J. Yeatman.

Mrs. Anne Wolfe for *The British Journalist* from *The Uncelestial City* by Humbert Wolfe, and *When Lads Have Done With Labour* from *Lampoons* by Humbert Wolfe.

Patrick Ryan for an extract from *Blood* (first published in *New Scientist*).

Penguin Putnam, Inc. for conundrums from *Word Play* by Hubert Phillips.

Clerihews from *Clerihews Complete* by E C Bentley reproduced with permission of Curtis Brown Group Ltd, London on behalf of the Estate of E C Bentley. Copyright © E C Bentley 1951.

Little, Brown and Co. for an extract from "The Cliché Expert Testifies on Love" from *A Pearl In Every Oyster* by Frank Sullivan. Copyright 1935 by Frank Sullivan; originally published in *The New Yorker*.

Sydney ("Steak") T. Kendall for extracts from *Up The Frog* (Wolfe Publishing Ltd.).

The Literary Trustees of Walter de la Mare and the Society of Authors as their representative for *The Elephant, Or The Force of Habit* and *When Adam Day By Day* by A. E. Housman.

An extract from *The American Language, 4th Ed.* by H. L. Mencken, copyright © 1936 by Alfred A. Knopf, Inc. and renewed 1964 by August Mencken and Mercantile-Safe Deposit and Trust Co. Used by permission of Alfred A. Knopf, a division of Random House, Inc.

An extract from *Finnegan's Wake* by James Joyce, copyright © 1939 by James Joyce, copyright renewed © 1967 by Giorgio Joyce and Lucia Joyce. Used by permission of Viking Penguin, a division of Penguin Group (USA) Inc.

Doubleday & Company, Inc. and Putnam & Company, Ltd. for extracts from *Fractured French* by Fred Pearson II and Richard Taylor. Copyright 1950 by Fred Pearson II and Richard Taylor.

The New Yorker and Howard Moss for *Geography: A Song* by Howard Moss. Copyright © 1968 The New Yorker Magazine, Inc.

Mary Ann Madden for double dactyls from *New York Magazine* (now published in *Thank You for the Giant Sea Tortoise* by The Viking Press, Inc. Edited by Mary Ann Madden. © 1971.

Justin Richardson for *High-Life Low-Down* from *Verse Come Verse Served* (published by Hugh Evelyn Ltd. London) © Justin Richardson, 1966.

Peter Dickinson for *I Arise From Dreams of Steam Publishing*. Copyright Peter Dickinson.

A. P. Watt Ltd. on behalf of Jocelyn Hale and Teresa Elizabeth Perkins for *I Can't Think What He See In Her* by A. P. Herbert. (Originally published in *Punch*.)

CONTENTS

Introduction

ANY fair-minded person must concede that words are not tools of communication in the way that, say, frowns and kisses are. In childhood we communicate by screaming, chuckling, sticking fingers into eyes and pulling hair. Our parents communicate with us by suckling, hugging, changing diapers, spanking and sending us to bed without our suppers.

A few years later teachers communicate with us by putting gold stars after our names, or standing us in corners. We answer by turning our hair into blackberry bushes and, these days, knocking the teachers down and stomping them.

In college, we communicate by locking the president in his office and bombing the library. The president communicates by calling in the constabulary, who communicate by means of truncheons, Mace, tear gas and, occasionally, gunfire. The meaning of these exchanges is perfectly understood by everyone involved, though an observer would not be able to recognise any words at all in the din, except for a continuous chant of 'Motherf—', which does not count, since it does not appear in either Webster's or the *Oxford English Dictionary*.

By the time we marry and settle down we are locked for life into the Manichean fallacy. Everything we do not like about the world is the result of someone's deliberate evildoing. So we have no reason for verbal expression. One does not hold a dialogue with the wicked; and as for the good (that is, those who are on our side) one communicates very satisfactorily simply by grunting.

The working man communicates with his boss by striking, arriving late, getting messages wrong, disarranging the cards in the computer and forgetting to flush the toilet. The boss talks back by flaunting a Cadillac or Mercedes-Benz, taking winter holidays and having no money left over for a Christmas bonus. Politicians communicate by waving their arms, shaking their fists and glaring into the television camera. Nations communicate by stockpiling, and at times using, napalm, atom bombs, submarines, missiles and poison gas.

These forms of communication outrank words because they are far more effective. Sticks and stones may break my bones, but words will never hurt me. Promises are pleasant, but diamonds are a girl's best friend. Speak softly, but carry a big stick. I'll brave the thunder if you'll brave the lightning.

The pretence that words make a difference in human affairs is one of the oldest and dirtiest tricks of English teachers and the ruling classes. Long before we emerged from our caves it had become clear that if one man could fool another one into arguing instead of throwing a rock, he—the first man, that is—had it made. Marie Antoinette did not say, 'Let them eat cake'. She said, 'Keep them talking'. When people stop talking, they are becoming dangerous.

This granted, you may wonder why I have written a book not only made up of words (it is really very difficult to avoid them in writing), but actually *about* words. The reason is simple: I have nothing whatever to communicate, and words are the best means of non-communication I know.

You will notice, though, that I do not treat them as equals, but as pets, to be stroked or kicked according to their desert and my whim. Go thou and do likewise. Housebreak your words while they are still too young to know better. When you take one for its exercise, curb it, or the neighbours will become angry. Be considerate but firm. Teach your words to sit, lie, stay, fetch. Reward them for obedience and cleverness with a dog biscuit or, in the case of catty words, with a sardine.

You may be one of those persons whom words frighten. If so, never let them know it. The instant you shrink back, they will rush at you and take a piece out of your trouser leg. Thereafter, they will ignore your commands.

But if they respect you, they will like you, and if they like you, there is nothing in their power that they will not do for you.

For a few rare people they not only roll over and play dead, but walk on their hind legs. For an even tinier number, they soar up to Heaven and play angel, or God himself.

This book is a friendly salute to the utterly unimportant Game of Words. Since you will go on playing this game, willy-nilly, as long as you live, you may as well learn to relax and enjoy it. I offer you, as a starter, a share in some of the wordplay *I* have enjoyed, from pig Latin to palindromes (horrible stuff, some of it), and some of the word games I have played (always badly), from *Bouts Rimés* to Guggenheim. You can take it from there.

Do not try to arrive at a deep reason for my helter-skelter inclusion of light verses by other writers. They are here simply as wordplay which happened to strike my fancy.

My own effusions aside, everything you will find here is lost, strayed or stolen from some other pasture. 'When you steal from one author,' says Wilson Mizner, 'it is plagiarism; when you steal from many, it is research.' This book is research.

But please do not think it lacks serious purpose. It is a reminder to you of something the world seems to be fast losing, and for lack of which we all may perish. That something is irrelevance. If Alexander Woolcott had not been there before me, my title would have been 'While Rome Burns'. *The Game of Words* is uniquely useful because you cannot put it to any good use whatever, except perhaps as a horrible example. On irrelevance I give myself high marks.

Elsewhere I make acknowledgement to the many writers and publishers who graciously acceded to my thievery. Here I wish to express special gratitude to Louise, my wife, who located many of the sources I have used. I also owe a debt to the long-defunct magazine *Notes and Queries*, which I was able to consult at the British Museum. Many of the language oddities represented here first came to my attention in its pages.

My thanks also to two Victorian gentlemen: William Dobson, an Englishman, and C. C. Bombaugh, an American. Both spent the best and, no doubt, happiest part of their lives locating and preserving obscure and outrageous examples of wordplay. Often, indeed, their findings overlapped. Mr. Dobson wrote *Literary Frivolities* and *Poetical Ingenuities* in the 1880s. At about the same time, Mr. Bombaugh was writing *Gleanings for the Curious from the Harvest Fields of Literature*, which Dover Publications reissued in 1961 as *Oddities and Curiosities of Words and Literature*, with

Martin Gardner as editor. I have shamelessly ghouled both graves.

Finally, I hope the following pages may provide you with a few hours' irrelevant entertainment, and perhaps tempt you to do a little wordplaying of your own. Words may be an inferior means of communication, but they are fun.

W. R. E.

THE GAME OF WORDS

For Alexander, Elliott, Jeremy, and Medora the Sixth,
with this special note for the last:

> I christened my daughter Medora,
> She christened her daughter the same.
> Medorable, dorable daughters;
> Medorable, durable name.

> 'The question is,' said Alice, 'whether you *can* make words mean so many different things.'
>
> 'The question is,' said Humpty Dumpty, 'which is to be master—that's all.'
>
> LEWIS CARROLL

A, B, C, D, J, K, M, P, Q and Z Shall Overcome, with a Little Help from L

Some 794 letters make up the words for the numbers from one through to ninety-nine. Among them all, I notice, there are only two *l*'s. In an effort to determine the significance of this blatant alphabetical discrimination, I checked the frequency of the other letters in the same set of words. How many *a*'s are there? None! How many *b*'s? None! How many *c*'s? None! How many *d*'s? None! Clearly, first-grade arithmetic is a club which arbitrarily excludes some of the finest letters in the alphabet. Where is *j*? *k*? *m*? *p*? *q*? *z*? All outside looking in.

I maintain that *l* is not being permitted to make anything like its full contribution to our understanding of arithmetic. And just imagine what might be accomplished for a better world, without racism, poverty, pollution, or war, by a full infusion of *a*, *b*, *c*, *d*, *j*, *k*, *m*, *p*, *q*, and *z*! Why not give these deserving, disadvantaged letters a chance, instead of spending all that money on sending a man to the moon?

ABC Language

ABCD GOLDFISH

Abey takes one side of the following argument. Who takes the other side is not recorded:

> AB C D goldfish!
> L M N O goldfish!
> O S A R 2 goldfish.

Abey also figures in a provocative line which has come without explanation down the years:

> AB C D FEG!

He appears as a greengrocer in the following:

> AB, F U NE X?
> S V F X.
> F U NE M?
> SV F M.
> OK L F M N X.

The following ABC communication is part rebus:

> YY U R
> YY U B
> I C U R
> YY 4 me.

One solves by treating YY as two Ys.

The same system is at work in:

> If U eat TT
> I shall have TT U.

To write in ABC, begin by listing all digits and letters that have the approximate sound of words. Cheat by counting, for instance, D or Z for *the*, E for *he*, F for *if* and *have*, L for *hell*, M for *am*, *him* and *them*, N for *an*, *Ann*, and *in*, S for *is*, *as*, *ass*, and *yes*, V for *we*, X for *eggs*, and so on. ME is *Emmy*, MU *emu*. You now have a vocabulary in ABC about the size of a bushman's, though less practical. I hope it serves you well.

LAMENT OF A 4SAKN LOVER

U 4N female K9's son,
U KG CD flea,
My heart CCCC its hope's DK;
Your AAAA on my QT may
Have B10 me, I C.

U C me 2 N N8 worth
Be W, no less;
Your MT BD glances bore
My II; had I IIIIIIIII more,
They'd bore me 2 XS.

Y 1 should fall 4 U S hard
4 NE 1 2 C;
Your PP never fit U L;
N this, N all, I U XL;
Yet o's left 4 me.

With NRG and EZ skill,
U 1 1 I love well.
I NV U that 1 B9,
U 4N S, and hourly pine
4 U 2 B N L.

W. R. E.

ANSWER

You foreign female canine's son,
You cagey, seedy flea,
My heart foresees its hope's decay;
Your forays on my cutie may
Have beaten me, I see.

You see me to in innate worth
Be double you, no less;
Your empty, beady glances bore
My two eyes; had I ten eyes more,
They'd bore me to excess.

Why one should fall for you is hard
For anyone to see;
Your toupees never fit you well;
In this, in all, I you excel;
Yet nothing's left for me.

With energy and easy skill,
You won one I love well.
I envy you that one benign,
You foreign ass, and hourly pine
For you to be in Hell.

Acronyms

An acronym is a word formed of the initials of other words. WASP, for instance, is an acronym for 'white Anglo-Saxon Protestant'—an odd notion, since it is hard to conceive of a non-white Anglo-Saxon Protestant. Were there such, a black one would be a BASP; a red one a RASP; a yellow one a YASP.

Tantum Ergo, meaning 'So great, therefore', a familiar expression to Roman Catholics, is an acronym for the words of the last two stanzas of a hymn sung when the Eucharist is borne in procession.

Posh, for 'elegant, luxurious', is probably short for 'polished', but some say is an acronym for 'Port Out, Starboard Home', the preferred ship accommodations for the families of nineteenth-century civil servants on their way to and from India.

The common opinion that SOS is an acronym for 'Save our ship' is incorrect; it is simply three call letters of the Morse code, the quickest and simplest that can be transmitted by one in distress.

Equally unfounded is the legend that *cabal*, meaning a 'conspiratorial group', is an acronym for Clifford–Ashley–Buckingham–Arlington–Lauderdale, a clique of cabinet ministers under Charles II. They probably conspired no more than others of their ilk. *Cabal* actually derives from Hebrew *cabala*, 'an occult theosophy, full of hidden mysteries'. The first letters of the ministers' names just happened to fit.

World War II saw the rise of such acronyms as WAC (in the United States, Woman's Army Corps); loran (long range navigation); sonar (sound navigation ranging); and radar (radio detecting and ranging).

Technically, a combination of initials does not become an acronym until it is accepted as a word in its own right. Loosely, however, the term acronym is applied to any series of first letters of the words in a given phrase, even when these letters do not themselves form accepted words. I give you two sets of such informal acronyms, the first drawn from nursery rhymes and the second from Shakespeare.

Nursery rhyme acronyms

1. Omhwttctghpdab
2. Dddmsj
3. Twalmahhalg
4. Wwwrttt
5. Ssmapgttf

Shakespearean acronyms

1. Tbontbtitq
2. Ftniw
3. Arbaonwsas
4. Nitwoodmgsbtsoy
5. Ahahmkfah
6. Orrwatr

ANSWERS

Nursery rhyme acronyms

1. Old Mother Hubbard went to the cupboard to get her poor dog a bone.
2. Diddle diddle dumpling my son John.
3. There was a little man and he had a little gun.
4. Wee Willy Winkie runs through the town.
5. Simple Simon met a pieman going to the fair.

Shakespearean acronyms

1. To be or not to be, that is the question.
2. Frailty, thy name is woman.
3. A rose by any other name would smell as sweet.
4. Now is the winter of our discontent made glorious summer by this sun of York.
5. A horse! a horse! my kingdom for a horse!
6. O Romeo, Romeo! Wherefore art thou Romeo?

INITIALLY SPEAKING

The substitution of initials for familiar word combinations goes on apace. This may not always be a service. Sometimes the initials take longer to say, if not to write, than the words themselves. Often, too, they lose their meaning as the expressions for which they stand lose their currency. It is doubtful whether our grandchildren will instantly identify an R.L.S., F.D.R., G.B.S., or J.F.K.* Many of the following phrases are products of World War II that are already fading from memory.

---

* Robert Louis Stevenson; Franklin Delano Roosevelt; George Bernard Shaw; John Fitzgerald Kennedy.

Others, however, are so common that we know what the initials mean even if we do not know the words they stand for. See how many you can identify.

1. A1, A.A.A.S., A.B.C., A.D., AFL-CIO, AID, A.M., ANZAC, AP, ARC, AWOL.
2. BBC, B.E., B.I.S., B.L.E., C.I.A., C.I.D., C.I.F., C.O.
3. COD, CORE, C.P.A., C.S.C., CSC, C.S.O., D.S.C., D.S.T., D/W, ENE, E.E.C., E.R.V.
4. FBI, F.O.B., FM, G.H.Q., G.P.O., H.M.S.
5. i.e., I.N.S., IOU, I.Q., KO, K.P., L.C.L., L.C.M., LP, LSD.
6. MC, MP, Nato, N.C.O., NEA, N.F., N.G., N.S.P.C.C., N.A.A.C.P., O.B.E., O.D., O.G., O.K.
7. P.A.U., P.D.Q., P.M., P.O.D., P.S., P.T.A., Q.E.D., Q.M.C., QT, R.A.F., R.A.A.F., RFD.
8. R.I.P., R.O.T.C., R.S.V.P., Scuba, SHAPE, snafu, SOB, S.R.O., SWALK, TB, TNT, TV, TVA, VC, V.D., V.I.P., W.B., WC, YMCA.

ANSWERS

1. First rate (at Lloyd's); American Association for the Advancement of Science; Argentina, Brazil, and Chile; Anno Domini; American Federation of Labor-Congress of Industrial Organizations; Agency for International Development; *ante meridian* (before noon); Australian and New Zealand Army Corps; Associated Press; American Red Cross; Absent Without Official Leave.
2. British Broadcasting Corporation; bill of exchange; Bank for International Settlements; Brotherhood of Locomotive Engineers; Central Intelligence Agency; Criminal Investigation Department; Cost, Insurance and Freight; Commanding Officer (or conscientious objector).
3. Cash (or collect) on delivery; Congress of Racial Equality; Certified Public Accountant; Conspicuous Service Cross; Civil Service Commission; Chief Signal Officer; Distinguished Service Cross; Daylight Saving Time; dock warrant; east-northeast; European Economic Community; English Revised Version (of the Bible).
4. Federal Bureau of Investigation; free on board; Frequency Modulation; General Headquarters; General Post Office; Her Majesty's Ship.
5. That is; International News Service; I owe you; intelligence quotient; knockout; kitchen police; less than carload lots; lowest, or least, common multiple; long-playing; lysergic acid diethylamide.

INTERCOM IN NASAKOM

The poem below appeared in the *Sunday Telegraph* on December 24, 1967. The author did not explain his acronyms, but most of them are familiar to any newspaper reader.

'Euratom!' cried Oiccu, sly and nasa,
'I'll wftu in the iscus with my gatt.'
'No! No!' the Eldo pleaded, pale with asa.
'My unctad strictly nato on comsat.'

The Oiccu gave a wacy little intuc,
He raft and waved his anzac oldefo.
'Bea imf!' he eec, a smirk upon his aituc,
And smote the Eldo on his ganefo.

The Eldo drew his udi from its cern,
He tact his unicet with fearless fao.
The Oiccu swerved but could not comintern;
He fell afpro, and dying moaned, 'Icao!'

The moon came up above the gasbiindo,
The air no longer vip with intercom.
A creeping icftu stirred the maphilindo
And kami was restored to Nasakom.

'O kappi gum!' the fifa sang in cento,
'O cantat till the neddy unficyp.'
The laser song re-echoed through the seato,
As the Eldo radar home to unmogip.

Towyn Mason

Acrostic Verses

Poets, particularly when in love, are apt to conceal messages in their verses. In the simplest such code the first letters of the lines, taken together, form a complete word or sentence, but most frequently a name. Or the poet may use the first letter of the first line, the second letter of the second line, and so on; or the first letter of the first word of the first line, the second letter of the second word of the second line . . . the combinations are limited only by ingenuity. If he uses the last letter of the last word of each line, the result is not an acrostic but a *telestich*.

Admirers of the French actress Rachel once presented her with a diadem, so arranged that the initials of the name of each stone in the proper order formed both her name and the initials of some of her principal roles, thus:

Ruby	Roxana
Amethyst	Amenaide
Cornelian	Camille
Hematite	Hermione
Emerald	Emilie
Lapis lazuli	Laodice

---

7. Pan American Union; pretty damned quick; *post meridian* (afternoon; also prime minister and post mortem); Post Office Department; postscript; Parent-Teacher Association; *quod erat demonstrandum* (which was to be proven); quartermaster corps; quiet; Royal Air Force; Royal Australian Air Force; Rural Free Delivery.

8. *Requiescat in pace* (rest in peace); Reserve Officers Training Corps; *répondez s'il vous plaît* (please reply); S(elf) C(ontained) U(nder-water) B(reathing) A(pparatus); Supreme Headquarters, Allied Powers, Europe; situation normal all fouled up; son of a bitch; standing room only; sealed with a loving kiss; tuberculosis; trinitro-toluene, or trininitrotoluol; television; Tennessee Valley Authority; Viet Cong (or Victoria Cross); venereal disease; very important person (one given priority for transportation in World War II); waybill; water closet; Young Men's Christian Association.

Here is a brief sampling of acrostic verses:

1

Beauty to claim, among the fairest place,
Enchanting manner, unaffected grace,
Arch without malice, merry but still wise,
Truth ever on her lips as in her eyes;
Reticent not from sullenness or pride,
Intensity of feeling but to hide;
Can any doubt such being there may be?
Each line I pen, points, matchless maid, to thee!

Planche's *Songs and Poems*

2

Cursèd, ugly moustache; I forgot
That it was bound to not
Tickle only my kissee, but *me*—
Frequently, frequently me.

W. R. E.

3

Unite and untie are the same—so say you.
Not in wedlock, I ween, has the unity been
In the drama of marriage, each wandering *goût*
To a new face would fly—all except you and I
Each seeking to alter the *spell* in their scene.

Author unknown

ANSWERS

1. The first letters of each line: BEATRICE.
2. The first letters of the first and second words of each line: CUT IT OFF.
3. Unless you are sharper than many, this one fooled you. It is both an acrostic and a telestich. The opening letters of the lines form UNITE; the closing letters, UNTIE.

Additives

An infinite variety of words can be created by adding words or letters to existing words or letters or, contrariwise, subtracting. Here are some examples:

1. Add a tree to *h*; may your sloop answer to its.
2. Drop the *n* from gun; add a home for swine; better hold on to your hat.
3. Drop the *t* from count; add effort; it has less pollution than the city.
4. Add a tree to *s*; often mine needs stiffening.
5. Drop the final *l* from bell and add to cook in hot fat, not ordinarily in a church tower.
6. Take your dog in your automobile, and you have a floor covering.
7. Add a tree to *b*, and it shows you are no longer a youth; but you can't do much about it.

ANSWERS

1. Helm	4. Spine	7. Balder
2. Gusty	5. Belfry	
3. Country	6. Carpet	

'C'?

By adding *c*'s to the entries below, you will create complete sentences. The numbers indicate how many *c*'s are required.

1. ANELONERTEDESAPADESSUHAOMPLISHINALULA BLEINDISRETIONSIRREONILEABLETOIVIHARATE R (17).
2. AORDINGTOSIKHOLERITYOONSTHEALORIAPAIT YOFONOTIONSINONRETEROKSISRYPTIANDHAOT I (21).
3. LUKLUKLUKAKLEDTHEORNEREDHIKTOTHEROW INGOKSUHONUPISENEISSARELYONEIVABLE (23).
4. OURAOPHONOUSOUSINLARAOLLETSINALULABLE ARETIONSOFATIINOHINHINAASTLES (16).

28

ANSWERS

1. Cancel concerted escapades. Such accomplish incalculable indiscretions irreconcilable to civic character.
2. According to sick choleric tycoons, the caloric capacity of concoctions in concrete crocks is cryptic and chaotic.
3. 'Cluck, cluck, cluck!' cackled the cornered chick to the crowing cock. 'Such concupiscence is scarcely conceivable.'
4. Our cacophonous cousin Clara collects incalculable accretions of cacti in Cochin China castles.

'HE HATH SUFFERED A C CHANGE . . .'

There is one lone *c* in my passage below; it requires many. Put a *c* before each capitalised word except those that begin the sentences, and the message will clear up.

The Optic Reed has a Haste Harm. It Hose, one assumes, not to be Lever; it neither Heats the Ripple, nor Hides the Razed sinner for his Rude Rime; it is not Old. Then Leave to it; ere thy grave Loses, thou mayst find here the Hart to the Rest thou Ravest to Limb.

ANSWER

The Coptic creed has a chaste charm. It chose, one assumes, not to be clever; it neither cheats the cripple, nor chides the crazed sinner for his crude crime; it is not cold. Then cleave to it; ere thy grave closes, thou mayst find here the chart to the crest thou cravest to climb.

All 26 Letters of the Alphabet

EZRA VII, 21

This is supposed to be the only verse of the Bible that contains every letter of the alphabet; but it does not. It lacks *j*, a latecomer on the alphabetical scene.

And I, even I Artaxerxes the king, do make a decree to all the treasurers which are beyond the river, that whatsoever Ezra the priest, the scribe of the law of the God of heaven, shall require of you, it be done speedily.

All 26 Letters in Four Lines
MALE CHAUVINIST

Though I enjoy the zeal of Women's Lib,
It's quite a comfort knowing Adam's rib
Is long re-fixed, and waits there in reserve
Should God opine the first one's ceased to serve.

W. R. E.

All 26 Letters in Two Lines
PEACE IN OUR TIME

God be his judge: that passive, zealous Quaker
Who first yields Country: Kindred next; then Maker.

W. R. E.

EACH LETTER USED ONCE

It is not particularly difficult to write a four-line, or even a two-line, verse containing all the letters of the alphabet. Try cutting back to a one-line sentence, though, and the difficulty waxes. And anyone who tries to compose a sensible line which contains each of the 26 letters of the alphabet only once has his work cut out for him. Here is how various forgotten puzzlers have crept up on the goal:

A quick brown fox jumps over the lazy dog. (33)
Pack my bag with five dozen liquor jugs. (32)
Quick wafting zephyrs vex bold Jim. (29)
Waltz, nymph, for quick jigs vex Bud. (28)

Augustus DeMorgan, a nineteenth-century mathematician, reached the 26-letter goal through a ruse: he substituted *u* for *v* and *i* for *j*. (In alphabetic genealogy, *u* descends from *v* and *j* from *i*.) The result was:

I, quartz pyx, who fling muck beds.

Others emulated him, but so far nobody has been able to squeeze in the *v* or the *j*. Some examples:

Dumpy Quiz, whirl back fogs next.
Get nymph; quiz sad brow; fix luck.
Export my fund! Quiz black whigs.

It is hard to accept the impossibility of composing a sensible line which contains every letter of the alphabet once and only once. There are 403,000,000,000,000,000,000,000,000 possible combinations of those 26 letters; surely *some* of them should make sense.

ALPHABETICAL ADVERTISEMENT

TO WIDOWERS AND SINGLE GENTLEMEN.—WANTED by a lady, a SITUATION to superintend the household and preside at table. She is Agreeable, Becoming, Careful, Desirable, English, Facetious, Generous, Honest, Industrious, Judicious, Keen, Lively, Merry, Natty, Obedient, Philosophic, Quiet, Regular, Sociable, Tasteful, Useful, Vivacious, Womanish, Xantippish, Youthful, Zealous, &c. Address X. Y. Z., Simmond's Library, Edgware-road.

The Times, 1842

ALPHABETICAL LOVER

Cervantes wrote that the whole alphabet is required of every good lover, and proceeded to list the qualities he had in mind. For some reason, though, he left out *u* and *x*. 'Understanding' would have been a good choice for *u*, it seems to me. So would 'useful'. As for *x*, there is nothing wrong with 'xenial', meaning 'hospitable'.

Make your own alphabetical list of the qualities you expect of a lover, and see how often you agree with Cervantes.

ANSWERS

Agreeable, bountiful, constant, dutiful, easy, faithful, gallant, honourable, ingenious, just, kind, loyal, mild, noble, officious,* prudent, quiet, rich, secret, true, valiant, wise, young, zealous.

---

* This word has gone downhill with the years. It once meant 'disposed or eager to serve or do kind offices'.

AN ANIMAL ALPHABET

Alligator, beetle, porcupine, whale,
Bobolink, panther, dragon-fly, snail,
Crocodile, monkey, buffalo, hare,
Dromedary, leopard, mud-turtle, bear,
Elephant, badger, pelican, ox,
Flying-fish, reindeer, anaconda, fox,
Guinea-pig, dolphin, antelope, goose,
Humming-bird, weasel, pickerel, moose,
Ibex, rhinoceros, owl, kangaroo,
Jackal, opossum, toad, cockatoo,
Kingfisher, peacock, anteater, bat,
Lizard, ichneumon, honey-bee, rat,
Mocking-bird, camel, grasshopper, mouse,
Nightingale, spider, cuttle-fish, grouse,
Ocelot, pheasant, wolverine, auk,
Periwinkle, ermine, katydid, hawk,
Quail, hippopotamus, armadillo, moth,
Rattlesnake, lion, woodpecker, sloth,
Salamander, goldfinch, angleworm, dog,
Tiger, flamingo, scorpion, frog,
Unicorn, ostrich, nautilus, mole,
Viper, gorilla, basilisk, sole,
Whippoorwill, beaver, centipede, fawn,
Xantho, canary, polliwog, swan,
Yellowhammer, eagle, hyena, lark,
Zebra, chameleon, butterfly, shark.

Author unknown

GEMINI JONES

At several times the speed of light,
Astronaut Gemini Jones took flight,
Buzzing about, now to, now from,
All the constellations of God's kingDOM:

Ácrux, Ras Álgethis, Tarf, Acanár;
Bénetnasch, Kítalpha, Sąlm, Giansár;
Cástor, Hercúlis, Skat, Úrsae Majóris,
Délta, Kids, Ádib, Cor, Úrsae Minóris;
Eléctra, Dracónis, Poláris, Mizár;
Fúrud, Austrális, Pleióne, Dog Star;
Goméisa, Ed Ásich, Scheḍár, Sulafát,
Hámal, Kaus Áustralis, Áldhaf'ra, Skat;
Ízar, Sagíttirri, Spíca, Meróper;
Júga, Giánsar, Homám, Asteróper;
Kitálpha, Mekbúda, Yed Pósterior,
Lesáth, Vinddemístrix, Zaurák, Yed Priór;
Mintáka, Porríma, Rasálas, Wasŋt,
Náshiri, Présepe, Taygéte, Andrát;
Oriónis, Alcyóne, Pegási, Alyá,
Pherkád, Nair al Zúrak, Al Chiba, Alschá;
Rastában, Suzlócin, Canópis, Mwnkár,
Seginis, Algénib, Alphécca, Schedár;
Talítha, Taygéte, Ruchbáh, Scheat, Kocháb,
Unúk al H, Piscium, Altair, Arkáb;
Véga, Peiádum, Graffiés, Leónis,
Wézen, Tarízed, Virgínis, Dracónis;
Yíldun, Angétenar, Kaus Boreális;
Záurak, Antáres, Alúla Austrális:

Buzzing about, now to, now from,
All the constellations in God's kingDOM.

W. R. E.

Alliteration

Alliteration—what the *Encyclopaedia Britannica* calls 'the jingle of like beginnings', by contrast with Milton's definition of rhyme as 'the jingling sound of like endings'—is everywhere in English. Early English poetry, indeed, had no rhyme, but was held together entirely by a pattern of alliteration, as in these lines from Beowulf:

> . . . then friendship he awaited,
> Waned under the welkin, in worship throve,
> Until each one of those outdwelling
> Over the whale-road, must hearken to him,
> Gold must give him; that was a good king.

Piers Plowman was an alliterist:

> In a somer seson when soft was the sonne,
> I shope me in shroudes as I a shepe were.
>
> A depe dale benethe, a dongeon there-inne,
> With depe dyches and derke and dredful of sight.

So was Chaucer:

> But of the fyr and flaumbe funeral
> In which my body brennen shal to glede.

Some familiar alliterative lines:

Shakespeare:

> After life's fitful fever.
> Full fathom five thy father lies.

Coleridge:

> The fair breeze blew, the white foam flew,
>   The furrow followed free;
> We were the first that ever burst
>   Into that silent sea.

Tennyson:

> Fly o'er waste fens and windy fields.

Swinburne, famous for his alliterative poetry, sometimes parodied himself:

From the depth of the dreamy decline of the dawn through a notable number of nebulous noonshine.

We alliterate without noticing it, as we breathe. 'Like Louise?' I might exclaim; 'I love that lady!'. Many expressions continue to be the small change of our small talk simply because of the way they trip off the tongue.

Some of these are defined below—see if you can identify them.

1. In good shape, generally referring to one who has been through a misadventure.
2. Through good and bad.
3. New and fresh; neat and trim.
4. Neither one thing nor another.
5. Friends and relatives.
6. Without attachments that impede freedom of action.
7. Uncivilised; rough in manner.
8. Most important.
9. Meticulous in what does not matter, careless in what does.
10. Completely extinct.

ANSWERS

1. Safe and sound.
2. Through thick and thin; through weal or woe; through fair or foul.
3. Spick and span.
4. Neither fish, flesh, nor fowl.
5. Kith and kin.
6. Footloose and fancy free.
7. Wild and woolly.
8. First and foremost.
9. Penny wise, pound foolish.
10. Dead as a doornail (or dodo).

SPANKER

The advertisement below for the sale of a horse appeared in a Manchester paper in 1829.

SPANKER:
The Property of O—— D——

Saturday, the 16th September next, will be sold, or set up for sale, at Skibbereen:

A strong, staunch, steady, sound, stout, safe, sinewy, service-able, strapping, supple, swift, smart, sightly, sprightly, spirited, sturdy, shining, sure-footed, sleek, smooth, spunky, well-skinned,

sized, and shaped sorrel steed, of superlative symmetry, styled
SPANKER; with small star and snip, square-sided, slender-
shouldered, sharp-sighted, and steps singularly stately; free from
strain, spavin, spasms, stringhalt, staggers, strangles, surfeit,
seams, strumous swellings, scratches, splint, squint, scurf, sores,
scattering, shuffling, shambling-gait, or sickness of any sort.
He is neither stiff-mouthed, shabby-coated, sinew-shrunk, saddle-
backed, shell-toothed, skin-scabbed, short-winded, splay-footed,
or shoulder-slipped; and is sound in the sword-point and stifle-
joint. Has neither sick-spleen, sleeping-evil, snaggle-teeth, sub-
cutaneous sores, or shattered hoofs; nor is he sour, sulky, surly,
stubborn, or sullen in temper. Neither shy nor skittish, slow,
sluggish, or stupid. He never slips, strips, strays, starts, stalks,
stops, shakes, snivels, snaffles, snorts, stumbles, or stocks in his
stall or stable, and scarcely or seldom sweats. Has a showy,
stylish switch-tail, or stern, and a safe set of shoes on; can feed
on stubble, sainfoin, sheaf-oats, straw, sedge, or Scotch grass.
Carries sixteen stone with surprising speed in his stroke over a
six-foot sod or a stone wall. His sire was the Sly Sobersides, on a
sister of Spindleshanks by Sampson, a sporting son of Sparkler,
who won the sweepstakes and subscription plate last session at
Sligo. His selling price is sixty-seven pounds, sixteen shillings
and sixpence sterling.

VERSE BY GERARD MANLEY HOPKINS

No poet loved wordplay more than Gerard Manley Hopkins;
nor did any alliterate more angelically. Almost any Hopkins line
will serve as an example; I lift three from *Henry Purcell*:

The thunder-purple seabeach, plumed purple-of-thunder,
If a wuthering of his palmy snow-pinions scatter a colossal smile
Off him, but meaning motion fans fresh our wits with wonder.

These are from the more familiar *Pied Beauty*:

Glory be to God for dappled things—
        For skies of couple-colour as a brindled cow;
                For rose-moles all in stipple upon trout that swim;
Fresh-firecoal chestnut-falls; finches' wings;

Landscape plotted and pieced—fold, fallow, and plough;
  And all trades, their gear and tackle and trim.

All things counter, original, spare, strange;
  Whatever is fickle, freckled (who knows how?)
  With swift, slow; sweet, sour; adazzle, dim;
He fathers-forth whose beauty is past change:
              Praise him.

THE SIEGE OF BELGRADE

It is a shame that no-one seems to know who wrote this, one of
the cleverer examples of alphabetical alliteration. (The author
couldn't work in the *j*, though.)

An Austrian army, awfully arrayed,
Boldly, by battery, besieged Belgrade;
Cossack commanders cannonading come—
Dealing destruction's devastating doom;
Every endeavour, engineers essay,
For fame, for fortune—fighting furious fray:—
Generals 'gainst generals grapple—gracious God!
How honours Heaven, heroic hardihood!
Infuriate,—indiscriminate in ill,
Kindred kill kinsmen,—kinsmen kindred kill!
Labour low levels loftiest, longest lines—
Men march 'mid mounds, 'mid moles, 'mid murderous mines:
Now noisy, noxious, noticed nought
Of outward obstacles opposing ought:
Poor patriots, partly purchased, partly pressed;
Quite quaking, quickly quarter, quarter quest,
Reason returns, religious right redounds,
Suwarrow stops such sanguinary sounds.
Truce to thee, Turkey—triumph to thy train!
Unjust, unwise, unmerciful Ukraine!
Vanish vain victory, vanish victory vain!
Why wish ye warfare? Wherefore welcome were
Xerxes, Ximenes, Xanthus, Xaviere?
Yield! ye youths! ye yeomen, yield your yell!
Zeono's, Zapater's, Zoroaster's zeal,
And all attracting—arms against acts appeal.

America Speaks

There are almost as many varieties of spoken American as there are of speaking Americans. In the *Saturday Review*, Cleveland Amory presents a common, or field, variety in an account called 'Our Gray Nashnul Pastime', signed Jim Barnett and submitted by James Bonnell. After an introduction listing the major league baseball teams (in one league the Allanna Brays, the Pissburgh Pyruss, the Los Angeles Dahjers, the Sane Louis Carnals, the Monreal Espos and the Cincinnaai Res; in the other, the Ballimore Orioles, the Washinton Senaturs, the Deetroy Tigers, the Cleeland Indians, and the Minnesota Twins) the story, which I judge to be jotted down from a television announcer's report, begins:

Each mannijer signs the car showing his lineup for the day and joins the daily huddle arown home plate to learn the groun rules . . .

(As the batteen order appears before us on the screen, we are told that certain named players are in leff, senner an rye feels. Others are at the traditional spots of firss, secun an thirr base, an shorestop.)

The pisher no longer goes inna wineup, but a stresh. The firss pish is stry one, followed by ball one. Then stry two, ball two, ball three—the full cown. The ba—er fouls one inna the stanns an the cown remains aa three an two. Finally he flies deep to the senner feeler who makes a long run anna fine runnen catch up againssa wall, beyonna warneen track.

Another ba—er goes to one an one, then pulls one downa leff feel line, where the feeler plays it offa wall an fires to secun. But the ba—er, with a hook sly, slies in safely at secun with a double. He calls for time while he duss off his suit, or at leass his pans.

The game moves along. It develops into a real pishers ba—l.

The nex ba—er grouns to shore, anna runner on firss slies inna secun, to break up the du-ul play.

Three weeks from necks Sa–arday is Ole Timers' day, so get your tickus early at onea the many convenion box offices. Come ow an see baseball's grays, including several memmers of the Hall a Fame.

38

Anagrams

ANAGRAM EXERCISE

Not only does the quatrain below contain three unrelated sets of anagrams, but one anagram combination is broken into two words. Start solving by rhyming 'commend it'.

My *******'s low, my ***** is high,
A ***** with little to commend it;
Of ******, ****** few have I;
I ***** **.

But on second thought, I am more interested in pointing out the elegance of the verse than in making the solution difficult for you. So if you wish to take the easy way out, play with any one of the three variants below without looking at the others. Solving one solves them all.

My *******'s low, my taste is high,
A state with little to commend it.
Of specie, pieces few have I;
I ***** **.

Or

My stipend's low, my ***** is high,
A ***** with little to commend it.
Of specie, pieces few have I;
I spend it.

Or

My stipend's low, my taste is high,
A state with little to commend it.
Of ******, ****** few have I;
I spend it.

W. R. E.

ANAGRAMS from *Punch*
Drinking Song

He **** for gold,
As I for ale;
I've **** of this:
Of that has he.
For me a kiss
**** Holy Grail;
He'd go cuckold
To **** a fee.
Yet, ****! I wist
(And I'd **** bail)
He'd pay fourfold
To be like me.

W. R. E.

ANSWER: Opts, pots, tops, spot, stop, post.

Highland Fling

Sweet Molly MacDougal, in labour,
Warned her sister, 'It hurts like a *****.
Sin ***** a high price,
So a girl should think twice
What she ***** on the ***** for a neighbour.'

W. R. E.

ANSWER: Sabre, bears, bares, braes.

I Hope to Meet my Bartender Face to Face

'Twould much ****** you to me if, when I
Have ****** my fatal moment, and must die,
You'd share one well ****** drink, and pray there are
Some more to come across that final bar.

W. R. E.

ANSWER: Endear, neared, earned.

History Revisited: *The Mayflower*

********* and repainting and refitting,
Rescraping, -calking, -binding and -bowspritting,
They patched the little vessel, with the notion
Of ********* oppression . . . and the ocean.
When she was shipshaped, holystoned and gleaming,
Aboard the pilgrim ********* came *********.

W. R. E.

ANSWER: Remasting, mastering, emigrants, streaming.

Minatory Note to my Unborn Son

Asleep in your ******** pad,
You dream of future joys ********.
Don't be in such a hurry, lad;
******** bills are monumental.

W. R. E.

ANSWER: Prenatal, parental, paternal.

Ugly Does as Handsome Is

Though flowers need tending to survive,
While weeds get on alone,
The *****'s loved by all alive,
While ***** are loved by none.
Man ***** the horse above the mule,
Although the mule is abler;
At pretty girls we ***** and drool,
Though ugly ones are stabler.
  I say through *****, I wish I could
  Be much more handsome, and less good.

W. R. E.

ANSWER: Aster, tares, rates, stare, tears.

41

We Mean a Lot to Each Other

When I am ******* and in bliss,
While Death my mortal clay *******
Beneath some ******* stone, I'll miss
The softer parts of my remains.
My bones will last, but who *******
Will **** ** * do liver, brains,
And other organs best unsaid?
I'll miss my vitals when I'm dead.

W. R. E.

ANSWER: Sainted, detains, stainèd, instead, tend as I.

I HATE YOU, JOHN RIDDS
A Tirade in Five Bursts

BURST THE FIRST

I hate my neighbour, ***** John Ridds,
As superegos hate their ids.
If e'er he turns his back, then zip!
I'll smite that neighbour, ***** and hip;

And, laughing as he lies *****,
***** John Ridds beneath the dirt.

My loathing has the mass, the *****,
The permanence of planet Earth.
Dear reader, you've a ***** to know
Why I despise this fellow so.

BURST THE SECOND

My ****** hangs upon a ******
So stout that none can shear it:
John ever ******, where I dread;
He shames my ****** of spirit.

John's big and bold; he ******* nought
From wave or wind or weather.
But I am small and ill begot,
And frightened by a *******.

A ******* John is to the end,
While I equivocate;
If battles are in store, my friend,
I'd rather pull my *******.

When John's besieged and sorely pressed,
He most delights in being.
In fact, he's ******* quite his best
Precisely when I'm *******.

*And since I run from **** of fray,*
*I **** you, John, because you stay.*

BURST THE THIRD

The fair sex scorn me for my *****;
While John, *preux chevalier*,
In matters amorous, one hears,
***** better every day.

While I can barely foist my kisses
On spinster aunts and cousins,
John's ******** with a hundred misses,
And ******** with dozens.

*Now why, ******, should such as he*
*Win hearts and hands ****** to me?*

43

Do not ***** that I pronounce
John Ridds a paragon;
I am, in all that really counts,
A ***** man than John.

True, John is ******, good to touch,
A natural for pairing;
It's not his girls I ****** so much,
But rather his not sharing.

John's ******* lies in hoarding beauties
As misers hoard their winnings.
He's overloaded with his duties,
And I deserve my *******.

*The *** truth is, I hate John for*
*Excelling me in love and ***.*

So here I sit, my **** before,
And brood, as embers cool;
If John were wood, how I'd adore
To throw him on for ****.

If God ******, I'll toll the bell
Some morning for John Ridds;
And as he's sliding down to Hell,
I'll gladly ****** the skids.

But if to Heaven he's conveyed,
I'll picket, jeer, and carp;
And when the angels' ***** are played,
I'll pray that John's plays *****.

W. R. E.

Burst the First: Hight, Thigh; Inert, Inter; Girth, Right

Burst the Second: Hatred, Thread, Dareth, Dearth; Feareth, Feather; Fighter, Freight; Feeling, Fleeing; Heat, Hate

Burst the Third: Fears, Fares; Flirting, Trifling; Indeed, Denied

Burst the Fourth: Infer, Finer; Rugged, Grudge; Sinning, Innings; Raw, War

Burst the Fifth: Flue, Fuel; Agrees, Grease; Harps, Sharp

MILTON, THOU SHOULD'ST BE RE-VERSING AT THIS HOUR

W. S. Gilbert wrote:

> If this young man expresses himself
> In terms too deep for *me*,
> Why, what a singularly deep young man
> This deep young man must be!

Unplumbable depths are the hallmark of some present-day poets. The reversal verse below is simple by comparison with theirs; every word is a real and common one. If you don't care for it this way, turn each word around and you will get the second version.

> won ma I
> a keels, gums, live rail, am?
> on,
> ton I. I garb ton, reel ton, lever ton.
> o,
> snug yam time tips; slag era diva; a eros lived yam knits;
> tub I,
> on dam flow
> ward laud drawer:
> I flog, I peels. ogre,
> I ma ton deliver,
> tub trams.

W. R. E.

(ANSWER OVERLEAF)

ANSWER

now am I
a sleek, smug, evil liar, ma?
                    no,
not I. I brag not, leer not, revel not.
                              o,
guns may emit spit; gals are avid; a sore devil may stink;
        but I,
            no mad wolf,
draw dual reward,
I golf, I sleep. ergo,
                    I am not reviled,
but smart.

REVERSE VERSES

Each of the couplets below defines two words, the first the reverse
of the second in spelling but otherwise unrelated to it. Guess the
words.

I

Without her I know that there wouldn't be me;
Turn her around, she's a word from 'to be'.

2

Detractors will say I'm too greedy by far;
Turn me around, I'm an opera star.

3

If I bore you by boasting and putting on airs,
Turn me around, and I'm something one wears.

4

A tinker's is worthless, it's often opined,
But worse turned around, for it's out of its mind.

5

It's used on your luggage to fasten about;
Turn it around, and your clothes may fall out.

46

6

Its meaning is kingly, a word to revere;
Turn it around, and it's rather small beer.

7

A river will do this, though shallow, though deep;
Turn it around, and it likes eating sheep.

W. R. E.

ANSWERS

1. Ma, am
2. Avid, diva
3. Brag, garb
4. Dam, mad

5. Strap, parts
6. Regal, lager
7. Flow, wolf

WHAT'S IN A NAME?

The following names have all given birth to well-known anagrams. If you don't recall the anagrams off-hand, you may enjoy anagramming the names yourself before looking at the time-honoured transpositions which follow.

1. Horatio Nelson
2. Adolf Hitler
3. Henry Wadsworth
   Longfellow

4. Florence Nightingale
5. Robert Louis Stevenson
6. Dante Gabriel Rossetti
7. Oliver Wendell Holmes

ANSWERS

1. Honor est a Nilo.
2. Hated for ill.
3. Won half the New World's glory.
4. Flit on, cheering angel!

5. Our best novelist, señor!
6. Greatest idealist born.
7. He'll do in mellow verse.

Anguish Languish

LADLE RAT ROTTEN HUT

Professor Howard Chace, Department of Romance Languages, Miami University, Oxford, Ohio, had a hobby of reducing folk tales to what he called 'Anguish Languish' by replacing all the words of the story with others, similar in sound but unrelated in meaning. The following example of his art appeared in *Word Study*, May 1953.

Wants pawn term dare worsted ladle gull hoe lift wetter murder inner ladle cordage honor itch offer lodge dock florist. Disc ladle gull orphan worry ladle cluck wetter putty ladle rat hut, end fur disc raisin pimple caulder ladle rat rotten hut. Wan moaning rat rotten hut's murder colder inset: 'Ladle rat rotten hut, heresy ladle basking winsome burden barter an shirker cockles. Tick disc ladle basking tudor cordage offer groin murder hoe lifts honor udder site offer florist. Shaker lake, dun stopper laundry wrote, end yonder nor sorgum stenches dun stopper torque wet strainers.'

'Hoe-cake, murder,' resplendent ladle rat rotten hut, end tickle ladle basking an sturred oft. Honor wrote tudor cordage offer groin murder, ladle rat rotten hut mitten anomalous woof.

'Wail, wail, wail,' set disc wicket woof, 'evanescent ladle rat rotten hut! Wares or putty ladle gull goring wizard ladle basking?'

'Armor goring tumor groin murder's,' reprisal ladle gull. 'Grammars seeking bet. Armor ticking arson burden barter end shirker cockles.'

'O hoe! Heifer blessing woke,' setter wicket woof, butter taught tomb shelf, 'Oil tickle shirt court tudor cordage offer groin murder. Oil ketchup wetter letter, an den—O bore!'

Soda wicket woof tucker shirt court, end whinney retched a cordage offer groin murder, picket inner widow an dore debtor port oil worming worse lion inner bet. Inner flesh disc abdominal woof lipped honor betting adder rope. Zany pool dawn a groin murder's nut cup an gnat gun, any curdle dope inner bet.

Inner ladle wile ladle rat rotten hut a raft attar cordage an ranker dough ball. 'Comb ink, sweat hard,' setter wicket woof, disgracing is verse. Ladle rat rotten hut entity bet rum end stud buyer groin murder's bet. 'Oh grammar,' crater ladle gull, 'Wart bag icer gut! a nervous sausage bag ice!' 'Butter lucky chew whiff, doling,' whiskered disc ratchet woof, wetter wicket small. 'Oh grammar, water bag noise! A nervous sore suture anomalous prognosis!' 'Buttered small your whiff,' inserter woof, ants mouse worse wadding. 'Oh grammar, water bag mousey gut! A nervous sore suture bag mouse!'

Daze worry on forger nut gull's lest warts. Oil ofter sodden throne offer carvers an sprinkling otter bet, disc curl an bloat Thursday woof ceased pore ladle rat rotten hut an garbled erupt.

Mural: Yonder nor sorghum stenches shud ladle gulls stopper torque wet strainers.

DARN BODY OAT MEAL STREAM

Darn body oat meal stream,
 Wear a first mate shoe,
Ouija eyesore blue
 Dresden gingham, too.
It was there anew
 Thatch a loft me too.
You were sixteen,
 Marvel itch Queen,
Darn body oat meal stream!

Dave Morrah

APPLESAUCE

The Apple which the Snake supplied
Arrived complete, with Worm inside.
Child, shun this Sequence of the Snake:
First Fruit, then Worm, then Belly-Ache.

W.R.E.

Animal Noise

The cry of a cat's a ****,
And an **** is the **** of a hog;
And a *** is the **** of a cow,
And a **** is the *** of a dog;

And a ***** is the **** of a horse,
And a *******'s an elephant's ****;
And the ******** of lions are *****,
And the **** of a donkey's a ****;

And the **** of a duck is a *****,
And the ***** of a snake is a ****;
And if that doesn't take you aback,
You may be confounded by this:

The **** of a sheep is a ***,
And a hyena's *** is a *****;
And the ***** of a babe is a ****,
And the **** of a . . . say a . . . giraffe
  Is so small
    It is nothing
      Nothing at all.

                          W. R. E.

ANSWER

The cry of a cat's a meow,
And an oink is the meow of a hog;
And a moo is the oink of a cow,
And a bark is the moo of a dog;

And a neigh is the bark of a horse,
And a trumpet's an elephant's neigh;
And the trumpets of lions are roars,
And the roar of a donkey's a bray;

And the bray of a duck is a quack,
And the quack of a snake is a hiss;
And if that doesn't take you aback,
You may be confounded by this:

The hiss of a sheep is a baa,
And a hyena's baa is a laugh;
And the laugh of a babe is a waah,
And the waah of a . . . say a . . . giraffe
   Is so small
     It is nothing
      Nothing at all.

Animal Offspring

A cow has a ****, but the **** of a mare
Is a ****, and a *** is the **** of a bear;
A **** is the *** of a deer, while the ****
Of a beaver's a ******, and, carrying on,
The *** of a sheep is a ****, and the ****
Of a wolf is a *****, while the ***** of madame
Is a ****, and the **** of a dog is a ***,
And I thought for awhile this would wind the thing up,
But the *** of a goat is a ***, and, Mon Dieu!
A ****'s the *** of a kangkangaroo.

W. R. E.

ANSWER

A cow has a calf, but the calf of a mare
Is a foal,* and a cub is the foal* of a bear;
A fawn is the cub of a deer, while the fawn
Of a beaver's a kitten, and, carrying on,
The kit of a sheep is a lamb, and the lamb
Of a wolf is a whelp, while the whelp of Madame
Is a babe, and the babe of a dog is a pup,
And I thought for awhile this would wind the thing up,
But the pup of a goat is a kid, and, Mon Dieu!,
A joey's the kid of a kangkangaroo.

* Or colt.

As I Lay Dying

You are asked to develop an appropriate deathbed statement for past or present notables. (The *New Statesman* performed the same service for beasts. The flea, for instance, said, 'And now for Abraham's bosom'; the ostrich, 'Where's that sand?'; the Phoenix, 'It's my wish to be cremated'.)

Some last words of record:

The British statesman Henry Labouchere, noting the flaring of the oil lamp beside the bed where he lay dying, said, 'Flames? Not yet, I think.'

Hugh Latimer, the Protestant martyr, told Nicholas Ridley, Bishop of London, as the lighted fagots touched their pyres: 'Be of good comfort, Master Ridley, and play the man. We shall this day light such a candle, by God's grace in England, as I trust shall never be put out.'

Louis XIV: 'When I was King . . .'

Lady Mary Wortley Montagu: 'It has all been very interesting.'

William Palmer, the poisoner, told to step out on the gallows trap: 'Are you sure it's safe?'

Anna Pavlova: 'Get my swan costume ready.'

Heinrich Heine: 'God will pardon me—it's his profession.'

A. E. Housman (after being cheered by his doctor with a risqué story): 'Yes, that's a good one and tomorrow I shall be telling it on the Golden Floor.'

Disraeli (asked whether he would like Queen Victoria at his deathbed): 'Why should I see her? She will only want to give a message to Albert.'

Auguste Comte, the positivist: 'What an irreparable loss!'

Michael Restuzhev-Ryumin, the Russian revolutionary whose first rope broke at his hanging: 'Nothing succeeds with me. Even here I meet with disappointment.'

Anne Boleyn, approaching the guillotine: 'The executioner is, I believe, very expert; and my neck is very slender.'

Buffalo Bill (William Frederick Cody), on being told his remaining time was short: 'Well, let's forget about it and play high five.'

Thoreau, asked if he had made his peace with his God: 'I was not aware that we had ever quarrelled.'

W. C. Fields: 'On the whole, I'd rather be in Philadelphia.'

Nero's mother, to the assassins sent by her son: 'Smite my womb!'

P. T. Barnum: 'How were the circus receipts today at Madison Square Garden?'

Clarence Walker Barron, publisher of the *Wall Street Journal*: 'What's the news?'

Clifton Fadiman has suggested deathbed utterances for the notables listed below. To make sure you know how As I Lay Dying should be played, write down your own last words for each of these men and women. Then see how yours compare with Mr. Fadiman's.

1. Gypsy Rose Lee, ecdysiast.
2. Henry Luce, founder of *Time* and *Life*.
3. Sam Goldwyn, cinema producer.
4. Mary Baker Eddy, founder of Christian Science.

ANSWERS

1. Gypsy Rose Lee: 'Are those wings detachable?'
2. Henry Luce: 'It's time, life.'
3. Sam Goldwyn: 'I never thought I'd live to see the day.'
4. Mary Baker Eddy: 'Impossible!'

AUTHOR'S QUERY

William Cole, in *Pith and Vinegar*,* asked who wrote the couplet which follows. As far as I know, he has received no reply. If you send me the answer, it will put me one up on William Cole.

> Do you love me or do you not?
> You told me once but I forgot.

*Simon and Schuster, New York

B

Basic English

'What is the difference between visiting a man and going to see him, extracting a tooth and taking it out, forbidding a person solid food and saying he may not have it, preparing a meal and getting one ready, retiring at 10 and going to bed at that hour, rising at 7 and getting up then, dispatching a message and sending one, maintaining silence and keeping quiet, assisting your friends and helping them, commenting on something they do and making an observation about it, enlisting in one of the services and joining up, occupying a house and living in it, concentrating on your work and putting your mind to it?'

The question is put by Mr. I. A. Richards and Miss Christine Gibson, advocates of Basic English, a simplified form of the language. Anyone reasonably proficient in English can master the basics of Basic English in a few days, or even a few hours, though it is not clear why one should. But to a person born to any of the other 1700 languages in the world, Basic affords perhaps the easiest possible entry to English.

There are only 850 words to learn. As one might suspect, many of these become portmanteau words; *seat*, for instance, is used for such particular kinds of seats as settees, couches, settles, thrones, stalls, divans, hassocks, tripods, taborets, and woolsacks. This Liberty Hall does not make for precision of speech.

Still, if you know Basic you can make yourself understood wherever English is spoken, and there is nothing to stop you from adding less basic words as you go along.

One of the reasons Basic is easy to learn is that it has only sixteen verbs: *come, get, give, go, keep, let, make, put, seem, take, be, do, have, say, see,* and *send.* These may be combined with *may, will,* and a number of prepositions.

I have given here only a very sketchy idea of the way Basic works. It would not be surprising, though, if you could figure out the rest for yourself. Below is a Basic English exercise. If your answers agree with those which follow the exercise, you don't need to take the course.

1. When we *enter* a room, we———.
2. When we *leave* it, we———.
3. If an army *advances*, it———.
4. If an army *retreats*, it———.
5. If a man *hurries*, he———.
6. If he *dawdles*, he———.
7. If you *ascend* steps, you———.
8. In *descending*, you———.
9. If a man *precedes* another, he———.
10. If he *follows* him or *pursues* him, he———.
11. If you *forget* a thing, it———.
12. If you *recollect* it, it———.
13. If you *visit* someone, you———.
14. If you *inherit* money, you———.
15. When the sun *rises*, it———.
16. When it *sets*, it———.
17. If it *disappears* behind a cloud, it———.
18. If it *reappears*, it———.

ANSWERS

1. come *or* go into it.
2. go out.
3. goes forward.
4. goes back.
5. goes quickly.
6. goes slowly.
7. go up them.
8. come down.
9. goes before him.
10. goes after him.
11. goes out of your mind.
12. comes back to you.
13. go to see him *or* go to his house.
14. come into it.
15. comes up.
16. goes down.
17. goes under it, *or* out of view.
18. comes out again.

HOW COMMON CAN YOU GET?

Ten English words, according to advocates of Basic English, make up a full fourth part of all our reading. When you have guessed which ones they are, check your list with the one given below.

ANSWER

The ten most frequent words in English are *the, of, and, to, a, in, that, it, is, I.*

Beasts at Bay

CREATURES IN COUPLETS

1 There's a word that holds a cat, and means a social class;
2 There's a word that holds a cow, and means a silly ass.
3 One that holds a goat's a mighty giant, David's menace.
4 One that holds a dog was once a magistrate in Venice.

5 There's a word that holds a horse, and means an incubus;
6 One that holds a bear, and bore me, you, him, her, and us;
7 One that holds a lion is a medal oversize;
8 One that holds a seagull means to lock up, penalise.

9 One that holds a kind of fish, a kind of pattern, too;
   I must stop this game before I use up all the zoo.

W. R. E.

ANSWERS

1. Caste.	4. Doge.	7. Medallion.
2. Clown.	5. Nightmare.	8. Intern.
3. Goliath.	6. Forebear.	9. Herringbone.

TALE OF THE NAKED RABBI

If the night had not been so dark, the two unfortunate rabbis whose adventures are related below would have found a number of animals concealed in the haunted wastes they were traversing —one, in fact, to a line. Once you have located the first beast, you should have no trouble flushing out the others.

1	Two naked rabbis, one black night,
2	Not local folk, but strangers,
3	Called on a German for a light.
4	One said, 'O God, such dangers!
5	In such black ink a journey ne'er
6	Was planned till now, or taken;
7	Drab ruins ring me everywhere;
8	'Neath each stele, phantoms waken.
9	Would that wide Erie flowed e'en now
10	Betwixt those shapes and me!
11	They made a most terrific row;
12	One sobbed and wailed, on key.
13	And one would sigh, or seem to sigh,
14	And one would yell amain,
15	And one, with blust'ring oath and cry,
16	Would grab, bite, kick, and pain.
17	Dear God! It rushes to attack!
18	I struck it ten times three;
19	A spirit moans, while striking back,
20	"I'm vile—O, pardon me!"
21	Th' avowal rustles to an end;
22	What rout or final victory befell
23	This naked rabbi and his friend
24	'Twould take a sadder, wiser pen to tell.

W. R. E.

(ANSWERS OVERLEAF)

1. Bison. 2. Calf. 3. Onager. 4. Dog. 5. Kinkajou. 6. Wasp. 7. Bruin. 8. Elephant. 9. Deer. 10. Ape. 11. Crow. 12. Donkey. 13. Horse. 14. Llama. 15. Goat. 16. Rabbit. 17. Stoat. 18. Kitten. 19. Asp. 20. Leopard. 21. Walrus. 22. Trout. 23. Snake. 24. Serpent.

TROJAN HORSE WORDS

Some creatures slip into words as slyly as the Trojan horse slipped into Troy. Each of the phrases below holds a clue to a word in which another word is hidden.

1. Alas for this beautiful vanishing heron!
2. Such an insect might blow its own horn.
3. Poor Fido! In the soup!
4. Who, a-hunt by night? Who?
5. When hunted it hasn't sense enough to do what it's part of.
6. At the farthest end from the squeal is the whole hairstyle.
7. Not a bully, anyhow.
8. Even the Augean stables never stank like this.

ANSWERS

	The container	*The contained*
1.	Regret	Egret
2.	Bugle	Bug
3.	Chowder	Chow
4.	Prowl	Owl
5.	Scoot	Coot
6.	Pigtail	Pig
7.	Coward	Cow
8.	Maremma	Mare

Berlitz School

Say 'Donkey field mice' to a Viennese, and he will think you speak excellent German; for that is the Viennese pronunciation of 'Danke viel mals', 'Thank you very much'.

Charles F. Berlitz, on an opposite tack, once published a list of foreign words that sound like English. Some of these international homonyms are the subjects of the verses below.

I

'Good day,' said I to Jap chauffeur.
'Ohio,' was his sequitur.
I thanked him for the motor ride;
'Don't touch my moustache, sir,' he cried.
'You're wanting manners, man,' said I;
He deeply bowed, and said, 'High, high.'
I said, 'My mother is in town.'
'Ha ha,' said he. I knocked him down.

2

How 'how' resounds in every nation!
How different its interpretation!
In Hawaiian, 'how' 's 'to smoke';
'Greetings' 'tis to redskin bloke;
'Aristocrat' to Japanese;
'Good' to neighbouring Chinese.
To a German in a twit
It's imperative for 'hit'.

3

'I beg a Mere lighthearted Sin,'
Said I to Moscow maid;
'Peace be to you and me,' said she,
'But no Son, I'm afraid.'
'A Brat you are to treat me so!'
I cried out angrily;
'I'll be your sister,' she replied,
'A Brother I can't be.'
'My brother's name is Bill,' I said;
'He was?' said she to me.
'I call him Billy,' I went on.
'They were? How nice!' said she.

W. R. E.

(ANSWERS OVERLEAF)

ANSWERS

1. The name of the American state means 'good morning' in Japanese. 'You are welcome' is '*Do itashimash'te*'—as near as makes no difference to 'Don't touch my moustache'. 'High, high,' is 'No, no'. 'Ha ha' is 'mother'.
2. Self-explanatory.
3. 'Mere' in Russian means 'peace' or 'world'; 'sin' means 'son'; 'brat' means 'brother'; 'Bill' means 'was'; 'Billy' means 'were'.

IMPERIAL ENGLISH

The English-speaking peoples may (or may not) be losing rank in the councils of the mighty, but their language continues to spread. Sometimes, to be sure, it is hard to recognise; one has to think a moment before realising that 'Oossmaheel' is simply the Puerto Rican way of pronouncing 'U.S. mail'. The Puerto Ricans have similarly turned the baseball term 'home run' into 'jonron'. The Japanese call the afternoon rush hour 'rushewawa'.

'Le week-end' is one of hundreds of English expressions that have slipped past the guard of the wary and indignant French. I note, for instance, that French engineers working on the faster-than-sound Concorde aircraft say 'broque' for 'broke'. A fashion advertisement in Germany says, 'Was ist IN, was ist OUT?' another, 'Auf in den Winter mit Country Boots'! Politicians in the western countries accept unchanged such Anglo-American words and phrases as appeasement, escalation, rollback, comeback and 'no comment'.

*

BUSTS AND BOSOMS

Busts and bosoms have I known
Of various shapes and sizes,
From grievous disappointments
To jubilant surprises.

Author unknown

*

Bogus is to Borghese as Phoney is to Forney

Some of the best stories about word origins suffer from the minor disadvantage of being lies. Among these bogus, phoney reports are those on *bogus* and *phoney*.

Bogus is allegedly a corruption of Borghese, the name of a man who in the nineteenth century made a good thing of drawing cheques on fictitious banks. His name, according to the story, came to be used as a description of any such worthless bills. At about the same time, one Mr. Forney was happily selling fake jewellery to buyers who knew no better. Again, *phoney* is said to be corrupted from his name.

Messrs. Borghese and Forney may well have existed, but at best their names could only have reinforced words already in existence. *Bogus* comes from an old dialectal term in south-west England, *tankerabogus*, 'a goblin'. (Its tail end survives in *bogey*.) As to *phoney*, it is a corruption of the British underworld term *fawny*, in turn a corruption of Irish *fainne*, meaning 'finger-ring' —hence ring-switching and cheating in general.

While Borghese and Forney were playing their games, a man named Colonel Booze was distilling whisky and selling it in a bottle bearing his name. For this reason, it is said, *booze* came to mean hard liquor. But again, his name can only have reinforced an existing word: *booze* goes back to Middle English *bousen*, 'to carouse'.

Corsair may have become a common word because so many privateers lurked in the harbours of Corsica, the French island in the Mediterranean; but this common tradition does not alter the fact that the true origin of the word is Latin *correre*, 'to run'.

Gibberish is probably a corruption of *jabber*. Yet it was once called 'the mystic language of Geber, used by chymists', by no less a lexicographer than Samuel Johnson. The Geber he referred to was Jabir ibn Hayyan, an eighth-century alchemist who is reputed to have written more than 2000 books. The likely explanation is that other medieval alchemists borrowed his name to give authority to their works.

Blazer is often credited to the captain of H.M.S. *Blazer*, who ordered his officers to spruce up by wearing blue jackets with metal buttons. But probably the name simply refers to the blazing colour of the jacket.

Thomas Costain says in one of his novels that a man named Blanket, famous as a weaver of fine wools, dwelt long ago in Britain, and gave his name to the common bedcover. Actually, 'blanket' is simply an anglicisation of French *blanc*, 'White'. Once more, I do not rule out the possibility that Mr. Blanket gave the term currency by association; if he had been Mr. White, we might today be calling blankets 'whites'.

Tom Stoppard, in *Lord Malquist and Mr. Moon*, says: 'In the 13th century Sir John Wallop so smote the French at sea that he gave a verb to the language. But there must be less energetic ways of doing that.' But as far as I can learn, Sir John exists only in Mr. Stoppard's mind. *Wallop* comes from an old French word meaning 'gallop'.

My friend Irwin Shapiro once told me with a straight face that *pumpernickel* was named for Napoleon's horse. According to Irwin, the Emperor was offered a piece of this dark, sourish rye bread by a peasant while on one of his recurrent military expeditions in Eastern Europe. He tasted it, made a face, and gave the bread to his horse, Nicole, with the comment, 'Bon pour Nicole'. Hence, by corruption, *pumpernickel*. The true story is even odder. The bread gets its name because it is so hard to digest. The word is early New High German *Pumpern*, 'a fart', + *Nickel*, 'the devil': 'the devil's fart'.

Marmalade is traced by some to *Marie malade*, 'sick Mary'. The reason given is that this jam, then a rarity, was among the few foods that Mary, Queen of Scots, could hold on her stomach during an illness. The true source, though, is Greek *melimelon*, 'sweet apple'.

Russell Baker, a tongue-in-cheek newspaper columnist, once attributed the word *pragmatism* to Giovanni Pragma, whom he described as a nineteenth-century Florentine councilman and bungler. When I raised an eyebrow, he insisted that the provenance was authentic, coming to him by way of his friend Nino, who manages a trattoria in Washington, D.C. He wrote that Nino would be glad to confirm the derivation for me in person if I would first buy him a bottle of Bollo to loosen his tongue.

If the lexicographers take Mr. Baker seriously, you may find in some future *OED* a definition starting like this:
prag.ma-tism (prag'ma-tizm), n. [G. Pragma, It. statesman.] A philosophy holding that the truth is pre-eminently to be tested by the practical consequences of belief . . .

Burlesque and Parody

A parody is a comic imitation of a serious poem, and a burlesque is a particularly ludicrous form of parody.

The English seem to take special pleasure in parodies, perhaps because so many Englishmen had to write compositions after the manner of classical poets when in public school.

HUSH, HUSH

Hush, hush,
Nobody cares;
Christopher Robin
Has
Fallen
Down-
Stairs.

'Beachcomber' (J. B. Morton)

THE TENTH DAY OF CWTHMAS

On the tenth day of Cwthmas,* the Commonwealth brought to me
Ten Sovereign Nations
Nine Governors General
Eight Federations
Seven Disputed Areas
Six Trust Territories
Five Old Realms
Four Present or Prospective Republics
Three High Commission Territories
Two Ghana-Guinea Fowl

One Sterling Area
One Dollar Dominion
One Sun That Never Sets
One Maltese Cross
One Marylebone Cricket Club
One Trans-Arctic Expedition
And a Mother Country up a Gum Tree.

from *The Economist*

---

* Contraction of 'Commonwealthmas'.

HOW I BROUGHT THE GOOD NEWS FROM
AIX TO GHENT

(or Vice Versa)

I sprang to the rollocks and Jorrocks and me,
And I galloped, you galloped, we galloped all three.
Not a word to each other: we kept changing place,
Neck to neck, back to front, ear to ear, face to face:
And we yelled once or twice, when we heard a clock chime,
'Would you kindly oblige us, *is that the right time?*'
As I galloped, you galloped, he galloped, we galloped, ye
    galloped, they two shall have galloped: *let us trot.*

I unsaddled the saddle, unbuckled the bit,
Unshackled the bridle (the thing didn't fit)
And ungalloped, ungalloped, ungalloped, ungalloped a bit.
Then I cast off my buff coat, let my bowler hat fall,
Took off both my boots and my trousers and all—
Drank off my stirrup-cup, felt a bit tight,
And unbridled the saddle: it still wasn't right.

Then all I remember is, things reeling round,
As I sat with my head 'twixt my ears on the ground—
For imagine my shame when they asked what I meant
And I had to confess that I'd been, gone and went
And *forgotten* the news I was bringing to Ghent,
Though I'd galloped and galloped and galloped and galloped
    and galloped
And galloped and galloped and galloped. (Had I not would
    have been galloped?)

ENVOI

So I sprang to a taxi and shouted 'To Aix!'
And he blew on his horn and he threw off his brakes,
And all the way back till my money was spent
We rattled and rattled and rattled and rattled and rattled
And rattled and rattled—
And eventually sent a telegram.

Walter Carruthers Sellar
and Robert Julian Yeatman

OH, POE!

Few poets are more tempting to parodists than Edgar Allen Poe, described by James Russell Lowell as 'three-fifths genius, two-fifths fudge'. Here is a happy take-off by Bret Harte:

> But Mary, uplifting her finger,
>   Said, 'Sadly this bar I mistrust—
>   I fear that this bar does not trust.
> Oh, hasten—oh, let us not linger—
>   Oh, fly—let us fly—ere we must!'
> In terror she cried, letting sink her
>   Parasol till it trailed in the dust,—
> In agony sobbed, letting sink her
>   Parasol till it trailed in the dust,—
>   Till it sorrowfully trailed in the dust.
>
> Then I pacified Mary and kissed her,
>   And tempted her into the room,
>   And conquered her scruples and gloom;
> And we passed to the end of the vista,
>   But were stopped by the warning of doom,—
> By some words that were warning of doom.
>   And I said, 'What is written, sweet sister,
>   At the opposite end of the room?'
> She sobbed as she answered, 'All liquors
>   Must be paid for ere leaving the room.'

*

THE BRITISH JOURNALIST

> You cannot hope
>   To bribe or twist
> (Thank God!) the British
>   Journalist;
> But, seeing what
>   The man will do
> Unbribed, there's no
>   Occasion to.

Humbert Wolfe

*

PARODIES BY LEWIS CARROLL

As a boy I always had the feeling there was something that just escaped me about the verses in *Alice and Wonderland* and *Through the Looking-Glass*. Probably I had read in passing the verses that inspired them, and sensed some indefinable reminiscence in the lines. A parody cannot be effective—as a parody, that is—if the original has been forgotten. Since most of the originals from which Mr. Carroll worked *have* been forgotten, the 'Alice' verses have become immortal not as burlesques, but as nonsense.

Below are some stanzas of verse familiar to every Victorian child, followed by excerpts from Lewis Carroll's takeoffs.

1. Dr. Isaac Watts: *Against Idleness and Mischief*
   How doth the little busy bee
     Improve each shining hour,
   And gather honey all the day
     From every opening flower! . . .

   In works of labour or of skill,
     I would be busy too;
   For Satan finds some mischief still
     For idle hands to do . . .

   1A. *Lewis Carroll's rendition*
   How doth the little crocodile
     Improve his shining tail,
   And pour the waters of the Nile
     On every golden scale!

   How cheerfully he seems to grin,
     How neatly spreads his claws,
   And welcomes little fishes in
     With gently smiling jaws!

2. Robert Southey: *The Old Man's Comforts and How He Gained Them*
   'You are old, Father William,' the young man cried;
     'The few locks which are left you are grey;
   You are hale, Father William—a hearty old man:
     Now tell me the reason, I pray.'

66

'In the days of my youth,' Father William replied,
  'I remembered that youth would fly fast,
And abused not my health and my vigour at first,
  That I never might need them at last . . .'

2A. *Lewis Carroll's rendition*

'You are old, Father William,' the young man said,
  'And your hair has become very white;
And yet you incessantly stand on your head—
  Do you think, at your age, it is right?'

'In my youth,' Father William replied to his son,
  'I feared it might injure the brain;
But now that I'm perfectly sure I have none,
  Why, I do it again and again . . .'

3. Jane Taylor: *The Star*

Twinkle, twinkle, little star
How I wonder what you are!
Up above the world so high,
Like a diamond in the sky.

3A. *Lewis Carroll's rendition*

Twinkle, twinkle, little bat!
How I wonder what you're at!
Up above the world you fly,
Like a teatray in the sky.

*

BLOOD

A scientific humourist named Patrick Ryan makes the following comments on blood:

To the human mind there is more to blood than its mere chemical content. . . . For example, blood must essentially be thicker than water, impossible to get out of stones, indelible in its staining. . . . When apparent on heads, it should leave them unbowed; and should have the capacities to combine formidably with toil, tears and sweat; and to attain boiling-point when its host faces frustration.

WHEN LADS HAVE DONE WITH LABOUR

When lads have done with labour
In Shropshire, one will cry,
'Let's go and kill a neighbour,'
and t'other answers 'Aye!'

So this one kills his cousins,
and that one kills his dad;
And, as they hang by dozens
at Ludlow, lad by lad,

Each of them one-and-twenty,
all of them murderers,
The hangman mutters: 'Plenty
even for Housman's verse.'

Humbert Wolfe

WISE SAWS AND MODERN INSTANCES
(OR POOR RICHARD IN REVERSE)

Saw, *n.* A trite popular saying, or proverb. (Figurative and colloquial.) So called because it makes its way into a wooden head. The following are examples of old saws fitted with new teeth.

A penny saved is a penny to squander.
A man is known by the company that he organises.
A bad workman quarrels with the man who calls him that.
A bird in the hand is worth what it will bring.
Better late than before anybody has invited you.
Example is better than following it.
Think twice before you speak to a friend in need.
What is worth doing is worth the trouble of asking somebody to
  do it.
Least said is soonest disavowed.
He laughs best who laughs least.
Speak of the Devil and he will hear about it.
Of two evils choose to be the least.
Strike while your employer has a big contract.
Where there's a will there's a won't.

Ambrose Bierce

C

Chain Verse

A curious literary form, in which little of note has been accomplished, is the chain verse—an arrangement in which the last word or phrase of each line becomes the beginning of the next. Here is such a one:

AD MORTEM

The longer life, the more offence;
The more offence, the greater pain;
The greater pain, the less defence;
The less defence, the greater gain—
Wherefore, come death, and let me die!

The shorter life, less care I find,
Less care I take, the sooner over;
The sooner o'er, the merrier mind;
The merrier mind, the better lover—
Wherefore, come death, and let me die!

Come, gentle death, the ebb of care;
The ebb of care, the flood of life;
The flood of life, I'm sooner there;
I'm sooner there—the end of strife—
The end of strife, that thing wish I—
Wherefore, come death, and let me die!

Author unknown

Charades

1. I am a word of 12 letters.
   My 12, 4, 7, 2, 5 is an Eastern beast of burden.
   My 1, 8, 10, 9 is a street made famous by Sinclair Lewis.
   My 11, 3, 6 is past.
   My whole is a person suffering from delusions of greatness.

2. I am a word of 11 letters.
My 7, 3, 8, 4, 5 is what the little girl did when her cat died.
My 9, 10, 6, 2 is an obscuring smudge.
My 1, 11 is an abbreviation for that is.
My whole is as little as it can get.

3. I am a word of 11 letters.
My 4, 9, 5 is worn on the head.
My 10, 9, 1, 11 is a narrow road.
My 11, 2, 3, 4, 5 is a number.
My 8, 6, 7 is a spirit.
My whole is an excellent songster.

ANSWERS: 1. Camel, Main, ago; megalomaniac.
             2. Cried, blur, i.e.; irreducible.
             3. Hat, lane, eight, gin; nightingale.

The following three charades are by Hubert Phillips.

1

My first wears my second; my third might be
What my first would acquire if he went to sea.
Put together my one, two, three
And the belle of New York is the girl for me.

2

No hard decode. And, in this case,
A solid answer you can claim.
It has (I'm told) a different face
For every letter of its name.

3

Execration perhaps—though it seems very wrong
On request to the dog to oblige with a song.

ANSWERS

1. Manhattan.
2. Dodecahedron (a 12-sided solid; anagram of 'no hard decode').
3. Cur-sing.

A CENTURY OF CHARADES

William Bellamy's *Century of Charades*,* a book of an even
hundred unsolved charade verses, appeared in 1894. It was
followed a year later by another book, *Open Sesame*,† also in
rhyme, which gave the solutions. But the second book was not by
Mr. Bellamy—it was by Harland H. Ballard, whom Bellamy had
never so much as laid eyes on.

I give three of the Bellamy charades below.

I

My first endured a hundred years,
A progeny of logic and of wit;
My last the faro banker fears,
King Solomon was not arrayed like it.
My whole, dear reader, you'll divine
When you peruse this book of mine.

2

No longer for the Roman dame
My second from my first is brought;
Where once the Roman legions fought
No terror has the Roman name.
My whole is master of the soil,
And reaps in peace the fruits of toil.

3

A product of coniferous trees,
A hardy toiler of the seas;
These make when joined and matched
A Russian scratched.

I make this statement wholly on
The authority of Napoleon.

(ANSWERS OVERLEAF)

---

* Riverside Press, Cambridge, 1894.
† Colonial Press, Boston, 1895.

ANSWERS (by Ballard)

1

Have you heard of the wonderful 'one-hoss *shay*',
    That ran a century to a day,
Then stopped and shivered as if af*raid*?
    Aha! But I've answered the first *charade*.

2

No galleys now bring *myrrh* from *far*
    To stately dames of Rome;
Where Caesar drove his conquering car
    Now stands the *farmer*'s home.

3

Tar is the blood of pine trees, shed
    To save the gallant *tar*.
Napoleon had cause to dread
    The '*Tartars*' of the Tsar.

CHARISMA AT THE OCTAGONAL ROUND TABLE

When I to tell a Howler thirst,
I soften up my Hearers first,
And get them in a Laughing Mood,
For otherwise they might be Rude,
And say to Wait till after Lunch,
Or drown my Punch line in the Punch.
I offer to hang up their Hats,
Put out their Dogs and walk their Cats.
I pour Martinis in their Beers,
And tickle them behind the Ears.
And when I have that little band
Right in the Hollow of my Hand,
I spring my Masterpiece of Wit. . . .
They never see the point of it.

W. R. E.

My first last line for 'Charisma' read: 'and laugh until they think
I'll split'. Was I wrong in substituting 'They never see the point
of it'?

Chronograms

In the days when Roman numerals for the Year of Our Lord were more common than they are now, they were occasionally used in wordplay. XL, for instance, in sound is *excel*, in sense 'forty'. MIX is both *mix* and 1009. Holofernes is indulging in this sort of word game when he says in *Love's Labour's Lost*:

If sore be sore, then L to sore makes fifty sores;
O sore L!
Of one sore I an hundred make, by adding but one more L.

'This kind of wit,' Addison wrote in *The Spectator*, 'appears very often on modern medals, especially those of Germany, when they represent in the inscription the year in which they were coined. Thus we see on a medal of Gustavus Adolphus the following words—*ChrIstVs DuX ergo triVMphVs*'. If you take the pains to pick the figures out of the several words and range them in their proper order, you will find they amount to MDCXVVVII, or 1627, the year in which the medal was stamped; for, as some of the letters distinguish themselves from the rest and overtop their fellows, they are to be considered in a double capacity, both as letters and as figures.'

It is said that Michael Stifelius, a Lutheran minister at Wirtemberg, predicted that the world would end on October 3, 1533, at ten o'clock. He had figured this out by analysing John xix, 37— 'They shall look on Him whom they pierced.' The Latin of this is *Videbvnt In qvem transfixervnt*, which the good divine rendered *VIDebVnt In qVeM transfIXerVnt*, making MDXVVVVIII, or 1533. How he arrived at the day, month and hour is not revealed. At any event, that year, month, day, and hour did arrive, and as Stifelius was preaching to the congregation, a violent storm arose, convincing many that the prophecy was coming true. Fortunately for us, but perhaps unfortunately for Stifelius, the rage in the sky passed quickly, only to reappear in the hearts of the congregation, who dragged Stifelius from his pulpit and thrashed him.

One more note, and I think we shall have had enough of chronograms:

The death of Queen Elizabeth gave rise to the line
  'My Day Closed Is In Immortality'

The initial letters, in order, are MDCIII, or 1603, the year she died. A perfect chronogram, but I doubt whether by exhuming it I have resurrected the art.

Clerihews

Before the first world war, an English journalist named Edmund Clerihew Bentley developed the novel verse form which bears his middle name. A clerihew is an irreverent, unscanned rhyming quatrain upon a fanciful biographical theme, always beginning with the name of its subject. For instance:

Sir James Jeans
Always says what he means;
He is really perfectly serious
About the Universe being Mysterious.

The four men listed below are among the subjects of Mr. Bentley's sly attentions. Try writing your own clerihews about them; then compare your proficiency with Mr. Bentley's.

1. Alfred de Musset
2. George the Third
3. John Stuart Mill
4. Sir Christopher Wren

ANSWERS

1

Alfred de Musset
Used to call his cat Pusset.
His accent was affected.
This was to be expected.

2

George the Third
Ought never to have occurred.
One can only wonder
At so grotesque a blunder.

3

John Stuart Mill
By a mighty effort of will
Overcame his natural bonhomie
And wrote 'Principles of Practical Economy'.

4

Sir Christopher Wren
Said 'I am going to dine with some men.
If anyone calls
Say I am designing St. Paul's.'

74

Clichés, Platitudes and Proverbs

The other day a book reviewer wrote of a novelist: 'If she can think of a handy epithet that will do the work, she appropriates it, even if it *is* worn by time. Damsels are fair, waves are mountainous, doom imminent, chases merry, vows silent and people are in a brown study. Correspondence is regular, and is maintained, too; problems are turned over in the mind, rooms tastefully furnished; hope soars and death's breath is icy.'

He was having at the cliché, as common a target for erudite attack as the pun. 'A cliché,' says Partridge, 'is an outworn commonplace; a phrase (or virtual phrase) that has become so hackneyed that scrupulous speakers and writers shrink from it because they feel that its use is an insult to the intelligence of their auditor or audience, reader or public . . . They range from fly-blown phrases (*explore every avenue*) through soubriquets that have lost all point and freshness (*the Iron Duke*) to quotations that have become debased currency (*cups that cheer but do not inebriate*), metaphors that are now pointless, and formulas that have become mere counters (*far be it from me to . . .*).'

All very well. Yet Partridge's own 'fly-blown phrase' is next door to being a cliché. Not, perhaps, for the purposes of literature, but certainly for those of everyday intercourse, I suggest that the job is rather to be clear than to be brilliant. Clichés, for most of us, including fine writers, are like old clothes, useful for everyday, even if we hastily change when we see the rector approaching the house.

If there is a fault of language worse than a cliché, and I can think of several, it is a tortured effort to *avoid* a cliché. The results are less often funny than embarrassing. Most of us, in the first place, do not have the kind of facility that is required for verbal gymnastics; or, even if we have, we are not going to make the effort twenty-four hours a day, any more than the world's fastest runner is going to do hundred-yard sprints all day long. We are not so stupid.

Agreed that most clichés have long lost their lustre (if they are supposed to shine) or their cutting edge (if they are supposed to be sharp). Yet they have endured because no better statement of the case has come along. When one does, it will become a cliché in its turn.

The poem below is built around a series of proverbs so hackneyed that I suspect you will scarcely notice that key words are missing. But does that make the poem itself hackneyed? Bosh!

THE LADDY WHO LIVED BY THE BOOK

O sad is the story of Reginald Rory, a laddy who lived by the book;
If the longest way round was the ******** *** ****, why, the
   longest way Reginald took.
No chickens he counted before they were *******, nor yet wasted
   his tears on spilt ****,
Nor lopped with his shears at a lady pig's ears as a way to make
   purses of ****.

His best monologue was 'Love me love my ***,' although once in
   awhile he'd exclaim,
'It isn't the winning or ****** that counts, but the manner of
   playing the ****.'
He ran the good **** and he fought the good *****, and he
   thought an extremely good think;
He often led horses to *****, but never insisted they *****.

Well, all roads lead to **** as their ultimate home, and our
   Reginald's led him there too;
And he well understood that in Rome it is good to do as the
   good ****** **.
When he found they cohabit as fast as a rabbit, he resolved to
   leave no stone ********
To match their example; he tried a free sample, and got himself
   horribly burned.

Moral:
One *should* sometimes **** a gift horse in the *****, inasmuch as
   to *** is but human.
He wouldn't have trusted a ***** bearing gifts, but he thought
   the Greek girl was a Roman.

W. R. E.

ANSWER
Shortest way home; hatched; milk; silk; dog; losing; game; race; fight;
water; drink; Rome; Romans do; unturned; look; mouth; err; Greek.

THE CLICHÉ EXPERT TAKES THE STAND

The best evidence that the cliché is indestructible is that it has withstood even the assaults of Frank Sullivan, who all his life has been fouling clichés in their own nests and hoisting them by their own petards. For *The New Yorker* he created Mr. Arbuthnot, the cliché expert, who was regularly grilled in the pages of the magazine along the lines below.

Q. Mr. Arbuthnot, as an expert in the use of the cliché, are you prepared to testify here today regarding its application in topics of love, sex, matrimony and the like?
A. I am.
Q. Very good. Now, Mr. Arbuthnot, what's love?
A. Love is blind.
Q. Good. What does love do?
A. Love makes the world go round.
Q. Whom does a young man fall in love with?
A. With the Only Girl in the World.
Q. They are then said to be?
A. Victims of Cupid's darts.
Q. And he?
A. Whispers sweet nothings in her ear.
Q. Describe the Only Girl in the World.
A. Her eyes are like stars. Her teeth are like pearls. Her lips are ruby. Her cheek is damask, and her form divine.
Q. Haven't you forgotten something?
A. Eyes, teeth, lips, cheek, form—no, sir, I don't think so.
Q. Her hair?
A. Oh, certainly. How stupid of me. She has hair like spun gold.
Q. Very good, Mr. Arbuthnot. Now will you describe the Only Man?
A. He is a blond Viking, a he-man, and a square-shooter who plays the game. There is something about him that rings true, and he has kept himself pure and clean so that when he meets the girl of his choice, the future mother of his children, he can look her in the eye.
Q. How?
A. Without flinching.
Q. Now, Mr. Arbuthnot, when the Only Man falls in love, madly, with the Only Girl, what does he do?

77

A. He walks on air.

Q. Yes, I know, but what is it he pops?

A. Oh, excuse me. The question, of course.

Q. Than what do they plight?

A. Their troth.

Q. Mr. Arbuthnot, your explanation of the correct application of the cliché in these matters has been most instructive, and I know that all of us cliché-users here will know exactly how to respond hereafter when, during a conversation, sex—when sex—ah—

A. I think what you want to say is 'When sex rears its ugly head', isn't it?

Q. Thank you, Mr. Arbuthnot. Thank you very much.

A. Thank *you*.

Cockney

FRAMED IN A FIRST-STOREY WINDER

Framed in a first-storey winder of a burnin' buildin'
Appeared: A Yuman Ead!

Jump into this net, wot we are 'oldin'
And yule be quite orl right!

But 'ee wouldn't jump . . .
And the flames grew Igher and Igher and Igher.
(Phew!)

Framed in a second-storey winder of a burnin' buildin'
Appeared: A Yuman Ead!

Jump into this net, wot we are 'oldin'
And yule be quite orl right!

But 'ee wouldn't jump . . .
And the flames grew Igher and Igher and Igher
(Strewth!)

Framed in a third-storey winder of a burnin' buildin'
Appeared: A Yuman Ead!

78

Jump into this net wot we are 'oldin'
And yule be quite orl right!
Honest!
And 'ee jumped . . .
And 'ee broke 'is bloomin' neck!

Anonymous

EPITAPH ON A MARF

Wot a marf 'e'd got,
Wot a marf.
When 'e was a kid,
Goo' Lor' luv'll
'Is pore old muvver
Must 'a' fed 'im wiv a shuvvle.

Wot a gap 'e'd got,
Pore chap,
'E'd never been known to larf,
'Cos if 'e did
It's a penny to a quid
'E'd 'a' split 'is face in 'arf.

Anonymous

RHYMING SLANG

In my childhood, 'See you later alligator' was considered the height of wit. If we had thought to condense the expression to plain 'alligator', we should have been using something like rhyming slang.

In this light-hearted Cockney locution, the speaker substitutes a rhyming word or phrase for the one that is meant. 'Fire' becomes 'Anna Mariah'; 'stairs', 'apples and pears'; 'tram', 'baa-lamb'; 'ticket', 'bat and wicket', and so on. To make matters still more difficult for the uninitiated, the rhyming expressions are often condensed, so that the rhyme itself disappears. Thus, a man may say, 'You'd 'ardly Adam it; 'is trouble's going to have another Gawdfer.' Here 'Adam' is short for 'Adam and Eve', 'trouble' for 'trouble and strife', and 'Gawdfer' for 'God forbid'. The intended

79

words are 'believe', 'wife', and 'kid'. In 'Shut yer north, yer a Dunlop', further complications are introduced: 'North' is the opposite of 'south', which rhymes with 'mouth'; 'Dunlop' is a kind of tyre, which rhymes with 'liar'. So: 'Shut your mouth, you're a liar.'

Rhyming slang was developed by London pickpockets and vagabonds in the nineteenth century to outwit the police. The following examples are from the book *Up the Frog*, by Sydney ('Steak') T. Kendall.

1. Up the *apples and pears* to *lemon squash* me *Ramsgate Sands*.
2. D'yer want any *fisherman's daughter* wiv yer *pimple and blotch*?
3. 'E's only got one *mince pie* and 'e's as *Mutt an' Jeff* as anyfink.
4. I've got to take the *cock sparrer* up the *Dolly Varden* fer some *rosebuds*.
5. Shove this *saucepan lid* in your *sky rocket*.

(The shorthand versions of the foregoing expressions would be considerably more difficult to translate. They are: 1. Up the apples to lemon me Ramsgates; 2. D'yer want any fisherman's wiv yer pimple?; 3. 'E's only got one mince and 'e's mutt'n as anyfink; 4. I've got to take the cock sparrer up the Dolly for some roses; and, 5. Shove this saucepan in yer sky.)

ANSWERS

1. Upstairs to wash my hands.
2. Do you want any water with your Scotch?
3. He's only got one eye and he's as deaf as anything.
4. I have to take the barrow up to Covent Garden for some potatoes (spuds).
5. Shove this quid in your pocket.

UP THE FROG

I was taking the cherry 'og for a ball o' chalk up the frog and toad the other night, when I met a China plate o' mine. We 'ad a few dicky birds an' then 'e suggested we 'ad a tumble dahn the sink together.

Well, instead of going into the Red Lion, we went into the first rub-a-dub we comes to. I sez 'what are you going to 'ave?' 'E sez, 'I'll 'ave a drop o' pig's ear,' so I gets a pint o' pig's ear for 'im an' I 'ad a drop of needle and pin, just for a start.

We got chatting an' one fing led to a-uvver when we 'ears the Guv'nor calling 'Time, gents please!'

I could 'ardly Adam and Eve it that we 'ad bin at it so long. So I gets an Aristotle of In-and-out for the plates and dishes, picks up the cherry 'og an' orf we Scarpa Flow.

As it's so 'Arry Tate I gets on a trouble an' fuss, an' when I gets 'ome, I find the plates 'n' dishes is out 'avin' a butcher's 'ook round the rub-a-dubs for me and the cherry 'og. So I gets up the apples and pears an' into the ol' Uncle Ned and when she comes in, there I am wiv me loaf o' bread on the weeping willow, readin' the linen draper. She starts a few early birds but I don't want no bull and cow, so I turns over an' in a couple o' cock linnets I'm Bo-Peep.

Sydney T. Kendall

ANSWER

I was taking the dog for a walk up the road the other night, when I met a mate of mine. We had a few words and then he suggested we had a drink together.

Well, instead of going into the Red Lion, we went into the first pub we came to.

I said, 'What are you going to have?' He said, 'I'll have a drop of beer,' so I got a pint of beer for him and I had a drop of gin, for a start.

We got chatting and one thing led to another, when we hear the landlord calling, 'Time, Gents, please!'

I could hardly believe that we had been at it for so long, so I got a bottle of stout for the missus, picked up the dog and off we go.

As it's so late I got on a bus and when I got home, I found the missus is out having a look round the pubs for me and the dog. So I got upstairs and into bed, and when she came in, there I was with my head on the pillow, reading the paper.

She started having a few words but I didn't want a row, so I turned over, and in a couple of minutes I was asleep.

Colourful Words

The opening letters of each of the words defined below spell a colour, which may or may not have anything to do with the meaning of the whole word.

1. A disease
2. A flower
3. A goblin
4. An insect
5. A keep
6. Lessen
7. An old man
8. Used in school
9. A weapon

ANSWERS

1. Pinkeye
2. Bluebell
3. Brownie
4. Bluebottle
5. Dungeon
6. Reduce
7. Greybeard
8. Blackboard
9. Bayonet

Controlling the Language Explosion

I have an acquaintance who is writing quite an important paper on the threat of unbridled population growth, which he calls 'pollulation': very clever, and I can see why he finds the word irresistible. But are all these new words really necessary?

Why do so many people worry about the population explosion, and so few about the language explosion? Words, like people, when they multiply too fast, crowd into slums, lose their innocence in the hour of their birth, and decay before they have time to mature. Charles W. Ferguson points out that Dr. Samuel Johnson's *Dictionary*, published in 1755, contained but 58,000 words; Noah Webster's, in 1828, offered 70,000; and the current Webster's *Unabridged* carries well over 600,000, with another 400,000 technical terms waiting in the wings. Professor Albert H. Marckwardt of the University of Michigan adds that the next two centuries may see an increase of the total English vocabulary to more than two million words.

There is probably no author in the language from whose works, however voluminous, as many as 10,000 words could be collected. Few of us use as many as 5000 in conversation. Our dictionaries are bulked out with words that are useless save to the specialist, and not always to him. As Bombaugh remarks, 'What man in his senses would use zythepsary for a brewhouse, and zymologist for a brewer; would talk of a stormy day as procellous and himself as madefied; of his long-legged son as increasing in procerity but sadly marcid; of having met with such procacity from such a one; of a bore as a macrologist; of an aged horse as macrobiotic; of important business as moliminous, and his daughter's necklace as moniliform; of some one's talk as meracious, and lament his last night's nimiety of wine at that dapatical feast, whence he was taken by ereption?'

The language explosion has become ridiculous. I suggest an end to sentimentality. Let us begin throwing unwanted words out into the snow to perish, as the Spartans did with their girl babies.

Better still, let us carry out a verbal vasectomy on all writers, excepting only two or three dozen selected poets. I should be tempted to include even them, but the ones I have excepted are long dead.

Crossing Jokes

David Frost, the television interviewer, has a speciality called 'crossing jokes'. He puts two names together to get a third. If you can solve the crossing jokes below, he may invite you to appear on his programme. Then again he may not. Anyhow, here are the three jokes.

1. Cross a cowboy with a gourmet and you get a . . .
2. Cross Jimmy Durante with an employment agency and you get a . . .
3. Cross a zebra with an ape-man and you get . . .

ANSWERS: 1. Hopalong Casserole. 2. Nose job.
3. Tarzan Stripes Forever.

Cryptograms

A cryptogram being merely a coded message, it can scarcely be considered a literary form; a sonnet would have to be written in the clear before it could be encoded. Still, cryptograms do pop up

83

in books and stories, especially when international hanky-panky is involved. The following substitution cipher is from Poe's *The Gold-Bug*:

'53##+305))6*;4826)4#.)4#);806*;48+8%60))85;1#(;:#*8+
83(88)5*+;46(;88*96*?;8)*#(;485);5*+2:*#(;4956*2(5*−
4)8%8*;4069285);)6+8)4##;1(#9;48081;8;8#1;48+85;4)485+
528806*81(#9;48;(88;4(#?34;48)4#;161;:188;#?;'

William LeGrand, who solved the cryptogram in Poe's story, started with the knowledge that by far the most common letter in English is e, followed in order, as he thought, by a o i d h n r s t u y c f g l m w b k p q x z. (*The World Book Encyclopaedia* agrees on the primacy of e, but puts the other letters in quite a different order: t r i n o a s d l c h f u p m y g w v b x k q j z. Poe forgot the letters j and v altogether.)

The most common character in the cryptogram was 8, which appeared thirty-three times. LeGrand therefore concluded that 8 represented e.* He next listed each set of three characters ending in 8. The most frequent of these trios was ;48. LeGrand assumed that these represented the word 'the.' He now had three of his letters—e, t, and h—as well as an indication of the beginning and end of several words. Continuing in this fashion, he soon arrived at his solution. I trust that you, building on the clues already given (and bearing in mind that Poe treats #), +1, 92, :3 and −. as single characters) can do as well. In any event, you will find the solution on the next page.

Morse code is a form of cryptogram; so is journalistic cable-ese; so is shorthand. Francis Bacon developed a substitution cipher in which each letter of the alphabet is represented by five letters, each of which is either a or b. Thus the letter a becomes aaaaa; b, aaaab; c, aaaba; and so on. You can attain the same result by substituting for a and b a long and short straw, a circle and triangle, or any other symbol you find convenient.

In a substitution cipher the letters of the message remain in their proper order. In a transposition cipher they are rearranged.

---

* If the man who wrote the puzzle had held down his e's deliberately, or even omitted them, as in a lipogram, the solution would have been more difficult, though far from impossible.

There is nothing to prevent the cryptogrammer from employing both transposition and substitution in the same code, or piling one substitution on another. For me, however, the most elementary substitution code is quite difficult enough to riddle. The expert will solve these two at a glance:

1. NW SHQW EVHOWP OSHUBWR YA STBS WDEVYRTQW LJPWU WQWUC YJW YA KSW GUTPBWR VWHPTJB AUYI KSW KYNJ NSWJ NW UWOWTQW NYUP AUYI CYL NW NTVV GVYN KSWI LE HJP KSLR TRYVHKW KSW OTKC AYU ALKLUW IWRRHBWR NW NTVV LRW KSW JWN OYPW.

2. BAY BQ WKY XOHMYHV KYHY RV GCRWY O LBBM VBHW BQ QYIIBX R OT VCHY WKOW KY XRII KYIU TY WB YVNOUY RQ R NOA LHYOVY KRV UOIT XRWK QRQWE GCRM RQ EBC NOA HORVY WKY NOVK IYW TY JABX OAM R VKOII OHHOALY QBH KRT WB LYW RW QHBT EBC.

ANSWERS

The 'Gold-Bug' cryptogram reads:

'A good glass in the bishop's hostel in the devil's seat forty-one degrees and thirteen minutes northeast and by north main branch seventh limb east side shoot from the left eye of the death's-head a bee-line from the tree through the shot fifty feet out.'

I am aware that the solution may appear almost as impenetrable as the cryptogram. For clarification, and considerable entertainment, I suggest that you re-read *The Gold-Bug*.

As for the other cryptograms (taken from *One Hundred Problems in Cipher*, by Louis C. Mansfield), here are the messages conveyed:

1. We have placed charges of high explosive under every one of the bridges leading from the town. When we receive word from you we will blow them up and thus isolate the city. For future messages we will use the new code.

2. One of the warders here is quite a good sort of fellow. I am sure that he will help me to escape if I can grease his palm with fifty quid. If you can raise the cash, let me know, and I shall arrange for him to get it from you.

Cumulative Verses

In the days when most American newspapers had 'funny' departments, it was not uncommon for one paper to print a few lines built around printers' marks, to which other papers would add. For instance:

THE ARAB AND HIS DONKEY

An Arab came to the river side,
  With a donkey bearing an †;
But he would not try to ford the tide,
  For he had too good an *.
Boston Globe

So he camped all night by the river side,
  And remained till the tide had ceased to swell,
For he knew should the donkey from life subside,
  He never would find its ‖.
Salem Sunbeam

When the morning dawned, and the tide was out,
  The pair crossed over 'neath Allah's protection
And the Arab was happy, we have no doubt,
  For he had the best donkey in all that §.
Somerville Journal

You are wrong, they were drowned in crossing over,
  Though the donkey was bravest of all his race;
He luxuriates now in horse-heaven clover
  And his master has gone to the Prophet's em ⌒.
Elevated Railway Journal

These asinine poets deserve to be 'blowed',
  Their rhymes being faulty, and frothy and beery;
What really befell the ass and its load
  Will ever remain a desolate ?
Paper and Print

Our Yankee friends, with all their ——
  For once, we guess, their mark have missed;
And with poetry *Paper and Print* is rash
  In damming its flow with it's editor's 👉

In parable and moral leave a # between
  For reflection, or your wits fall out of joint;
The 'Arab', ye see, is a printing machine,
  And the donkey is he who can't see the .
                    British and Colonial Printer

For those unfamiliar with the ways of proof-readers, † is an obelisk; * is an asterisk; ‖, parallel; §, section; ⁀, brace, bring together; ?, query; ——, dash; 👉, fist; #, space, put a space between; and . , of course, full point.

D

Defiant Definitions

Name each of the words defined here. The words are given below.

1. A fraudulent abstraction of money.
2. Ornamental open work in fine gold or silver wire.
3. The camelopard.
4. To put to death by fixing on a stake.
5. A minute parasitic fungus that causes decay in vegetable matter.
6. To withdraw from a purpose.
7. A buttery.
8. An elevated, broad, flat area of land.
9. Easily rubbed down, crumbled, or pulverised.
10. The forepart of a ship.
11. To compose or write; to direct or dictate.

12. To charge with a crime or misdemeanour in due form of law.
13. State appointed or predetermined; fate, invincible necessity.
14. To talk familiarly.
15. To arise or come; to be added.
16. An absurd story; a false rumour.
17. Sending out a flood of light; gleaming; splendid.
18. An Egyptian peasant
19. Vast grassy plains in South America.
20. A person with full power to act for another.

ANSWERS

1. Defalcation	11. Indite
2. Filigree	12. Indict
3. Giraffe	13. Destiny
4. Impale	14. Confabulate
5. Mildew	15. Accrue
6. Resile	16. Canard
7. Pantry	17. Effulgent
8. Plateau	18. Fellah
9. Friable	19. Llanos or pampas
10. Prow	20. Plenipotentiary

Disemvowelled Proverbs

In each of the following lines, insert the same vowel the number of times indicated to restore a proverb.

1. ASTTCHNTMESAVESNNE (4).
2. ABRDNTHEHANDSWORTHTWONTHEBUSH (4).
3. GFURTHERDWRSE (3).
4. ERLYTOBEDNDERLYTORISEMKESMNHELTHYWE LTHYNDWISE (9).
5. BTTRLATTHANNVR (5).
6. ALLSWLLTHATNDSWLL (3).

ANSWERS

1. A stitch in time saves nine. 2. A bird in the hand is worth two in the bush. 3. Go further, do worse. 4. Early to bed and early to rise makes a man healthy, wealthy and wise. 5. Better late than never. 6. All's well that ends well.

Double-entendres

W. H. Auden recently noted that Miss Rose Fyleman, a child's author, best known for her *There Are Fairies at the Bottom of My Garden*, is responsible for such bemusingly innocent *double-entendres* as:

> There are no wolves in England any more;
> The fairies have driven them all away

and

> My fairy muff is made of pussy-willow

and

> The best thing the fairies do, the best thing of all
> Is sliding down steeples—you know they're very tall.
> Climb up the weather-cock, and, when you hear it crow,
> Fold your wings, and clutch your things, and then—
>   Let go!

Dutch Widows, Irish Beauties, Scotch Warming-pans

Do you recall how, in 1968, the Republican candidate for the Vice-Presidency of the United States was roundly scolded by the Press for referring to a newsman of Japanese background as a 'fat Jap'? The furore reflected the increased sensitivity of English-speaking people to the feelings of persons belonging to alien or minority groups. We may tell it like it is in matters of sex and defaecation, but increasingly we withdraw the savour from the salt in describing those who differ from ourselves in appearance, accent or background. This inhibition is, as President Hoover said of Prohibition, an experiment noble in purpose; but it may not be altogether a good thing.

   Language reflects attitudes. At their lowest ebb, members of a despised group pay little attention to the epithets used to describe them; they are too busy staying alive. As they make their inevitable way into the mainstream, however, they become self-conscious, and ask for relief from terms that remind them of their earlier state. Once they are completely accepted by society, the whole thing becomes a joke; the president of a department store chain no longer rages when called a Mick, but chuckles.

If members of any minority or outside group object to what they are called, I am all for changing the epithet to whatever they prefer. No epithet, however, can be dissociated from its unspoken meaning to the one who says it and the one who hears it.

According to H. L. Mencken in *American Language*:

One may say *Chinese*, but not *Chinaman, Chink*, or *Chinee*; *German*, but not *squarehead, boche, heinie, hun, kraut*, or *sausage*; *Hungarian* or *Bohemian*, but not *Hunky* or *Bohunk*; *Japanese*, but not *Jap* or *Nip*; *Korean*, but not *gook*; *Vietnamese*, but not *geek*; *Greek*, but not *greaseball*. Nor may one call an East Indian by our fathers' epithet, *wog*, acronym for 'wily oriental gentleman'.

You are not to call a Frenchman a *frog*, nor to refer to *French leave*, the *French pox* (syphilis), or a *French letter* (condom). (The French, for their part, have the effrontery to call a condom a *capote anglaise*. They also call lice *Spaniards* and fleas *female Spaniards*. The Prussians, in turn, call lice *Frenchmen*, while other Germans call cockroaches *Prussians*.)

Ever since the seventeenth-century naval rivalry between the Dutch and the English, the English have used 'Dutch' as an epithet of derision. Under today's rules, though, one must drop all reference to *in Dutch* (in trouble); a *Dutch widow* (prostitute); a *Dutch bargain* (made in one's cups); *Dutch courage* (produced by alcohol); a *Dutch treat* (where each pays for himself); a *Dutch wife* (bolster); and *Dutch comfort* (no comfort at all).

Just dropping Irish pejoratives will leave a deep hole in your vocabulary. Farewell to *mick, harp, flannel mouth, biddy*! Never again can you call a woman with two black eyes an *Irish beauty*; or perjury *Irish evidence*; or a spade an *Irish spoon*; or thick legs *Irish legs*; or a police station an *Irish clubhouse*; or a demotion an *Irish rise*; or a fast an *Irishman's dinner*; or a wheelbarrow an *Irish chariot* ('the greatest of human inventions, since it taught the Irish to walk on their hind legs').

Who today would dare call an Italian a *guinea*, a *Tony*, or a *wop* (from *guappo*, a Neapolitan term for a showy, pretentious fellow)? Who would call a Mexican a *greaser*, or a Panamanian a *spick* ('No spik Inglis')?

Then there are the Jews. No longer is a *kike* a Jew who has left the room. No longer may one assert social superiority by referring to *yids, sheenies*, or *mockies*. No longer dare we 'jew the man down' when we are persuading him to reduce his asking price. Efforts have even been made to turn the humble *jews harp* into a *jaws harp*.

It is closed season on the Scots, too. That they allegedly do not like being called Scotch did not, until recently, prevent our referring to the itch as the *Scotch fiddle*; a loose girl as a *Scotch warming-pan*; hot water flavoured with burnt biscuit as *Scotch coffee*; or a two-quart bottle as a *Scotch pint*. To the English, Scotland was *Itchland*, *Scratchland*, or *Louseland*. Never more!

The Negroes in the United States are a special case. In the early nineteenth century, they were called *blacks* (as, in a curious historical echo, many wish to be called today); later, *Africans*; still later, *darkies* (not invidiously at the start); then briefly, and by very few, *Africo-Americans*; still more briefly, following the Civil War, *freedmen*; in the 1880s, as again today, *Afro-Americans*. There was an effort, now largely abandoned, to break them down into *mulattos* (halfbreeds), *quadroons* (quarter-breeds), and *octaroons* (eighth-breeds). They were also called *coons, shines, smokes, dinges, boogies, eightballs, jazzbos, jigaboos, snowballs, spades, jigs,* and *crows*.

Because of its association of contempt, blacks particularly hate the word *nigger*. Such once-common expressions as *nigger heaven* and *nigger in the woodpile* are now unmentionables.

Curiously, as some derogatory terms go on the Forbidden Index, others emerge. The G.I. in Vietnam, for instance, has become a *grunt*. To young demonstrators, police are *pigs*. Militant blacks call whites *ofay*, perhaps Pig Latin for 'foe'.

E

Echoing Words

Echoism and onomatopoeia mean the same thing—the formation of words by imitation of sounds, as in the *hiss* of a goose or the *click* of a camera. There once was a conjecture, called variously the 'bow wow theory', the 'pooh pooh theory', and the 'ding dong theory', that sounds from nature played a major part in the origin and growth of language; but no-one seems to take much stock in that notion any more.

Except when combined with other devices, onomatopoeia plays a rather trivial role in literature. An example of sorts is Shakespeare's

> Hark, hark!
> Bow-wow.
> The watch-dogs bark!
> Bow-wow.
> Hark, hark! I hear
> The strain of strutting chanticleer
> Cry 'Cock-a-doodle-doo!'

Here, *bark*, *bow-wow*, and *cock-a-doodle-doo* are onomatopoeic words, while *hark* reinforces *bark*. There are many other words whose sounds suggest their thrust; it has been pointed out, for instance, that in *flicker*, the *fl* suggests moving light, the *i* suggests smallness, the *ck* suggests sudden cessation of movement (as in *crack*, *peck*, *pick*, *hack*, and *flick*), and the *er* suggests repetition.

In each line below I have left out an onomatopoeic word. Using the clues (which are in no particular order) guess the missing words. (It may help to know that the second and fourth lines of each stanza rhyme.)

1

*****, whip!
Train, *****!
***, horse!
****-****!

2

Brook, ******!
Fountain, ******!
*******, faucet!
****, wash!

3
****, saw!
*****, glue!
****, train!
****-****!

4
***, sheep!
***, cow!
*****, frog!
(***-***!)

5
Bell, ****,
****-****!
(Gun: ****!
End of song.)

To solve the puzzle, look first for the sounds associated with: a bee (though there is no bee in the verse), a dog, a starting steam train, the train after starting, a gun, a sheep, a whip, a cow, a frog, a bell (two variants). Among the other onomatopoeias, one means a series of short, inarticulate, speechlike sounds (a verb here); another is a light, clear, metallic note; and a third is the cry of an owl. It is useful to remember that the same sound may have more than one source.

Of the words whose sounds somehow suggest their meaning, one means to pant; one, to dash water about; one, to adhere; one, to let drops of liquid fall; one, to run at a slow, steady trot; one, to drop in a thin, gentle stream.

ANSWERS:

1	3	5
Crack, whip!	Buzz, saw!	Bell, ring,
Train, chuff!	Stick, glue!	Ding-dong!
Jog, horse!	Hoot, train!	(Gun: BANG!
Puff-puff!	Choo-choo!	End of song.)

2	4
Brook, babble!	Baa, sheep!
Fountain, splash!	Moo, cow!
Trickle, faucet!	Croak, frog!
Drip, wash!	(Bow-wow!)

ECHOING TRIOLET

O, let me try a triolet!
O, let me try! O, let me try
A triolet to win my pet!
O, let me try a triolet,
And if the triolet's all wet,
I'll try a letter on the sly.
O, let me try a triolet!
O, let me try! O, let me try!

W. R. E.

*

THE ELEPHANT, OR THE FORCE OF HABIT

A tail behind, a trunk in front,
Complete the usual elephant.
The tail in front, the trunk behind,
Is what you very seldom find.

If you for specimens should hunt
With trunks behind and tails in front,
The hunt would occupy you long;
The force of habit is so strong.

A. E. Housman

*

Epigrams

An epigram is a brief comment, often in rhyme, which closes
with a sudden surprising or witty turn. A Latin poet laid down
its criteria as follows:

The qualities rare in a bee that we meet,
In an epigram never should fail.
The body should always be little and sweet,
And a sting should be left in the tail.

94

Coleridge's definition was more succinct:

> What is an epigram? A dwarfish whole,
> Its body brevity, and wit its soul.

Alexander Pope's best-remembered verse consists of such epigrammatic couplets as

> Why has not man a microscopic eye?
> For this plain reason—man is not a fly.

and

> Vice is a monster of so frightful mien
> As, to be hated, needs but to be seen;
> Yet seen too oft, familiar with her face,
> We first endure, then pity, then embrace.

Lord Rochester wrote this premature epigram-epitaph for King Charles II:

> Here lies our sovereign lord, the King,
> Whose promise none relies on;
> He never said a foolish thing,
> Nor ever did a wise one.

To which the witty monarch rejoined:

'My words are my own, and my actions are my ministers'.'

Some of the best-known modern epigrams are by Hilaire Belloc:

On Lady Poltagrue, a Public Peril

> The Devil, having nothing else to do,
> Went off to tempt My Lady Poltagrue.
> My Lady, tempted by a private whim,
> To his extreme annoyance, tempted him.

On a Dead Hostess

> Of this bad world the loveliest and the best
> Has smiled and said 'Good Night', and gone to rest.

On His Books

When I am dead, I hope it may be said:
'His sins were scarlet, but his books were read.'

Oscar Wilde's epigrams shocked and titillated late Victorian society. "I can resist everything,' he said solemnly, 'except temptation.' Fox-hunting he described as 'the unspeakable in full pursuit of the uneatable'.

Some Wilde epigrams have been scrambled below. Put the words back in order, and then check to see if you are right.

1. Seriously to talk important is ever a far thing about life too.
2. Charming and good people are absurd. To divide either into tedious or bad people is it.
3. Us we are are in at but all some the the stars gutter looking of.
4. The one play cards one winning has always fairly when should.
5. In a sense romance spoils a woman as so much the humour of nothing.
6. To be sure truth tells one later or if one is out the sooner found.
7. The mistakes are never regrets only one's one thing.
8. The nothing knows of everything and the price value of a man who is a cynic.

ANSWERS

1. Life is far too important a thing ever to talk seriously about.
2. It is absurd to divide people into good and bad. People are either charming or tedious.
3. We are all in the gutter, but some of us are looking at the stars.
4. One should always play fairly when one has the winning cards.
5. Nothing spoils a romance so much as a sense of humour in the woman.
6. If one tells the truth, one is sure, sooner or later, to be found out.
7. The only things one never regrets are one's mistakes.
8. A cynic is a man who knows the price of everything, and the value of nothing.

MACAULAY TELLS US

Macaulay tells us Byron's rules of life
Were: Hate your neighbour; love your neighbour's wife.

W. R. E.

ON AN AGEING PRUDE

She who, when young and fair,
Would wink men up the stair,
Now, old and ugly, locks
The door where no man knocks.

W. R. E.

Epitaphs

Laughter is as useful a weapon against death as any other, which
is why some of the funniest lines around are on gravestones. The
following epitaphs appear in various collections.

POOR MARTHA SNELL
HER'S GONE AWAY
HER WOULD IF HER COULD
BUT HER COULDN'T STAY;
HER HAD TWO SWOLN LEGS
AND A BADDISH COUGH
BUT HER LEGS IT WAS
AS CARRIED HER OFF

HERE LIES A FATHER OF 29:
THERE WOULD HAVE BEEN MORE
BUT HE DIDN'T HAVE TIME

Dorothy Parker, the wit, proposed for her gravestone the line:

THIS IS ON ME

or, as an alternative,

EXCUSE MY DUST

There is a spurious smell about this inscription, supposedly
from a hypochondriac's tombstone:

I TOLD YOU I WAS SICK

This epitaph for a waiter, too, is doubtless apocryphal:

GOD FINALLY CAUGHT HIS EYE

Occasionally the inscriptions prepared by a surviving spouse reflect something less than utter despair. A French example sets the tone:

> CI-GIT MA FEMME, AH! QU'ELLE EST BIEN
> POUR SON REPOS ET POUR LE MIEN

Similar sentiments of relief have appeared in English:

> HERE LIES MY WIFE
> IN EARTHY MOULD
> WHO WHEN SHE LIVED
> DID NAUGHT BUT SCOLD:
> GOOD FRIENDS GO SOFTLY
> IN YOUR WALKING
> LEST SHE SHOULD WAKE
> AND RISE UP TALKING

> ELIZA ANN
> HAS GONE TO REST;
> SHE NOW RECLINES
> ON ABRAHAM'S BREAST;
> PEACE AT LAST FOR ELIZA ANN
> BUT NOT FOR
> FATHER ABRAHAM

Mourners frequently punned on the name of the late lamented, thus:

On a spinster, Miss Mann:

> HERE LIES ANN MANN;
> SHE LIVED AN OLD MAID
> BUT DIED AN OLD MANN

On Jonathan Fiddle:

> ON THE 22ND OF JUNE
> JONATHAN FIDDLE
> WENT OUT OF TUNE

A gravestone makes an enduring billboard:

SACRED TO THE REMAINS OF
JONATHAN THOMPSON
A PIOUS CHRISTIAN AND
AFFECTIONATE HUSBAND
. . .
HIS DISCONSOLATE WIDOW
CONTINUES TO CARRY ON
HIS GROCERY BUSINESS
AT THE OLD STAND ON
MAIN STREET; CHEAPEST
AND BEST PRICES IN TOWN

It would be a shame if all tombstones tried to be funny, or
even if they were funny inadvertently. The following, one of my
favourites, has a touch of humour, but it is a gentle touch, done
by a gentle soul:

HERE LIE I
MARTIN ELGINBRODDE:
HAE MERCY O' MY SOUL
LORD GOD
AS I WAD SO
WERE I LORD GOD
AND YE WERE
MARTIN ELGINBRODDE

On Sir John Vanbrugh, Architect

Under this stone, reader, survey
Dear Sir John Vanbrugh's house of clay.
Lie heavy on him, earth! for he
Laid many heavy loads on thee.

Abel Evans

On Frank Pixley, Editor

Here lies Frank Pixley, as usual.

Ambrose Bierce

99

Equivocally Speaking

LOVE LETTER

An odd art indeed is 'Equivoque'—the creation of passages which may have quite opposite meanings, according to how you read them. If, after you have read the following letter straight, you go back over it, confining your attention to the odd-numbered lines, you will find that L—— is not really so annoyed with Miss M—— as he makes out to be.

To Miss M——

—The great love I have hitherto expressed for you
is false and I find my indifference towards you
—increases daily. The more I see of you, the more
you appear in my eyes an object of contempt.
—I feel myself every way disposed and determined
to hate you. Believe me, I never had an intention
—to offer you my hand. Our last conversation has
left a tedious insipidity, which has by no means
—given me the most exalted idea of your character.
Your temper would make me extremely unhappy
—and were we united, I should experience nothing but
the hatred of my parents added to the anything but
—pleasure in living with you. I have indeed a heart
to bestow, but I do not wish you to imagine it
—at your service. I could not give it to any one more
inconsistent and capricious than yourself, and less
—capable to do honour to my choice and to my family.
Yes, Miss, I hope you will be persuaded that
—I speak sincerely, and you will do me a favour
to avoid me. I shall excuse you taking the trouble
—to answer this. Your letters are always full of
impertinence, and you have not a shadow of
—wit and good sense. Adieu! adieu! believe me
so averse to you, that it is impossible for me even
—to be your most affectionate friend and humble servant.

L——

Espy's Fables

KING CARTH AND THE SUFFRTTE

Insert 'age' a hundred and some times in the passage below, and you will have the story.

I wr you are unaware that in one of the bygone s, there lived in a remote vill called Anchor a haughty suffrtte who much dispard all men, as if they were a menrie of uncd beasts. Yet she was the object of their er hom; for her vis was fair as the sun, and her cleav far from mer; she mand her men competently, and the meals she prepared were a tasty assembl of cabb, sauss, bls, from, pot, vint wines, and lr beer.

Now, Anchor was under the patron of King Carth of Carth, a Plantnet of ancient line, who by the lever of a few gold coins persuaded the girl's cy parents to pledge her to him in marri— for them an advantous match indeed, since Carth was known as a s and courous ruler.

During the engment, Carth brought her each day ps and ps of ardent ads, together with numerous corss, arriving before her cott at the reins of a mnta carri drawn by six milk-white onrs.

But the suffrtte was in a r; for Carth by this time was so d that he was in his dot. As he descended from the carri she would seize his onr-whip, shout 'Carth must be destroyed!' into his deaf ear, and fillate the poor old man savly. Nor could her umbr be assud. 'So you think I'll sell my herit for a mess of pott?' she would shout. 'Not I! I'll sabot this marri! I'll rav and pill your castle! I'll send you out to for for sil like an onr, and I'll take the reins of the carri myself!'

The king, unable to hear what she was saying, considered her comments only amusing persifl; but not so his entour. To them, the suffrtte's conduct had hopelessly damd her im. 'The bagg treats him like garb, nay, like sew!' they told one another. 'This press no good!'

They determined to salv the situation by taking advant of the girl's desire to drive onrs. To set the st, they camoufld their nts as milk-white onrs and, hitching them to the mnta carri, they invited the haughty suffrtte to take the reins. The onrs promptly broke from control and rampd across the till onto the pl, where the carri shattered in the deep sand. The carn was outrous. The suffrtte's bones, hair, and cartils were scattered about like spaghetti. She died of a haemorrh in the wreck, unmourned; no-one even bothered to apply a band.

The moral: If you have it on your nda to rav and pill Carth, first make sure your onrs are really asses.

ANSWER

I wager you are unaware that in one of the bygone ages, there lived in a remote village called Anchorage a haughty suffragette who much disparaged all men, as if they were a menagerie of uncaged beasts. Yet she was the object of their eager homage; for her visage was fair as the sun, and her cleavage far from meager (U.S.); she managed her menage competently, and the meals she prepared were a tasty assemblage of cabbage, sausages, bagels, fromage, potage, vintage wines, and lager beer.

Now, Anchorage was under the patronage of King Carthage of Carthage, a Plantagenet of ancient lineage, who by the leverage of a few gold coins persuaded the girl's cagey parents to pledge her to him in marriage —for them an advantageous match indeed, since Carthage was known as a sage and courageous ruler.

During the engagement, Carthage brought her each day pages and pages of ardent adages, together with numerous corsages, arriving before her cottage at the reins of a magenta carriage drawn by six milk-white onagers.

But the suffragette was in a rage; for Carthage by this time was so aged that he was in his dotage. As he descended from the carriage she would seize his onager-whip, shout 'Carthage must be destroyed!' into his deaf ear, and flagellate the poor old man savagely. Nor could her umbrage be assuaged. 'So you think I'll sell my heritage for a mess of pottage?' she would shout. 'Not I! I'll sabotage this marriage! I'll ravage and pillage your castle! I'll send you out to forage for silage like an onager, and I'll take the reins of the carriage myself!'

The king, unable to hear what she was saying, considered her comments only amusing persiflage; but not so his entourage. To them, the suffragette's conduct had hopelessly damaged her image. 'The baggage treats him like garbage, nay, like sewage!' they told one another. 'This presages no good!'

They determined to salvage the situation by taking advantage of the girl's desire to drive onagers. To set the stage, they camouflaged their agents as milk-white onagers and, hitching them to the magenta carriage, they invited the haughty suffragette to take the reins. The onagers promptly broke from control and rampaged across the tillage onto the plage, where the carriage shattered in the deep sand. The carnage was outrageous. The suffragette's bones, hair, and cartilages were scattered about like spaghetti. She died of a haemorrhage in the wreckage, unmourned; no-one even bothered to apply a bandage.

The moral: If you have it on your agenda to ravage and pillage Carthage, first make sure your onagers are really asses.

OLÉ, OLO!

Insert 'olo' as needed, and you need not turn to the completed version to read this thought-provoking story.

An old anthgy reveals how a Cmbian named Pnius, idegically unsound and a notorious gig, found himself bigically drawn to Madame Dres, a cratura from Crado who sang ss and blew the picc at the Cnial Opera House. Pnius put his fairest phrasegy into his suit, but wás so injudicious as to use calumnious termingy against La Dres's true love, a p-playing cnel from a Cgne regiment. Contemptuously rebuffed, the gig came in his dur to Master Hfernes, a well-known astrger, whom he prayed to use astrgical arts to eliminate the offending cnel. Hfernes, his mind on certain tautgies he wished to strike from a hgraph, absently lifted his cyes from a semicn in the cphon on the title page and suggested: 'Why not cut down the cnel with your b as he strolls with Dres along the Cnnade?' 'Absurd!' cried the contemptible gig. 'You give me a pain in the cn! You are full of bney! This cnel is a cssus of a man, a veritable Mch to his enemies! His rage borders on the mythgical! If I were to confront him, we all should perish in the hcaust!' 'That being so,' said the astrger, 'why come to me? I am no sn, much less a Smon. I can only suggest that you go to the cnel and apgise.' So saying, he picked up his hgraph and departed, insouciantly dancing the Pnaise.

ANSWER

An old anthology reveals how a Colombian named Polonius, ideologically unsound and a notorious gigolo, found himself biologically drawn to Madame Dolores, a coloratura from Colorado who sang solos and blew the piccolo at the Colonial Opera House. Polonius put his fairest phraseology into his suit, but was so injudicious as to use calumnious terminology against La Dolores's true love, a polo-playing colonel from a Cologne regiment. Contemptuously rebuffed, the gigolo came in his dolour to Master Holofernes, a well-known astrologer, whom he prayed to use astrological arts to eliminate the offending colonel. Holofernes, his mind on certain tautologies he wished to strike from a holograph, absently lifted his eyes from a semicolon in the colophon on the title page and suggested, 'Why not cut down the colonel with your bolo as he strolls with Dolores along the Colonnade?' 'Absurd!' cried the contemptible gigolo. 'You give me a pain in the colon! You are full of boloney! This colonel is a colossus of a man, a veritable Moloch to his enemies! His rage borders on the mythological; if I were to confront him, we all should perish in the holocaust!' 'That being so,' said the astrologer, 'why come to me? I am no solon, much less a Solomon. I can only suggest that you go to the colonel and apologise.' So saying, he picked up his holograph and departed, insouciantly dancing the Polonaise.

Euphemisms

DIRT IS A DIRTY WORD

An American visiting England discovers quickly that different words are under the ban on the two sides of the ocean. An Englishman restricts the use of *bug* to the *Cimex lectularius*, or common *bedbug*, and hence the word has highly impolite connotations.* All other crawling things he calls *insects*. The English aversion to *bug* has been breaking down of late, however, probably under the influence of such naturalised Americanisms as *jitterbug*, but it yet lingers in ultra-squeamish circles, and a *ladybird* is never called a *ladybug*. Not so long ago *stomach* was on the English *Index*, and such euphemisms as *tummy* and *Little Mary* were used in its place, but of late it has recovered respectability. *Dirt*, to designate earth, and *closet*, in the sense of a cupboard, are seldom used by an Englishman. The former always suggests filth to him, and the latter has obtained the limited use of *water closet*. But the Englishman will innocently use many words and phrases that have indecent significances in the United States, quite lacking in England, e.g., *to be knocked up* (to be tired), *to stay with* (to be the guest of), *screw* (as a noun, meaning salary or pay), *to keep one's pecker up*, *douche* (shower bath) and *cock* (a male

---

* Might not the English use of *bugger* for sodomite, rare in the United States, have something to do with the stigma? W. R. E.

chicken). The English use *bitch* a great deal more freely than Americans. Now and then an American, reading an English newspaper, is brought up with a start by a word or phrase that would never be used in the same way in the United States. I offer two examples. The first is from an advertisement of a popular brand of smoking tobacco in the *News of the World*: 'Want a good *shag*?' The second is from the *Times Literary Supplement*: 'On the whole we may congratulate ourselves on having chosen not to be born in that excellent and indispensable century when an infant of six could be hanged . . . and school boys were encouraged to match *cocks*.'

H. L. Mencken, *The American Language*

NICE-NELLYISMS

In my college days, one of my classmates wrote and produced a musical comedy. This I remember because I played the walk-on part of a buttons, and frequently missed my entrances. The hero of the play had to attract my attention by shouting at the top of his lungs, 'Where is that rascally page? Oh—I think I hear him coming now!' Anyhow, the Dean of Women took exception to a phrase in the theme song: 'He said to me, come on and be/ My woman.' *Woman*, she said, disregarding the slight on her own title, had vulgar connotations; the word must be changed to *sweetheart*. And changed it was.

It is curious that *woman* is considered by many, and even by some relatively literate persons, to be a term of disrespect. In America, a hundred years ago, *female* was frequently substituted for it, in effect lumping women with the females of all species. *Lady*, though, won the day. My grandmother, who was reared in Mexico as the result of a disagreement between her father and the Federal government as to who had won the Civil War, or, as he called it, the War Between the States, first heard *lady* used as a synonym for *woman* when she returned to the United States as a bride. The story goes that she burst into tears, and demanded of her husband, 'What kind of a country *is* this, where even washer-women are washer-*ladies*?'

The eventual effect of calling all women ladies was to debase the meaning of the word *lady* to that of *woman*. Such is the usual fate of Nice-Nellyisms.

As recently as World War II, Hollywood's Production Code strictly and successfully forbade the use in the cinema of such words as *broad* (for *woman*), *chippy, cocotte, courtesan, eunuch, fairy* (for *homosexual*), *floozy, harlot, hot mamma, hussy, madam, nance, pansy, slut, trollop, tart, wench, whore,* and even *sex* and *sexual.*

Nice-Nellyism is rampant today in the fertile field of under-garments, as is evident from a glance at advertisements for *step-ins, undies, undikins, roll-ons, campus briefs,* and *cup forms.*

Whore, still a shocker, is related to the Latin *carus* (dear), and, as Mencken points out, 'must once have been a polite substitute for some word now lost'.

F, G

False Rhyme

In assonance, or false rhyme, the vowels of one word correspond with those of another, but the consonants do not. *Name* is assonant with *Jane, scream* with *beach. Mad* as a *hatter, time* out of *mind, free* and *easy,* and *slapdash* are assonant expressions.

In consonance it is the consonants that correspond, as in *raid* and *red, staid* and *stood, odds* and *ends, short* and *sweet, stroke* of *luck, strut* and *fret.*

Assonance has triumphed over pure rhyme in Gaelic; the Irish poets writing in English who rhyme *Blarney* with *charming* are following an ancient tradition.

It is less popular, though far from unknown, in English. It seems most at home in Mother Goose and folk rhymes:

> And pray, who gave thee that jolly red nose?
> Cinnamon, Ginger, Nutmeg and Cloves.

> There was an old wife did eat an apple.
> When she had eat two she had eat a couple.

Famous Fakes and Frauds

I have not been able to authenticate, but consider likely, a story to the effect that a mischievous Englishman used to translate published verses into Greek or Latin and mail the translation to *The Times* as 'proof' that the poem had been outrageously expropriated from some ancient author. Just such a trick, in any event, was played on Sir Walter Scott by a correspondent who claimed the poet had stolen the address to 'Woman', in *Marmion*, from a Latin poem by Vida. Scott, suspecting nothing, told his friend Southey that truly the resemblance between the two poems was an astonishing one. His ended:

> When pain and anguish wring the brow,
> A ministering angel thou!

The purported lines from Vida were:

> Cum dolor atque supercilio gravis imminet angor,
> Fungeris angelico sola ministerio.

As Scott agreed, a more extraordinary example of casual coincidence could never have been pointed out. But when someone thought to check the Vida reference, it turned out not to exist.

A waggish friend of mine, Irish by inheritance, invited some friends of similar pedigree to a St. Patrick's day party, drenched them in martinis, and played them a record of what he claimed to be an ancient Gaelic song. Tears, composed largely of alcohol, rolled down Irish cheeks, and the guests cried nostalgically, 'Ah, that's the beautiful Gaelic!' But really it was Sophie Tucker singing 'Meine Yiddische Mamma'.

I mention this little hoax because it reminded me of a happening at a Boston Carlyle Club in the days when Carlyle devotees were more numerous and more fervent than they seem to be today. One Carlyle reading included the passage: 'Word-spluttering organisms, in whatever place—not with Plutarchean comparison, apologies, nay rather, without any such apologies—but born into the world to say the thought that is in them—antiphoreal, too, in the main—butchers, bakers, and candlestick makers; men, women, pedants. Verily, with you, too, it's now or never.' These lines evoked wild applause from the audience, and were hailed as a fresh instance of the master's genius, though in fact they were sheer fakery.

A remarkable literary forger was William Henry Ireland, who in 1799 published two plays, *Vortigern* and *Henry the Second*, which he claimed to be by Shakespeare himself. Sheridan accepted them as genuine, and even produced *Vortigern* at the Drury Lane theatre; but the play was a fiasco, and Ireland went to jail.

THE GREAT LONGFELLOW CAPER

In the 1930s the *Atlantic Monthly* fell victim to a literary hoax, unique in that it was unintentional. The magazine published a brief verse of four-line stanzas starting 'Softly, silently falls the snow', or something on that order (I really must look it up), credited to a college professor. *Atlantic* readers immediately leaped to the kill, with the terrible joy that inflates us all when we catch someone, particularly someone of high reputation, in a foolish error. The poem, they pointed out, was actually by none other than Henry Wadsworth Longfellow. Surely the *Atlantic*, of all magazines, might have been expected to know *that*.

Right they were; yet the professor was perfectly innocent. Mr. Longfellow's effusion had inspired him to create a verse of his own, in the same manner and on the same theme. He handed his poem, with Longfellow's stanzas at the top in italics, to his secretary to type and post. Unfortunately, she omitted his credit to Longfellow. The *Atlantic* editors, finding the italicised stanzas excellent but the rest trash, acted accordingly.

The bright side of the story is that Longfellow still stood up after nearly a hundred years, at least in his home town.

Finnegan's Wordplay

Finnegan's Wake, by James Joyce, must be one of the few classics in English for which the average reader requires a translation. It takes a good man to go through a passage like the example below without blinking.

—Rats! bullowed the Mookse most telesphorously, the concionator, and the sissymusses and the zozzymusses in their robenhauses quailed to hear his tardeynois at all for you cannot wake a silken nouse out of a hoarseoar. Blast yourself and your anathomy infairioriboos! No, hang you for an animal rurale! I am

superbly in my supremest poncif! Abase you, baldyqueens!
Gather behind me, satraps! Rots!

—I am till infinity obliged with you, bowed the Gripes, his
whine having gone to his palpruy head. I am still always having
a wish on all my extremities. By the watch, what is the time, pace?
Figure it! The pining peever! To a Mookse!

—Ask my index, mund my achilles, swell my obolum, woshup
my nase serene, answered the Mookse, rapidly by turning clement,
urban, eugenious and celestian in the formose of good grogory
humours. Quote awhore? That is quite about what I came on *my*
missions with *my* intentions *laudibiliter* to settle with *you*, bar-
barousse. Let thor be orlog. Let Pauline be Irene. Let you be
Beeton. And let me be Los Angeles. Now measure your length.
Now estimate my capacity. Well, sour? Is this space of our couple
of hours too dimensional for you, temporiser? Will you give you
up? *Como? Fuert it?*

*

LINES BY A MEDIUM

(in communication with the late L. Murray)

> I might not, if I could;
>   I should not, if I might;
> Yet if I should I would,
>   And shoulding, I should quite!

> I must not, yet I may;
>   I can, and still I must;
> But ah! I cannot—nay,
>   To must I may not, just!

> I shall, although I will,
>   But be it understood,
> If I may, can, shall—still
>   I naught, could, would, or should.

Author unknown

*

Franglish

If, given an English word, you proceed to name a synonym, this being identical in spelling to a French word of quite different meaning, you are playing Franglish. A synonym for 'calamitous', for instance, is 'dire'. 'Dire', in French, means 'to say'. Whet your appetite on the following examples, which come from 'Your Literary I.Q.', a department conducted by David M. Glixon in the *Saturday Review*.

The given word	*The French word for*	*The missing word*
Woo	Short	*Court*
Bastion	Strong	*Fort*
Crippled	Blade	*Lame*
Burn	Monkey	*Singe*
Depression	Tooth	*Dent*
However	Goal	*But*
Warbled	Blood	*Sang*
Penny	Corner	*Coin*
Chop finely	Slender	*Mince*
One	Year	*An*
Kind	Fate	*Sort*
Rows	Third	*Tiers*
Weary	Pull	*Tire*
Be ill	Garlic	*Ail*
Surety	Leap	*Bond*
Talk	Cat	*Chat*
Selected	Thing	*Chose*
Regret	Street	*Rue*
Precious fur	Sand	*Sable*
Candle	Typewrite	*Taper*

Doris Hertz and
Karin S. Armitage

RONDEAU: OOPS! YOU ALMOST PICKED UP THE BILL

English has bulled its way into many a language, and no-one complains more bitterly about its incursions than the French. In the matter of food, however, the situation is reversed. The following verse mentions a few of the scores of dishes which are commonly ordered in French, though perfectly good English equivalents are at hand or could be developed.

'I'll pay for lunch this time,' I bet you'll say,
'So join me in the best . . . What's good today?
Some *Escargots?* . . . *Saumon?* . . . *Palourdes Farcies?* . . .
Coquille Saint-Jacques? . . . or *Jambon de Paris?* . . .
Bisque de Homard? . . . or *Soupe de Trois Filets?*

Délices de sole might do for entremets . . .
Quiche? . . . *Fruits de Mer?* . . . Or *Foie de Veau Sauté?*
Escallopines de Veau? . . . It's all on me;
I'll pay for lunch this time.' (I bet!)

'And next . . . *Filet mignon?* . . . Or *Demi-Grain Grillé?* . . .
Chateaubriand? . . . *Paillard de Boeuf Vert-Pré?* . . .
With *Haut-Brion?* . . . Or *Haut-Lafitte?* Feel free:
I'll pay for lunch this time.

'We'll finish with . . . say *Mousse?* . . . Or *Crêpes Flambées?* . . .
And *Café Filtre*, topped off by *Pousse-Café?*'
(Again you murmur, reassuringly:
'I'll pay for lunch.')

But having lunched with you before, I'll stay
With tea and toast, and count my cash. The way
The record reads, it's sure as sure can be
I'll pay.

W. R. E.

S'IL VOUS PLAÎT'S NOT STERLING

It is obvious, when you stop to think about it, that 's'il vous plaît' is as close as the French can come to saying 'silver-plate'—i.e., 'not sterling'. Freddy Pearson stopped to think about it, and then proceeded to write a book, sinfully funny and condignly illustrated by R. Taylor, called *Fractured French*. In fractured French, 'de rigueur' can be nothing but a two-masted schooner, 'au contraire', 'away [in the country] for the weekend,' and 'a la carte', 'on the wagon'.

Even without the help of Taylor's saucy illustrations, I expect you can provide instant English versions of the French expressions below. Freddy did.

1. C'est à dire
2. Mal de mer
3. Faux pas
4. Carte Blanche
5. Coup de grâce
6. Tant pis, tant mieux
7. Louis Cinq
8. Mille fois
9. Pas de tout
10. J'y suis et j'y reste
11. Tout en famille
12. Pièce de résistance
13. Ile de France
14. Tête-á-tête
15. Endive
16. Hors de combat
17. N'est-ce pas
18. Pied-à-terre
19. Entrechat
20. Quelle heure est-elle?
21. Marseillaise
22. Legerdemain
23. Voici l'anglais avec son sang-froid habituel
24. Adieu, ma chérie

ANSWERS

1. She's a honey.
2. Mother-in-law.
3. Father-in-law.
4. For God's sake, take Blanche home!
5. Lawn mower.
6. My aunt is much happier since she made a telephone call.
7. Lost at sea.
8. Cold lunch.
9. Father of twins.
10. I'm Swiss, and I'm spending the night.
11. Let's get drunk at home.
12. Timid girl.
13. I'm sick of my friends.
14. A tight brassière.
15. A night club.
16. Camp followers.
17. Father robin.
18. The plumbing is out of order.
19. Let the cat in.
20. Whose babe is that?
21. Mother says okay.
22. Tomorrow's a holiday.
23. Here comes that Englishman with his usual bloody cold.
24. No English equivalent is given, but the picture is of a girl in her wedding gown.

THE WRECK OF THE *JULIE PLANTE*
A Legend of Lac St. Pierre

Henry Avery, of Canadian extraction, gave me not long ago a book
of French-Canadian dialect verses called *The Habitant*. Written
at the turn of the century by William Henry Drummond, it
memorialises a charming and rapidly vanishing tongue. The
following poem is typical of the book.

On wan dark night on Lac St. Pierre,
De win' she blow, blow, blow,
An' de crew of de wood scow *Julie Plante*
Got scar't an' run below—
For de win' she blow lak hurricane
Bimeby, she blow some more,
An' de scow bus' up on Lac St. Pierre
Wan arpent from de shore.

De captinne walk on de fronte deck,
An' walk de hin' deck too—
He call de crew from up de hole
He call de cook also.
De cook she's name was Rosie,
She come from Montreal,
Was chambre maid on lumber barge,
On de Grande Lachine Canal.

De win' she blow from nor'eas'-wes'—
De sout' win' she blow too,
W'en Rosie cry 'Mon cher captinne,
Mon cher, w'at I shall do?'
Den de captinne t'row de big ankerre,
But still the scow she dreef,
De crew he can't pass on de shore,
Becos' he los' hees skeef.

(CONTINUED OVERLEAF)

De night was dark lak' wan black cat,
    De wave run high an' fas',
W'en de captinne tak' de Rosie girl
    An' tie her to de mas'.
Den he also tak' de life preserve,
    An' jomp off on de lak',
An' say, 'Good-bye, ma Rosie dear,
    I go drown for your sak'.'

Nex' morning very early
    'Bout ha'f-pas' two—t'ree—four—
De captinne—scow—an' de poor Rosie
    Was corpses on de shore.
For de win' she blow lak' hurricane
    Bimeby she blow some more,
An' de scow bus' up on Lac St. Pierre,
    Wan arpent from de shore.

MORAL

Now all good wood scow sailor man
    Tak' warning by dat storm
An' go an' marry some nice French girl
    An' leev on wan beeg farm.
De win' can blow lak' hurricane
    An' s'pose she blow some more,
You can't get drown on Lac St. Pierre
    So long you stay on shore.

French Wordplay

After several tries, Clarkson Potter remembered these for me, though first, I think, his mother remembered them for him:

> Un train à l'aurore!
> Quelle horreur!
> C'est sans doute une erreur
> dans l'horaire!

The following lines were a teaching device for West Point cadets:

Jeanne portait l'armure
Jeanne portait le mur
Jeanne portait l'amour
Jeanne portait l'armoire

And finally:

La reine Didon
Dinà, dit-on,
Du dos d'un dodu dindon.

When challenged to write English poetry, Victor Hugo promptly replied:

Pour chasser le spleen
J'entrai dans un inn;
O, mais je bus le gin,
God save the Queen.

And I have this anonymous comment on the Biblical misadventure of Lot and his daughters:

Il but;
Il devint tendre;
Et puis il fut
Son gendre.

Fruits in Season

Two melons had an argument:
A lover's quarrel, too.
One melon said, 'I **********;'
The other, '********!'

W. R. E.

ANSWER

Two melons had an argument,
A lover's quarrel, too.
One melon said, 'I cantaloupe';
The other, 'Honeydew!'

GEOGRAPHY: A SONG

There are no rocks
At Rockaway,
There are no sheep
At Sheepshead Bay,
There's nothing new
In Newfoundland,
And silent is
Long Island Sound.

Howard Moss

*

H

Headline Hunters

Before me is a leader on the cost of the American farm subsidy programme. Its heading is '$4.5 Billion Ain't Hay'. The thrust of the entire 200-word essay is contained in the four words. Newspapers would be little less informative, and certainly more enjoyable, if they left out the stories and just ran the headlines.

Henry Kissinger, foreign affairs adviser to President Nixon, is a bachelor who boasts that 'power acts as an aphrodisiac', leaving unclear whether this effect is experienced by him or by the beautiful young women with whom he likes to spend his rare free evenings. A newspaper report on his tastes in this area is ambiguously headlined, 'Kissinger after dark'.

Below are the opening paragraphs of some news stories. Write the best headline you can for each of them, and then read on to see how your skill stacks up against that of the copy desk professionals.

1. PARIS—A French court has ruled that President François Duvalier of Haiti was libelled in the movie made from Graham Greene's novel *The Comedians*. It awarded him damages of one franc.

2. PIETERMARTIZBURG, South Africa—A Natal University couple claimed a world record after kissing for eight hours and 45 minutes nonstop.

3. LONDON—A fossil of a fish said to be 150 million years old was sold for £320 at Sotheby's auction yesterday.

4. NEW YORK—Rex Harrison and Richard Burton arrive here as two aging homosexuals when *Staircase* steps into the Penthouse theatre for its world premiere.

5. NEW YORK—The boost in the price of meat will cost New Yorkers $310 million this year.

6. NEW YORK—'Four boys!' George Schwab, proud father, marvelled. He smiled. 'Four boys! Apparently that's unprecedented.'

7. FONTANA, Wis.—Soviet scholars have been filibustering at the 20th Pugwash Conference in an effort to squelch all discussion of Russia's presence in Czechoslovakia.

8. WASHINGTON—With cigarette commercials banned from TV and radio, broadcasters are wondering whether they can continue to carry antismoking announcements without violating the 'fairness doctrine' requiring balanced presentation of controversial issues.

(ANSWERS OVERLEAF)

1. DUVALIER LIBELLED, FRANCLY
2. STUCK ON EACH OTHER
3. JUST CALL IT A GOLD FISH
4. 'STAIRCASE' SET TO SPIRAL IN
5. N.Y. HAS A BEEF ON MEAT PRICES
6. HE'S FATHER OF QUADS: BOY OH BOY OH BOY . . .
7. PUGWASH REDS TRY FOR CZECHMATE
8. ANTISMOKING ADS: SOME IFS & BUTTS

Hidden Words

In *Word Play**, Hubert Phillips asks his readers to find ten words containing cans (canopy, candour); ten containing discs (discussion, discretion); ten containing imps (imperious, impetuous); ten containing pens (penumbra, pentad); ten containing props (proportion, prophet); ten containing cities (mendacity, opacity); ten containing scents (obsolescent, adolescent); ten containing nations (damnation, coronation); ten containing rations (emigration, integration); and ten containing gents (indigent, tangent).

You may enjoy jotting down as many of these words as occur to you. I am not going to suggest answers, since the words meeting the specifications are easy to locate in the dictionary.

Higgledy-Piggledies

The double-dactyl verses I call Higgledy-Piggledies were invented by Paul Pascal and Anthony Hecht, and first made their mark in *Jiggery-Pokery*, edited by Mr. Hecht and John Hollander (Atheneum, 1966). The following examples of the genre are from Mary Ann Madden's column in *New York Magazine*.

* Ptarmigan Books, Penguin, 1945.

The first line of a Higgledy-Piggledy may be any nonsensical double dactyl—'Fiddledy faddledy', 'Niminy piminy', 'Jokery pokery', 'Hickory dickory', and the like. The second line names the subject of the composition. The fourth and eighth are the rhyme lines, curtailed double dactyls. The sixth line should be one double dactyl word, though sufficiently clever exceptions are forgiven. This contribution by James Lipton will give you the idea:

> Misericordia!
> College of Cardinals,
> Nervously rising to
> Whisper its will:
>
> 'Rather than being so
> Unecumenical,
> Can't we just quietly
> Swallow The Pill?'

The subjects of some of the other submissions are listed below. Work up a Higgledy-Piggledy about each. If you find that Higgledy-Piggledies are not your line of country, you can always copy the originals and tell your friends you wrote them yourself.

1. Yale University
2. Tom Tom the Piper's Son
3. Oedipus Tyrannos
4. Madame de Pompadour
5. Alice in Wonderland

ANSWERS

1

Higgledy Piggledy
Yale University
Gave up misogyny
Opened its door.

Coeducational
Extracurricular
Heterosexual
Fun is in store.
Fred Rodell

2

Higgledy Piggledy
Tom Tom the Piper's Son
Purloined a porker and
Forthwith he fled.

Passersby said this was
Incomprehensible
Due to the yarmulka
Worn on his head.
William McGuirk

(CONTINUED OVERLEAF)

3

Higgledy Piggledy
Oedipus Tyrannos
Murdered his father, used
Mama for sex.

This mad debauch, not so
Incomprehensibly
Left poor Jocasta and
Oedipus Wrecks.

Joan Munkacsi

4

Tiffety Taffety
Madame de Pompadour
Loved crême brulée, such ex-
Pansive desserts.

After developing
Steatopygia,
She was the one who in-
Vented hoop skirts.

Emily Barnhart

5

Tweedledum Tweedledee
Alice in Wonderland
First she was tiny and
Then she was tall,

Argued with animals
Anthropomorphical,
Didn't accept their con-
Clusions at all.

W. R. E.

*

HIGH-LIFE LOW-DOWN

To his Castle Lord Fotherday bore his young bride,
And he carried her over the drawbridge so wide,
Through the Great Hall, the Solar, the West Hall, the East,
And thirty-eight principal bedrooms at least.
Up seventeen stairways and down many more
To a basement twelve yards by a hundred and four,
And at last set her down—he was panting a bit—
In front of the sink and said, 'Kid, this is IT.'

Justin Richardson

*

Hobson-Jobsons

At the feast of Muharram, the Mohammedans raise the ritual cry of mourning, 'O Hasan! O Husein!', these being two murdered grandsons of Mohammed. The English substituted *Hobson-Jobson*, common surnames with no relation in meaning to the Arabic originals. A *hobson-jobson* is thus any word resulting from the corruption of a foreign expression. 'Compound', meaning 'a residence or group of residences set off by a barrier', is hobson-jobson for Malay 'kampong', 'village', as is 'forlorn hope' for Dutch 'verloren hoop', 'a lost expedition'. This kind of evolution goes on also inside the English language. The 'stark' in 'stark naked', for instance, does not come from 'stark', meaning 'bare, stripped of nonessentials', but from 'start', which once meant an animal's tail. 'Stark naked' is 'tail naked'.

See if you can reconstruct the origins of the words below.

1. Acorn	7. Helpmate
2. Belfry	8. Penthouse
3. Contredanse	9. Pickaxe
4. Curry favour	10. Reindeer
5. Greyhound	11. Saltcellar
6. Hangnail	12. Shamefaced

ANSWERS

1. Middle English *akern*, Old English *aecern* 'oak or beech mast'. Nothing to do with *corn*.
2. Middle English *berfrey*, 'tower'. Nothing to do with *bell*.
3. A French hobson-jobson that came back home. The French mistranslated *country dance*, and the English borrowed back the French word. Nothing to do with French *contre*, 'counter'.
4. In the fourteenth century French satirical poem *Roman de Favel*, Favel was a yellow horse, treated as a symbol of worldly vanity. He was soothed and lovingly tended by all classes of society. To *curry Favel* was thus to seek advancement by toadying. Folk etymology in England turned Favel into 'favour'.
5. Scandinavian *grey* 'dog' plus *hound*. Nothing to do with the colour grey.
6. Old English *ange* 'painful' plus *naegl* 'nail'. Nothing to do with *hanging*.

7. *Help* plus *meet* 'fitting'. Nothing to do with *mate*.
8. Middle English *pentis*, Old French *apentis*, connected with *pend* 'hang'. Nothing to do with either *pent* 'confined' or *house*.
9. Middle English *picois*, from Old French. Nothing to do with *axe*.
10. Scandinavian *hreinn*, the name of the animal, plus *deer*. Nothing to do with *rein*.
11. Middle English *saltsaler*, Old French *saliere*, Latin *salārium* (whose specific meaning 'money paid to soldiers for purchase of salt' accounts for *salary*). No connection with *cellar* 'basement'.
12. Old English *sceamfaest*, 'bound by shame'. Nothing to do with *face*.

Hoity-toities

There is a small family of words, often of folk origin and uncertain meaning, which command attention through a rhyme or near-rhyme within the word. Typical of the kind is 'hoity-toity', which can be interpreted according to taste as 'haughty, stuck-up' or 'an exclamation of surprise or disapprobation'.

The stanzas which follow, clearly dealing with a harum-scarum situation in a nursery, are built around a hodge-podge of familiar hoity-toities. Fill in the hoity-toities after studying the definitions.

*****-*****,[1] where is nanny?
There's some *****-*****[2] here.
******-*******[3] **********,[4]
*****-*****[5] ********-********,[6]
******-*****[7] ********-*******,[8]
-[9] ****-****,[10] ****-****,[11] queer,
Refrain: Beulah, set up one more beer.

*******-*******[12] *****-*****,[13]
******-*******[14] *****-*****,[15]
Have a ****-****,[16] *****-*****,[17]
*******-*****[18] don't ******-******,[19]
******-*****[20] *****-*****,[21]
*****-*****,[22] there's a dear.
Refrain: Beulah, set up one more beer.

*******_*******,²³ *******_******** ²⁴
*****_*****,²⁵ don't you worry:
*****_*****²⁶ plays by ear.
Pop's a *****_*****²⁷ *******_*******,²⁸
*****_*****²⁹ is dear muddy;
Pop's a *******_******³⁰ foola,
Muddy, she does ******_******;³¹
Be an *******_********,³² Beulah:
Refrain: Bring another round of beer!

W. R. E.

Definitions

1. Defined in the introduction.   2. Jugglery; trickery.
3. A step in a rustic dance; in this case, a bad situation.
4. A perfume imitating the odour of the red jasmine.
5. Upside down.   6. In a state of agitation.
7. A jumble.   8. In confusion.   9. Rabble.
10. Insincere sentiment designed to incite applause.
11. A reversal, as of opinion.
12. A diminutive or presumptuous person.
13. A lively expression.
14. Characterised by confused hurry.
15. A confection consisting of different kinds of preserved fruits.
16. A lively party.
17. King William IV.
18. At great speed (slang, U.S.).
19. Hesitate (usually the two halves are the other way around).
20. Finical.   21. Without choice; compulsory.
22. Nonsense intended to cloak deception.
23. In a hopping way.   24. Flustered haste.   25. Mummery.
26. An instrument of street music, played by turning a handle.
27. In a state of jitters.
28. One who is old-fashioned and fussy.
29. Weakly sentimental or affectedly pretty.
30. Quite to one's content.
31. Native Hawaiian dance.
32. An industrious, overzealous person.

(ANSWER OVERLEAF)

ANSWER

Hoity-toity, where is nanny?
There's some hanky-panky here.
Double-trouble, frangipani,
Topsy-turvy, jiggledy-wiggledy,
Hugger-mugger, higgledy-piggledy,
Rag-tag, clap-trap, flip-flop, queer.
Refrain: Beulah, set up one more beer.

Whipper-snapper, rooty-tooty,
Helter-skelter, tutti-frutti;
Have a wing-ding, silly Billy,
Lickety-split, don't shally-shilly,
Niminy-piminy, willy-nilly,
Hocus-pocus, there's a dear.
Refrain: Beulah, set up one more beer.

Hippety-hoppety, hurry-scurry,
Mumbo-jumbo, don't you worry;
Hurdy-gurdy plays by ear.
Pop's a jim-jam fuddy-duddy,
Namby-pamby is dear muddy;
Pop's a hunky-dory foola,
Muddy, she does hula-hula . . .
Be an eager-beaver, Beulah:
Refrain: Bring another round of beer!

Homonyms

Once, in an uncommon burst of egotism, I composed this anagram verse:

I don't mispell, as others ****,
But allways right each **** rite;
So I **** resounding hoops
At other righters' speling bloops.†

My verse was inspired by the extraordinary difficulty of mastering the spelling of many English words and, specifically, by the threat of lurking homonyms—words alike in sound, but different in spelling and meaning.

† The anagrams: mite, item, emit.

Test your homonymic skill on the couplets below.

1

Blest be that beast who, though he ***** on others,
Gives ****** to God, and ***** all beasts be brothers.

2

Food, if you diet, goes to *****;
And, if you try it, goes to *****.

3

I found a shaggy mare in *****.
With might and **** I trimmed her ****.

4

Say, **** man in thy ***** cot,
Art ****** pleased with thy lowly lot?

5

I met a wise antelope, born in a zoo;
And I wish that I knew what that *** *** ****.

W. R. E.

Definitions

1. That is, eats 'em; and well he might; the hypocrite!
2. . . . not, want not; very big on Falstaff.
3. An American State; reinforces might; hippy hairdo.
4. Three times before 'Lord God Almighty'; lets in the rain; completely.
5. A few hours old; the antelope in question; I already gave you this one.

<hr/>

ANSWERS

1. Preys, praise, prays.
2. Waste, waist.
3. Maine, main, mane.

4. Holy, holey, wholly.
5. New, gnu, knew.

HOMONYM LEXICON

A

Acclamation, acclimation
Ad, add
Adds, ads, adze
Aerie, airy
Ail, ale
Air, ere, heir
Aisle, I'll, isle
All, awl
Allowed, aloud
All together, altogether
All ways, always
Altar, alter
Analyst, annalist
Ant, aunt
Ante, anti
Arc, ark
Ate, eight
Auger, augur
Aught, ought
Auricle, oracle
Away, aweigh
Awful, offal
Aye, eye, I

B

Bad, bade
Bail, bale
Bait, bate
Balm, bomb
Band, banned
Banns, bans
Bard, barred
Bare, bear
Baron, barren
Based, baste
Bass, base
Be, bee
Beach, beech
Bearing, baring
Beat, beet
Beau, bow
Been, bean

Beer, bier
Bell, belle
Berry, bury
Berth, birth
Better, bettor
Bey, bay
Bight, bite
Billed, build
Bird, burred
Blew, blue
Bloc, block
Boar, bore
Board, bored
Boarder, border
Bode, bowed
Bold, bolled, bowled
Bolder, boulder
Bole, boll, bowl
Born, borne, bourn
Borough, burrow
Bough, bow
Bouillon, bullion
Boy, buoy
Brae, bray
Braise, brays, braze
Braid, brayed
Brake, break
Breach, breech
Bread, bred
Brewed, brood
Brews, bruise
Bridal, bridle
Bus, buss
But, butt
By, buy, bye
Byre, buyer

C

Cache, cash
Cane, cain
Cannon, canon
Cant, can't
Canvas, canvass

Homonym Lexicon

Carat, caret, carrot
Cart, carte
Cast, caste
Caudal, caudle
Cause, caws
Cedar, ceder, seeder
Ceiling, sealing, seeling
Cell, sell
Cellar, seller
Cense, cents, scents, sense, *SINCE*
Censer, censor
Cent, scent, sent
Cere, sear, seer, sere
Cereal, serial
Cession, session
Chantey, shanty
Chased, chaste
Cheap, cheep
Chews, choose
Choir, quire
Choler, collar
Choral, coral
Chronical, chronicle
Chute, shoot
Cite, sight, site
Clack, claque
Clause, claws
Cleek, clique
Climb, clime
Close, clothes
Clue, clew
Coal, cole
Coarse, corse, course
Coax, cokes
Coddling, codling
Coffer, cougher
Colonel, kernel
Complacence, complaisance
Complement, compliment
Coo, coup
Cord, cored, chord
Core, corps
Correspondence, correspondents
Council, counsel
Cousin, cozen
Coward, cowered

Creak, creek
Crews, cruise, cruse
Cue, queue
Currant, current
Currier, courier
Cygnet, signet
Cymbal, symbol

D
Dam, damn
Days, daze
Dear, deer
Dense, dents
Dependence, dependents
Desert, dessert
Devisor, divisor
Dew, due
Die, dye
Dire, dyer
Disc, disk
Discreet, discrete
Dissidence, dissidents
Doe, dough
Done, dun
Dost, dust
Dual, duel
Ducked, duct

E
Earn, erne, urn
Eau, oh, owe
Eave, eve
Elision, elysian
Ewe, yew, you
Eye, aye, I

F
Fain, fane, feign
Faint, feint
Fair, fare
Faker, fakir
Faro, Pharaoh
Faun, fawn
Fay, fey
Faze, phase
Feat, feet

Homonym Lexicon

Fete, fate
Filter, philtre
Find, fined
Fir, fur
Fisher, fissure
Fizz, phiz
Flair, flare
Flea, flee
Flecks, flex
Flew, flu, flue
Flo, floe, flow
Flocks, phlox
Flour, flower
Foaled, fold
For, fore, four
Foreword, forward
Fort, forte
Foul, fowl
Franc, frank, Frank
Frays, phrase
Frees, freeze, frieze
Friar, fryer
Fungous, fungus
Furs, furze

G

Gage, gauge
Gait, gate
Gamble, gambol
Genes, jeans
Gest, jest
Gild, guild
Gilder, guilder
Gilt, guilt
Gin, jinn
Gnu, knew, new
Gored, gourd
Gorilla, guerilla
Graft, graphed
Grater, greater
Grays, graze
Grill, grille
Grip, grippe
Grisly, grizzly
Groan, grown
Guessed, guest

Guide, guyed
Guise, guys

H

Hail, hale
Hair, hare
Hall, haul
Handsome, hansom
Hart, heart
Hay, hey
Hays, haze
Heal, heel, he'll
Heard, herd
He'd, heed
Heigh, hi, hie, high
Heir, air, e'er
Here, hear
Hew, hue
Hide, hied
Higher, hire
Him, hymn
Ho, hoe
Hoar, whore
Hoard, horde, whored
Hoarse, horse
Hoes, hose
Hold, holed
Hole, whole
Holey, holy, wholly
Hollo, hollow
Hoop, whoop
Hostel, hostile
Hour, our
Humerus, humorous

I

Idle, idol, idyl, idyll
Impassable, impassible
In, inn
Incidence, incidents
Indict, indite
Innocence, innocents
Instance, instants
Intense, intents
Invade, inveighed
It's, its

Homonym Lexicon

J
Jam, jamb

K
Key, quay
Knave, nave
Knead, need
Knight, night
Knit, nit
Knot, not
Know, no
Knows, noes, nose

L
Lacks, lax
Lade, laid
Lain, lane
Lam, lamb
Lapse, laps
Lay, lei
Lays, laze
Lea, lee
Leach, leech
Lead, led
Leaf, lief
Leak, leek
Lean, lien
Leas, lees
Leased, least
Lends, lens
Lessen, lesson
Levee, levy
Liar, lier, lyre
Lichen, liken
Licker, liquor
Lickerish, liquorice
Lie, lye
Limb, limn
Linch, lynch
Links, lynx
Literal, littoral
Lo, low
Load, lode, lowed
Loan, lone
Loch, lock
Locks, lox
Loon, lune

Loot, lute
Lumbar, lumber

M
Made, maid
Magnate, magnet
Mail, male
Main, mane
Maize, maze
Mall, maul, moll
Manner, manor
Mantel, mantle
Mare, mayor
Marshal, martial
Marten, martin
Massed, mast
Mead, meed
Mean, mien
Meat, meet, mete
Medal, meddle
Metal, mettle
Mewl, mule
Mews, muse
Might, mite
Mil, mill
Millenary, millinery
Mince, mints
Mind, mined
Miner, minor
Minks, minx
Missal, missile
Missed, mist
Moan, mown
Moat, mote
Mode, mowed
Mood, mooed
Moose, mousse
Morn, mourn
Mucous, mucus
Muscle, mussel
Mustard, mustered

N
Naval, navel
Nay, nee, neigh
None, nun

Homonym Lexicon

O

Oar, or, ore, o'er
Ode, owed
Oleo, olio
One, won

P

Paced, paste
Packed, pact
Paean, peon
Pail, pale
Pain, pane
Pair, pare, pear
Palate, palette, pallet, pallette
Pan, panne
Passed, past
Patience, patients
Pause, paws
Peace, piece
Peak, peek, pique
Peal, peel
Pearl, purl
Pedal, peddle
Peer, pier
Pend, penned
Per, purr
Pi, pie
Pistil, pistol
Place, plaice
Plain, plane
Plate, plait
Pleas, please
Pliers, plyers
Plum, plumb
Polar, poler
Poll, pole
Populace, populous
Pore, pour
Pray, prey
Prays, praise, preys
Presence, presents
Pride, pried
Prier, prior
Pries, prize
Prince, prints

Principal, principle
Profit, prophet
Pros, prose
Psalter, salter

Q

Quarts, quartz
Quean, queen

R

Rack, wrack
Raid, rayed
Rain, reign, rein
Raise, raze
Raiser, razor
Rancour, ranker
Rap, wrap
Rapped, rapt, wrapped
Ray, re
Read, reed
Read, red
Real, reel
Recede, reseed
Receipt, reseat
Reck, wreck
Reek, wreak
Residence, residents
Rest, wrest
Retch, wretch
Review, revue
Rheum, room
Rhyme, rime
Rigger, rigour
Right, rite, wright, write
Ring, wring
Road, rode, rowed
Roc, rock
Roe, row
Roes, rose, rows
Rôle, roll
Rood, rude, rued
Root, route
Rote, wrote
Rough, ruff
Rouse, rows
Rout, route

Homonym Lexicon

Rum, rhumb
Rung, wrung
Rye, wry

S
Sac, sack
Sail, sale
Sailer, sailor
Sane, seine
Scene, seen
Scull, skull
Seam, seem
Seas, sees, seize
Sequence, sequents
Serf, surf
Serge, surge
Sew, so, sow
Sewer, suer
Shake, sheik
Shear, sheer
Shier, shire, shyer
Shoe, shoo
Shone, shown
Sic, sick
Side, sighed
Sigher, sire
Sighs, size
Sign, sine, syne
Slay, sleigh
Sleight, slight
Slew, slough
Sloe, slow
Soar, sore
Soared, sword
Socks, sox
Sol, sole, soul
Soled, sold
Some, sum
Son, sun
Sou, sue
Staid, stayed
Stair, stare
Stake, steak
Stare, stair
Stationary, stationery

Steal, steel
Step, steppe
Stile, style
Straight, strait
Subtler, sutler
Succour, sucker
Suede, swayed
Suer, sewer
Suite, sweet

T
Tacked, tact
Tacks, tax
Tail, taille, tale
Taper, tapir
Tare, tear
Taught, taut
Tea, tee
Team, teem
Tear, tier
Teas, tease, tees
Tense, tents
Tern, turn
Their, there
Therefor, therefore
Threw, through
Throe, throw
Throne, thrown
Thyme, time
Tic, tick
Tide, tied
Timber, timbre
To, too, two
Toad, toed, towed
Tocsin, toxin
Toe, tow
Told, tolled
Ton, tun
Tongue, tung
Tool, tulle
Tooter, tutor
Tracked, tract
Tray, trey
Troop, troupe
Trussed, trust

Homonym Lexicon

U

Uncede, unseed
Undo, undue

V

Vail, vale, veil
Vain, vane, vein
Vary, very
Versed, verst
Vial, vile
Vice, vise
Villain, villein

W

Wade, weighed
Wain, wane
Waist, waste
Wait, weight
Waive, wave

War, wore
Ward, warred
Ware, wear
Warn, worn
Way, weigh
We, wee
Weak, week
Weal, we'll
Weather, wether
Weave, we've
We'd, weed
Weld, welled
We're, weir
Wind, wined
Wood, would
Worst, wurst

Y

Yoke, yolk
You'll, Yule

NOEL, NOEL

Virgin Mary, meek and mum,
Dominus is in thy tum.
What a jolly *jeu d'esprit*—
Christ beneath the Christmas tree!
W.R.E.

How to Tell the Birds from the Flowers

The wordplay poet Robert Williams Wood, a distinguished physicist, has been compared to Lewis Carroll for the virtuosity of his punning. After office hours, he specialised in a combination of ridiculous verse and misleading drawings. The latter are reminiscent of Edward Lear's in their mixture of subtlety and casual deliberate crudeness. I'm sorry I can't show the pictures.

The verses that follow are taken from his two slim collections: *How to Tell the Birds from the Flowers** and its sequel, *Animal Anatomies*.

The Clover. The Plover

The Plover and the Clover can be told apart with ease,
By paying close attention to the habits of the Bees,
For En-to-molo-gists aver, the Bee can be in Clover,
While Ety-molo-gists concur, there is no B in Plover.

The Pecan. The Toucan

Very few can
Tell the Toucan
From the Pecan—
Here's a new plan:
To take the Toucan from the tree,
Requires im-mense a-gil-i-tee,
While anyone can pick with ease
The Pecans from the Pecan trees.
It's such an easy thing to do,
That even the Toucan he can too.

The Elk. The Whelk

A roar of welkome through the welkin
Is certain proof you'll find the Elk in;
But if you listen to the shell,
In which the Whelk is said to dwell,
And hear a roar, beyond a doubt
It indicates the Whelk is out.

* Dover Publications, Inc., New York.

HIDE AND HAIR

Hides were man's first clothes. Eventually he learned to weave the hair from the hide into warm garments and coverings. Six products of hide or hair are defined below. Guess the words and the proper names that are their source.

1, 2. Two curly or wavy furs, comparable in desirability, made from the skins of young lambs.
3. Fine, downy wool growing beneath the outer hair of a Himalayan goat.
4. A soft, highly prized leather of goatskin tanned with sumac.
5. The skin of a sheep or goat, prepared for writing upon; paper made in imitation of this material.
6. Leather with a soft napped surface.

ANSWERS

1, 2. Caracul, astrakhan. Turkestan is dotted with lakes named Karakul, and with herds of sheep, also called karakul because they graze by the lakes. The fur of the karakul lambs, usually black, has the same name, differently spelled: *caracul*.

Astrakhan, in Russian Turkestan, is the home of the astrakhan sheep, a relative of the karakul, but having hair longer and with a more open curl. The name is applied to its fur, and to a fabric with a similar curled pile.
3. Cashmere. The name of the wool of the Kashmir goat; of a shawl made of it; and of a wool fabric of twill weave.
4. Morocco. This leather was first exported from Morocco, in northwest Africa.
5. Parchment. In the second century B.C., Eumenes II, ruler of the Asia Minor kingdom Pergamum, decided to build a grand new library, and asked the Egyptians to send him papyrus for his scribes to write on. The Egyptians refused, not caring to see a rival to their world-famous library at Alexandria. Eumenes therefore reverted to the earlier practice of writing on prepared skin, but cut down production costs by writing on both sides. The library was built in due course, and for a time did give Alexandria a run for its money. The writing skins came to be known as pergamene, after the country and its capital city. Later, however, Parthia became the dominant kingdom of Asia Minor,

and the name of the skins was changed to Particaminum—'Parthian leather'; in English, parchment.

6. Suede. French for Swedish, the Swedes being the earliest exporters of this kind of leather.

SAINTS IN MUFTI

The names of a number of saints have become vernacular for reasons that the saints probably would find surprising. The catherine wheel, for instance—either a firework similar to a pinwheel, or a circular rose window, as the case may be—derives from Catherine of Alexandria because, when the Roman emperor ordered the saint broken on the wheel, it miraculously shattered at her touch. The filbert is so named because the ripening season of the nut coincides with the feast day of St. Philibert. The pudenda are called after morbidly modest St. Pudentiana, who, according to one liturgical scholar, 'may simply be an adjective who became a saint'.

Below are definitions of six common words born of saints. Guess the words and the saints.

1. A little pig; the runt of the litter.
2. Noisy uproar and confusion; a lunatic asylum.
3. A bird sometimes seen in storms at sea.
4. (Slang.) Out of one's mind; crazy.
5. Gaudy and cheap; vulgarly ornamental.
6. Effusively sentimental.

ANSWERS

1. Tantony. St. Anthony, intercessor for swineherds, is generally pictured with a piglet trotting after him, so swineherds came to call the runt of each litter the 'St. Anthony pig'. The name was gradually shortened to its present form.
2. Bedlam. The hospital of St. Mary of Bethlehem in Lambeth, London, was a lock-up for lunatics as early as 1402. Cockneys corrupted Bethlehem to Bedlam, which was soon lowercased.
3. Petrel. The name derives from Peter's bootless try at walking on water (Matthew xiv, 29). His faith deserting him, he began to sink, and would have drowned if Jesus had not given him a lift. The birds are called after Peter because they fly so low that they sometimes seem to be walking on the sea.

4. Barmy. You have probably seen St. Bartholomew in Michelangelo's painting, flayed alive and holding his own skin in his hands. He is patron of the feebleminded, wherefore some assert, most plausibly, that 'barmy' is a corruption of his name. But the true source, one suspects, is 'barm', an old word for the froth on beer.

5. Tawdry. Ethelreda, daughter of a sixth-century king of East Anglia, lay dying of a tumour of the throat. She confided to her waiting women that God was punishing her for her girlhood love for pretty necklaces. Hundreds of years later, her name shrunken to Audrey, she became patron saint of Ely, Cambridgeshire, where the townfolk sold 'necklaces of fine silk' to celebrate her feast day, October 17. These 'Saint Audrey's laces' were soon manufactured all over England and, being of poor quality, gave their name to any trumpery stuff.

6. Maudlin. A contraction of magdalene, from Mary Magdalene, a devoted follower of Jesus who is painted with eyes swollen and red from weeping at His crucifixion.

SEX ON OLYMPUS

The ancient gods and demi-gods were noted for their interest in lively sex, and their amatory exploits gave rise to some of the more vivid expressions in today's sexual vocabulary. You will have no trouble identifying most of the seven words defined below, and recalling how they came into being.

1. One having the sex organ of both male and female.
2. A boy kept by a pederast.
3. A drug or food stimulating sexual desire.
4. Of or pertaining to sexual love or desire.
5. Of or pertaining to sexual intercourse.
6. A phallus.
7. A lecher.

ANSWERS

1. Hermaphrodite. Hermaphroditus, son of Hermes and Aphrodite, was named after both his parents. He was a shy, savage youth, whose chief pleasure was hunting. One day he chanced to take refuge from the heat in the fountain ruled by the nymph Salmacis. She, at the sight of him, was seized by ravening passion, and leaped into the water to embrace him. When he repulsed her, she cried out in anguish: 'O ye gods! Grant that nothing may ever separate him from me, or me from him!' On the instant, their two bodies were merged into one, neither man nor woman, yet both.

2. Catamite. A corruption of Ganymede, the name of a beautiful Trojan youth who so took Zeus's fancy that the god, assuming the form of an eagle, carried him off to Olympus where, when not cupbearing for the immortals, he performed more specialised functions impractical for his predecessor, the fair Hebe. A young bartender or waiter is referred to occasionally, with humorous intent, as a ganymede.

3. Aphrodisaic. Aphrodite, goddess of love, was no remote, unattainable vision; she was the epitome of sexually exciting beauty, and when she wanted a god, or a man, she got him. Her temple at Paphos was served by priestesses so carnally obliging that paphian became synonymous with strumpet. Aphrodite needed no aphrodisiacs.

4. Erotic. Eros, son of Aphrodite, was a winged youth, or boy, who wakened love by shooting arrows into the hearts of his victims. He specialised in physical rather than spiritual attraction. But Hesiod, a poet of the eighth century B.C., declares he was the earliest of all gods, born of Chaos, the cosmic egg. It is a pleasant conceit—love bringing order out of chaos.

5. Venereal. From Venus, the Roman version of Aphrodite. Venery connotes not just the pursuit of sexual delight but additionally the art of the chase, over which Venus also presided. The two sports have much in common; that venison as well as venereal disease comes down to us from the love goddess gives one to think. Venom likewise traces to her. It was a love potion originally; the changed meaning is a reminder that love gone rancid can be a poisonous brew indeed.

6. Priapus. Priapus, Aphrodite's son by Dionysus, was protector of herds, bees and fish, and personification of the male generative power. He was born with an extraordinary deformity, a tremendous phallus, the image of which was commonly placed as a protector in orchards and gardens. A priapus is a phallus of enormous proportions.

7. Satyr. Satyr, a sylvan deity, was much given to lasciviousness. He was often represented with the tail and ears of a horse, but sometimes with the feet and legs of a goat, short horns on his head, and his whole body covered with thick hair. Like Faunus, the Roman god of animals, he was multiple; there were as many Satyrs in Greece as Fauns in Rome. Satyriasis was the blessing bestowed on the world by Satyr; a nymphomaniac is his female equivalent.

A SHOT IN THE DARK

Not counting damascus steel, which can be pounded as easily into a plowshare as a sword, the bayonet, first produced at Bayonne, France, is the only killing tool in my files named after its place of origin. A number, however, have been named after people—and not always the people who invented them. Thus, the blunderbuss has a remote connection with Queen Bess; in

World War I British fliers called the German anti-aircraft guns 'archies' in allusion to a music-hall hit of the day, 'Archy, certainly not!'; the chassepot, a nineteenth-century French breech-loading rifle, is called after its inventor, as is the derringer, a short-barrelled pistol of the type used to slay Abraham Lincoln; the molotov cocktail of World War II was named for Russia's foreign minister. The six definitions below are of other devices named for people and intended primarily for slaughter. Give in each case the device and the person.

1. Fragments from a high-explosive shell.
2. A single-edged knife once popular in the American wilderness.
3. A large-bore, long-range German cannon of World War I.
4. The first practical revolver, still in wide use.
5. Underworld slang for a pistol.
6. A beheading machine.

ANSWERS

1. Shrapnel. In 1784, General Henry Shrapnel—or, as he then was, Lieutenant Shrapnel—began experimenting with the design of a hollow projectile containing a number of balls and a charge of powder to burst the shell. The British first fired shrapnel in anger in 1804, in Dutch Guiana. It reached its peak as an instrument of slaughter in World War I.
2. Bowie. Colonel James Bowie, an American adventurer and pioneer, fancied this ugly, single-edged knife, about fifteen inches long and curving at the tip. Whether the knife was actually designed by the Colonel or by his brother Rezin is in dispute.
   Bowie did not exactly die with his boots on, but he came close to it. When his heart stopped, in 1836, he was taking potshots from his sickbed at the Mexican attackers of the Alamo.
3. Big Bertha. The Germans in World War I used a massive long-range cannon to bombard Paris, and called it the Big Bertha in honour of Frau Bertha Krupp von Hohine un Hohlbach, head of the Krupp steel works.
4. Colt. Patented by Samuel Colt in 1835, this revolver became the universal handgun. In Wild West days it was a foolish cowboy indeed who would venture into a strange bar without his 'equaliser'.
5. Gat. In 1862, R. J. Gatling, a prolific inventor from North Carolina, perfected a gun that fired the then incredible total of 350 shots a minute. Within a few years, says the *Encyclopaedia Britannica*, the gatling gun was adopted 'by almost every civilised nation'. Gat, short for gatling, is established underworld usage for a pistol of any kind.

6. Guillotine. Dr. J. I. Guillotin developed this device just in time for the French Revolution. 'With my machine,' he informed the awestruck Assembly in 1789, 'I can whisk off your head in a twinkling and you suffer no pain.' But the guillotine was by no means the earliest tool of its kind. Holinshed's *Chronicles* reported in 1573 a great market-day attraction in Halifax—a blade that dropped in its frame 'with such violence that, if the neck of the transgressor were as big as that of a bull, it should be cut in sunder at a stroke and roll from the body by a huge distance'. And I believe an Edinburgh museum still displays the engine which in 1581 cut off the head of the regent Morton.

I

I ARISE FROM DREAMS

OF STEAM PUBLISHING

All night, from hush of thrush till rouse of rooster,
Simon and Schuster, Simon and Schuster, Simon and Schuster,
  The great expresses thundered through my dream
Or *Houghton Mifflin, Houghton Mifflin* panted
On gradients a bit more steeply canted,
  Or the implacable wheels took up the theme:
Lippincott, Lippincott, Lippincott they'd clink,
Lippincott, Lippincott, Doubleday and Company Inc,
  Lippincott, Lippincott till I could scream.
I turned to British books for my salvation:
The Rationalist Press Association
  Now all night long lets off its antique steam,
And all night long a shunted goods-train clanks
GOLLANCZ, *Gollancz, Gollancz, Gollancz, Gollancz.*

Peter Dickinson

Jealousy's an awful thing and foreign to my nature;
I'd punish it by law if I was in the Legislature.
One can't have all of any one, and wanting it is mean,
But still, there is a limit, and I speak of Miss Duveen.

> *I'm not a jealous woman,*
> *But I* can't *see what he sees in her,*
> *I can't see* what *he sees in her,*
> *I can't see what he* sees *in her!*
> *If she was something striking*
> *I could understand the liking,*
> *And I wouldn't have a word to say to that;*
> *But I can't see why he's fond*
> *Of that objectionable blonde—*
> *That fluffy little, stuffy little, flashy little, trashy little,*
> *creepy-crawly, music-hally, horrid little* CAT!

I wouldn't say a word against the girl—be sure of that;
It's not the creature's fault she has the manners of a rat.
Her dresses may be dowdy, but her hair is always new,
And if she squints a little bit—well, many people do.

> *I'm not a jealous woman,*
> *But I* can't *see what he sees in her,*
> *I can't* see *what he sees in her,*
> *I can't see what he* sees *in her!*
> *He's absolutely free—*
> *There's no bitterness in me,*
> *Though an ordinary woman would explode;*
> *I'd only like to know*
> *What he sees in such a crow*
> *As that insinuating, calculating, irritating, titivating,*
> *sleepy little, creepy little, sticky little* TOAD!

A. P. Herbert

I Dreamt of Couth

A few words thrive only in their antonyms. Why, if something is avoidable, do we go all the way around Robin Hood's barn to say it is *not inevitable?* The missing words in the verse below are forgotten positives. Fill them in to round out the quintain.

I dreamt of a **********,[1] *******[2] youth,
******,[3] ********,[4] and *****.[5]
A *****[6] and a *******[7] fellow, forsooth—
********,[8] *******,[9] *********,[10] ***[11], *****.[12]
A *******[13] fellow I dreamt.

W. R. E.

[1]Submissive to correction. [2]Hurtful. [3]Agile, handsome. [4]Contented. [5]Well-groomed. [6]Heartened, encouraged. [7]Straightforward. [8]Within reasonable bounds. [9]Capable of being uttered. [10]Tidy. [11]Dexterous. [12]Familiar, refined. [13]Forgettable.

ANSWER

I dreamt of a *corrigible, nocuous* youth,
Gainly, gruntled, and *kempt;*
A *mayed* and a *sidious* fellow, forsooth—
Ordinate, effable, shevelled, ept, couth;
A *delible* fellow I dreamt.

If -less were -ful, and -ful were -less

Just as some words are familiar only in their negative form (see 'I Dreamt of Couth'), so others commonly take '-less' but not '-ful' as a suffix, and vice versa. This is intolerable discrimination. The verse on the following page will set things straight.

A *******[1] dog, one ****-***[2] spring,
Set out for ********[3] foraging,
And as he dug in *******[4] sod,
Paid ********[5] tribute to his God.
At which, a *******,[6] *******[7] lass,
Whose ********[8] bodice charmed each pass-
Erby, cried out, 'O *******[9] sound!
O ******,[10] *******,[11] *******[12] hound!'

[1]Not curtailed. [2]Laminate, in a sense. [3]Clearly he had no need for dentures. [4]Very radical. [5]In full cry, as it were. [6]Efficient; strong. [7]Abounding in affection. [8]Referring to a safety feature for women, similar in concept to braces. [9]Because a dog's howl must come to an end. [10]Full of years; mortal. [11]Still alive, though. [12]A comforting reminder to the dog that his is not an endangered species.

ANSWER

A tailful dog, one leaf-ful spring,
Set out for toothful foraging,
And as he dug in rootful sod,
Paid voiceful tribute to his God.
At which, a feckful, loveful lass,
Whose strapful bodice charmed each pass-
Erby, cried out, 'O timeful sound!
O ageful, lifeful, peerful hound!'

Impossible Rhymes

Certain words in English have no true rhymes. It is always possible to approximate a rhyme, however, by fudging. To rhyme 'orange' here, I have bent the rules of syllabification and have accepted assonance instead of true rhyme in an unstressed syllable:

The fóur eng-
Ineers
Wear órange
Brassieres.

The only poet who completely solved the 'orange' problem was Arthur Guiterman, who wrote in *Gaily The Troubadour*:

Local Note

In Sparkill buried lies that man of mark
Who brought the Obelisk to Central Park,
Redoubtable Commander H. H. Gorringe,
Whose name supplies the long-sought rhyme
for 'orange'.

Below is a list of words difficult to rhyme. See what you can do with them before looking to see what others have done.

1. Orange and lemon
2. Liquid
3. Porringer
4. Widow
5. Niagara

ANSWERS

1. *Orange and lemon*

I gave my darling child a lemon,
That lately grew its fragrant stem on;
And next, to give her pleasure *more* range
I offered her a juicy orange,
And nuts—she cracked them in the door-hinge.

Author unknown

2. *Liquid*

After imbibing liquid,
A man in the South
Duly proceeds to stick quid
(Very likely a thick quid)
Into his mouth.

C. A. Bristed

3. *Porringer*

When nations doubt our power to fight,
We smile at every foreign jeer;
And with untroubled appetite,
Still empty plate and porringer.

Author unknown

4. *Widow*

The jury found that Pickwick *did* owe
Damages to Bardell's widow.

Author unknown

5. *Niagara*

Take instead of rope, pistol, or dagger, a
Desperate dash down the Falls of Niagara.

Tom Moore

SPELLING RHYMES

If word rhymes come hard to you, perhaps you will do better at verses in which the rhyme is provided not by the last word of the line, but by the last letter or two of the word. Here is the way it is done:

> 'Me drunk!' the cobbler cried, 'the devil trouble you,
> You want to kick up a blest r-o-w,
> I've just returned from a teetotal party,
> Twelve of us jammed in a spring c-a-r-t,
> The man as lectured now, was drunk; why bless ye,
> He's sent home in a c-h-a-i-s-e.'

Author unknown

Inflated Rhetoric

THE UNFIVETHREENNINE FIVETHREENE TELLER

That civilised understatement is extinct in America, and an endangered species in England, may or may not be an understatement. More and more, it seems, we emphasise by exaggerating. For *like* we substitute *love*; for *distaste, hate*; for *liberal, Red*; for *conservative, Fascist*; for *eccentricity, insanity*. We write, as it were, shouting, and hear others' shouts as whispers.

Victor Borge, the pianist and comedian, has popularised a game which illustrates this rhetorical inflation in a mathematical sort of way, and I have adapted his concept in the story below. You will notice that numbers are buried in a good many of the words. Reduce each number by one, and you will have the story as I originally wrote it.

If you decide to make this sort of puzzle yourself, you may prefer, if such is your direction in economics and rhetoric, to promote deflation rather than inflation by using in the puzzle a number just below, rather than just above, the approximation in the story as solved.

Twoce upon a time there lived in Threenisia a threetor who was a saturten, misbegoteleven ingrnine. This hnineful cnineiff fivethrightly abominnined his fivemer classeven sthreedent, the cele-brnined young potentnine Eightarola. Awnineing his oppor-threenity and opernineing without fivewarning, the trnineor initinined a devastnineing revolt. He fiveced Eightarola three fivefeit his estnines; three fivego his elevenure; three abdicnine his throne; and three haseleven to pull his frnine from his elevent fivethwith three fivestall annihilation.

Fnine has written that anytwo, even the most desolnine and fivelorn of men, still retains two elevenacious friend. Such was Eightarola's five-footed atelevendant Bedfived. This beten caten, a Grnine Dane, was antiqunined and superannunined, but he would not contemplnine fivesaking his master, who addressed him in the following despernine and aberrnined fashion:

'Two must fiveget two-time glories; two cannot yet affived three seek restithreetion. But two might, two calculnines, migrnine three fiveeign lands. Two might locnine in the fivebidden Black Fivest, threetling about preelevending three be a fivethreene teller.'

So off went the fivemer potentnine and the caten. Sad three relnine, however, Eightarola was not apprecinined in the Black Fiveest. No-two took his bnine. Through lack of atelevention, if not strnine asitenness, he had failed three fivearm, or even three fivefinger, himself with fivemulas five fivetelling the fnine of the fiveest dwellers.

By grnine luck, however, he two day met an intoxicnineing, tenteen-year-old ballet dancer, clad in an abbrevinined threethree. 'Threets,' cried Eightarola, 'it is my fivecefully articulnined conelevention that we three must become two.'

Threets agreed, and from that moment on he atelevended three his affairs as never befive. No longer at sevens and eights, he fiveced the fivemidable threetor three capithreelnine, two back his throne and elevent, and lived coneleventedly with his grnineful caten atelevendant and his elevender soulmnine fiveever after.

ANSWER

Once upon a time there lived in Tunisia a tutor who was a saturnine, misbegotten ingrate. This hateful caitiff forthrightly abominated his former classics student, the celebrated young potentate Sevenarola. Awaiting his opportunity and operating without forewarning, the traitor initiated a devastating revolt. He forced Sevenarola to forfeit his estates; to forgo his tenure; to abdicate his throne; and to hasten to pull his freight from his tent forthwith to forestall annihilation.

Fate has written that anyone, even the most desolate and forlorn of men, still retains one tenacious friend. Such was Sevenarola's four-footed attendant Bedford. This benign canine, a Great Dane, was antiquated and superannuated, but he would not contemplate forsaking his master, who addressed him in the following desperate and aberrated fashion:

'One must forget one-time glories; one cannot yet afford to seek restitution. But one might, one calculates, migrate to foreign lands. One might locate in the forbidden Black Forest, tootling about pretending to be a fortune teller.'

So off went the former potentate and the canine. Sad to relate, however, Sevenarola was not appreciated in the Black Forest. No-one took his bait. Through lack of attention, if not straight asinineness, he had failed to forearm, or even to forefinger, himself with formulas for foretelling the fate of the forest dwellers.

By great luck, however, he one day met an intoxicating, nineteen-year-old ballet dancer, clad in an abbreviated tutu. 'Toots,' cried Sevenarola, 'it is my forcefully articulated contention that we two must become one.'

Toots agreed, and from that moment on he attended to his affairs as never before. No longer at sixes and sevens, he forced the formidable tutor to capitulate, won back his throne and tent, and lived contentedly with his grateful canine attendant and his tender soulmate forever after.

Interminable Words

The longest word in English, says a riddle, is smiles, since there is a mile between the first and last letter. Shakespeare's longest word (27 letters) by no means matches this. In *Love's Labour's Lost* Costard the clown says to Moth the page: 'I marvel thy master hath not eaten thee for a word; for thou art not so long by the head as honorificabilitudinitatibus; thou art easier swallowed than a flap-dragon.'

Honorificabilitudinitatibus, if only it meant anything, would hold a respectable place in the ranks of the longer English words, even though it falls short of James Joyce's 34-letter *semperexcommuni-cambiambiambisumers*. Any such ranking would have to include also Henry Carey's

'*Aldiborontphosophorno*, (21)
Where left you *Chrononnotonthologos?*' (20)

146

But these words would be small fry in some countries. I have read, though I cannot attest the fact, that on p. 837 of Liddell & Scott's *Greek Lexicon* there appears a word of 176 letters meaning hash.

A nineteenth-century Flemish gentleman was inspired by the invention of the automobile to create the word *Snelpaardeloos-zonderspoorwegpatrolrijtuig*—41 letters meaning 'a carriage which is worked by means of petroleum, which travels fast, which has no horses, and which is not run on rails'.

It takes longer to say the names of some locations in Wales than to walk through them. The most impressive example in my records is *Llanfairpwllgwyngyllgogerychwyrndrobwllllantysili-ogogogoch*, 58 letters pronounced 'Klan-fire-pooth-gwin-geth-go-gerith-kwin-drooble-klan-dissileo-gogo-gok'. There may be a 59th letter missing, 13 letters from the end. The word means 'The church of St. Mary in a hollow of white hazel, near to the rapid whirlpool, and to St. Tisilio church, near to a red cave'. If you write to a friend there, you need use only the first 20 letters on the envelope; the Post Office will know what you mean.

The longest place name in the United States, from the Indian, is *Chargoggagoggmanchauggagoggchaubunaqwnaqungamangg*, the meaning of which is unknown to me. It is said to be a lake in south-central Massachusetts.

The Germans are compound-word addicts. A 57-letter whopper (and my version, according to authorities who do not bother to fill in the missing pieces, is seven letters short) is *Constantino-politanischerdudelsackpfeipenmachergsellschaft*, meaning 'Associ-ation of Constantinople bagpipe makers'.

Bismarck considered the word 'apothecary' insufficiently German, and coined a 71-letter replacement: *Gesundheitswieder-herstellungsmitterzusammenmischungsuerhaltnisskundiger*.

Some scientific terms in English stretch out interminably, but otherwise we are not in the same league with the Germans. Gladstone coined *disestablishmentarianism*, with 24 letters; *anti-* of course may be prefixed. *Floccinaucinihilipilification*, connected in some way with wool, has 29.

If you are an *antitransubstantiationalist* (27), you doubt that consecrated bread and wine actually change into the body and blood of Christ.

A 34-letter word popular with schoolboys and television comics is *supercalifragilisticexpialidocious*, a Walt Disney creation mean-ing, I suppose, superb.

A considerable company of words of 20 or more letters combine at least two words: *anthropomorphotheist* (20), *philosophicopsychological* (25), etc. Others grow through prefixing: *antianthropomorphism* (20), *hyperconscientiousness* (22), *superincomprehensibleness* (25) *semiprofessionalized* (20). There is no particular reason why there should not be an *antiantitransubstantiationalist* (31).

The words defined below are made up of 20 or more letters, and all occur more commonly than you might expect. Try guessing them before checking the answers.

1. Aptness to respond to a suggestion by doing the contrary.
2. State of being beyond the reach of the human mind.
3. One who seeks to upset a revolution.
4. Love of offspring.
5. Applying the attributes of man to God.
6. An opposite explanation.
7. Extreme deference to the dictates of conscience.
8. Opposition to freedom of thought and behaviour, especially in religion.

ANSWERS

1. Contrasuggestibility.
2. Incomprehensibleness.
3. Counterrevolutionary.
4. Philoprogenitiveness.
5. Anthropomorphilogical.
6. Counterinterpretation.
7. Hyperconscientiousness.
8. Antilatitudinarianism.

THE PRESCRIPTION

Said the chemist: 'I'll take some dimethyloximidomesoralamide
And I'll add just a dash of dimethylamidoazobenzaldehyde;
    But if these won't mix,
    I'll just have to fix
Up a big dose of trisodiumpholoroglucintricarboxycide.'

Author unknown

Irish Bulls

A ludicrous blunder of language is called an Irish bull, on the theory that Hibernians are particularly subject to this affliction. For instance:

An Irish member of Parliament, referring to a minister noted for his love of money, observed: 'I verily believe that if the honourable gentleman were an undertaker, it would be the delight of his heart to see all mankind seized with a common mortality, that he might have the benefit of the general burial, and provide scarfs and hat-bands for the survivors.'

A Hibernian gentleman, when told by his nephew that he had just entered college with a view to the church, said, 'I hope that I may live to hear you preach my funeral sermon.'

A poor Irishman offered an old saucepan for sale. His children gathered around him and inquired why he parted with it. 'Ah, me honeys,' he answered, 'I would not be afther parting with it but for a little money to buy something to put in it.'

'I was going,' said an Irishman, 'over Westminster Bridge the other day, and I met Pat Hewins. "Hewins," says I, "how are you?" "Pretty well," says he, "thank you, Donnelly." "Donnelly!" says I; "that's not *my* name." "Faith, no more is mine Hewins," says he. So we looked at each other again, and sure it turned out to be nayther of us.'

BULLS ABROAD

Irish bulls thrive far from the green fields of Ireland. Here are five lusty specimens of the breed, two from America and three from England.

The following resolutions were passed by the Board of Councilmen in Canton, Mississippi: 1. Resolved, by this Council, that we build a new Jail. 2. Resolved, that the new Jail be built out of the materials of the old Jail. 3. Resolved, that the old Jail be used until the new Jail is finished.

Wells & Fargo's Express, operating in Indian country, declared in its regulations that it would not be responsible as carriers 'for any loss or damage by fire, the acts of God, or of Indians, or any other public enemies of the government'.

George Selwyn, the missionary, once remarked that it seemed impossible for a lady to write a letter without adding a postscript. A lady present replied, 'The next letter you receive from me, Mr. Selwyn, will prove you wrong.' The letter arrived in due course, with the following line after the signature: 'P.S. Who is right now, you or I?'

Sir Boyle Roche is credited with two classic bulls:

'Mr. Speaker, I boldly answer in the affirmative—No.'

'Mr. Speaker, if I have any prejudice against the honourable member, it is in his favour.'

PARLIAMENTARY LETTER

The following letter, in Maria Edgeworth's *Essay on Irish Bulls*, is credited by her to one S——, an Irish member of Parliament at the time of the Rebellion:

My dear Sir:—Having now a little peace and quietness, I sit down to inform you of the dreadful bustle and confusion we are in from these blood-thirsty rebels, most of whom are (thank God!) killed and dispersed. We are in a pretty mess; can get nothing to eat, nor wine to drink, except whisky; and when we sit down to dinner, we are obliged to keep both hands armed. Whilst I write this, I hold a pistol in each hand and a sword in the other. I concluded in the beginning that this would be the end of it; and I see I was right, for it is not half over yet. At present there are such goings on, that everything is at a standstill. I should have answered your letter a fortnight since, but I did not receive it until this morning. Indeed, hardly a mail arrives safe without being robbed. No longer ago than yesterday the coach with the mails from Dublin was robbed near this town: the bags had been judiciously left behind for fear of accident, and by good luck there was nobody in it but two outside passengers who had nothing for thieves to take. Last Thursday notice was given that a gang of rebels were advancing here under the French standard; but they had no colours, nor any drums except bagpipes. Immediately every man in the place, including women and children, ran out to meet them. We soon found our force much too little; and we were far too near to think of retreating. Death was in every face; but to it we went, and by the time half our little party were killed we began to be all alive again. Fortunately, the rebels had no guns, except pistols, cutlasses, and pikes; and as we had plenty of guns and ammunition, we put them all to the sword. Not a soul of them escaped, except some that were drowned in an adjacent bog; and in a very short time nothing was to be heard but silence. Their uniforms were all different colours, but mostly green. After the action, we went to rummage a sort of camp which they had left behind them. All we found was a few pikes without heads, a parcel of empty bottles full of water, and a bundle of French commissions filled up with Irish names. Troops are now stationed all around the country, which exactly squares with my ideas. I have only time to add that I am in great haste.

Yours truly, ——

P.S.—If you do not receive this, of course it must have miscarried; therefore I beg you will write and let me know.

Isosceles Words

It is often possible to enlarge a word one letter at a time, each time rearranging the letters so as to create a word with a different root. It is equally possible to reverse the process. Try working out the four examples below before looking at the answers.

1. Build I into Flirters.
2. Reduce crotchets to O.
3. Build A into Drafting.
4. Reduce Befriends to I.

(ANSWERS OVERLEAF)

151

1	2	3	4
I	Crotchets	A	Befriends
If	Crochets	At	Definers
Fir	Torches	Tan	Refined
Rift	Throes	Rant	Finder
First	Short	Train	Diner
Strife	Shot	Rating	Rind
Trifles	Hot	Trading	Din
Flirters	To	Drafting	In
	O		I

J, K

Jargon

The following statement by a teacher is quoted exactly as it appeared in a school publication:

Totally obsolete teaching methods based on imprinting concepts instead of growthful actualising of potential have created the intellectual ghetto. If schools would stop labeling cooperation 'cheating', and adopt newer methods of student interaction, we wouldn't keep churning out these competitive isolates.

Which means, in plain English, 'Let the kids cheat'.

Thus ethics and English decay together. The teacher was impelled to conceal his thought in jargon, as an octopus might conceal itself in ink, either because he was not quite sure what he was saying; or he did not know how to say it; or he was apprehensive of saying it right out.

Jargon, even when used by learned physicists and noted educators, is, like Pig Latin, the in-language of the immature, who gladly sacrifice sense for secrecy. Specialised phraseology is acceptable as a tool of precise communication. When it obfuscates (as we jargoneers say) it is monstrous.

Fowler says jargon is 'the use of long words, circumlocutions, and other clumsiness'. Partridge calls it 'shop talk'. He is too kind; only the part of shop talk that is unnecessary, inappropriate, abstract, clumsy, passive and obscure deserves the dreadful label. Shop talk is shorthand; jargon has no purpose save perhaps to hint at some non-existent wisdom.

There are as many jargons as there are arts and professions. Politics, as the oldest profession but one, is encrusted with it. An article by David Steel, MP, in *Punch*, cites a number of examples of parliamentary jargon, from which I choose these:

'The problem is how to optimise the institutionalisation of the forecasting procedures.'

'If those sleeping peers who have not yet applied for the writ have not woken up to their possibilities, I should be disposed to think that they should be given quite a long *locus penitentiae* in which to reply.'

'Force . . . is the midwife of every society pregnant with the new. But in England, at any rate, is she not a somewhat outdated old body, doing her rounds in a few places, admittedly, but on the whole yielding to new obstetrical techniques—techniques which may be a bit impersonal but which are certainly a lot more painless? Such an unlikely duo as Mr. Enoch Powell and Mr. Tariq Ali seem both agreed that rivers of blood are flowing, or are going to be flowing somewhere, and both seem afraid of missing the boat.'

(On second look, I see that last passage is not jargon at all. It is, however, an example of the depths to which the language of Shakespeare can sink.)

A research chemist will accept as a truism the statement that chlorophyll makes food by photosynthesis. Say the same thing to a practical engineer, however, and his reaction may be a blank stare. Stuart Chase, after making this point, goes on: 'But if the statement is rephrased, "Green leaves build up food with the help of light", anyone can understand it. So, says [C. F.] Kettering, if we are going to surmount the boundaries between kinds of technical men: "The first thing to do is to get them to speak the same language".'

The man or woman who has scrambled about halfway up the intellectual slope, and has found a shaky toehold there, often finds the urge to use jargon irresistible. Louis Kronenberger recalls a recent article in one of the weightier American quarterlies which flaunted all these words, along with others as ill-begotten:

Rebarbarise, ephebic, totemic, semeiotics, thereiomorphic, biomorphic, developmental, authorial, theophany, catena, authentification, anamnesis, pseudocausality, eld, ludic, logoi, liminal, opsis, topos, sooth, psychotheology, liberative.

'What most enchants me,' says Mr. Kronenberger, 'is that the author, having inserted quotations from Emerson and Matthew Arnold in which every word and phrase is an easily understood and established one, must himself straightway refer to Emerson as a "comparatist" and to the "racial calculus" that Arnold is practising.'

The jargon of specialists at least has the excuse that special dialects are required for technical discussions. But what is *your* excuse when you use words, in the phrase of the philologist Wilson Follett, as 'mere plugs for the holes in one's thought'?

Among words commonly so used Mr. Follett lists the following:

NOUNS: *angle, approach, background, breakdown* (analysis), *concept, context, dimension, essentials, factor, insight, motivation, nature, picture* (situation), *potential, process.*

VERBS: *accent, climax, contact, de-emphasise, formulate, highlight, pinpoint, process, research, spark, trigger, update.*

MODIFIERS: *basic, bitter, crucial, cryptic, current(ly), drastic, essential, initial, key, major, over-all, realistic, stimulating, worthwhile.*

LINKS: *as of, -conscious, -free, in terms of, -wise, -with.*

Mr. Kronenberger gives examples in a different vein:

Life-style, value judgment, the human condition, charismatic, polarisation, paradigm, elitist, ecumenical, ambiance, graffiti, symbiosis, epiphany, extrapolate, archetype, analogue, concept, subsume, autonomy, dichotomy, viable.

All these words are legitimate when properly used. No-one asks you to discard them. They can give you loyal service. Just don't let them lead you into jargon.*

---

* Congressman Maury Maverick's word for the bureaucratic variety was 'gobbledygook'.

Jump or Jiggle

Somewhere in this book there is a poem that lists the young of animals, and somewhere else one that lists animal sounds. The poem below, by Evelyn Beyer, shows various animals animalbulating. I have jumbled the key words, just to stop you from reading too fast.

Frogs mpju
Caterpillars pmhu

Worms gligwe
Bugs glegij

Rabbits pho
Horses pocl

Snakes idsel
Seagulls eidlg

Mice ercpe
Deer plea

Puppies uncobe
Kittens uncope

Lions ktlas—
But—
I lwka!

ANSWERS

Frogs jump	Snakes slide	Lions stalk—
Caterpillars hump	Seagulls glide	But—
		I walk!
Worms wiggle	Mice creep	
Bugs jiggle	Deer leap	
Rabbits hop	Puppies bounce	
Horses clop	Kittens pounce	

L

THE LAMA

The one-l lama,
He's a priest.
The two-l llama,
He's a beast.
And I will bet
A silk pajama
There isn't any
Three-l lllama.*

Ogden Nash

Lesson in Address

This jingle might have been stretched out by including, among others, Mr. E., Aunty Quated, and Burl Esq., but it is tidier as it is.

Three pretty misses, partying they go:
Miss Creant,
Miss Anthrope,
Miss L. Toe.

Flirting with the gentry, fluttering their eyes:
Sir Cumvent,
Sir Cumspect,
Sir Cumcise.

W. R. E.

---

* Adds Mr. Nash: The author's attention has been called to a type of conflagration known as a three-alarmer. Pooh!

A LETTER FROM EDWARD LEAR TO EVELYN BARING, LORD CROMER

Thrippy Pilliwinx,—
   Inkly tinky pobblebockle able-squabs? Flosky! Beebul trimble flosky! Okulscratch abibblebongibo, viddle squibble tog-atog, ferry moyassity amsky flamsky damsky crocklefether squiggs.
                     Flinky wisty pomm,
                                Slushypipp

                     *

Lipograms

A Californian musician named Ernest Vincent Wright wrote a 50,000-word novel* without using the letter *e*. James Thurber wrote a story about a country in which no-one was permitted to use *o*. Any composition which thus rejects one or more letters, either vowel or consonant, is a lipogram. In this old lipogrammatic song, the letter *s* does not appear:

COME, LOVE, COME

Oh! Come to-night; for naught can charm
   The weary time when thou'rt away.
Oh! come; the gentle moon hath thrown
   O'er bower and hall her quivering ray.
The heather-bell hath mildly flung
   From off her fairy leaf the bright
And diamond dewdrop that had hung
   Upon that leaf—a gem of light.
                     Then come, love come.

(CONTINUED OVERLEAF)

* *Gadsby* (Wetzel, Los Angeles, 1939).

To-night the liquid wave hath not—
  Illumined by the moonlight beam
Playing upon the lake beneath,
  Like frolic in an autumn dream—
The liquid wave hath not, to-night,
  In all her moonlit pride, a fair
Gift like to them that on thy lip
  Do breathe and laugh, and home it there.
                Then come, love, come.

To-night! to-night! my gentle one,
  The flower-bearing Amra tree
Doth long, with fragrant moan, to meet
  The love-lip of the honey-bee.
But not the Amra tree can long
  To greet the bee, at evening light,
With half the deep, fond love I long
  To meet my Nama here to-night.
                Then come, love, come.

                        Author Unknown

There is another species of versification, the name of which
escapes me, in which every line begins or, as in the following
epitaph, ends, with the same letter.

The charnel mounted on the wall
Lets to be seen in funeral
A matron plain domesticall,
In pain and care continual.
Not slow, nor gay, nor prodigal,
Yet neighbourly and hospital.
Her children yet living all,
Her sixty-seventh year home did call
To rest her body natural
In hope to rise spiritual.

                        Author Unknown

THE FATE OF NASSAN

Each stanza of the following poem has been written so as to include every letter in the alphabet but the vowel *e*. The author is unknown.

Bold Nassan quits his caravan,
A hazy mountain grot to scan;
Climbs craggy rocks to spy his way,
Doth tax his sight, but far doth stray.

Not work of man, nor sport of child,
Finds Nassan in that mazy wild;
Lax grow his joints, limbs toil in vain—
Poor wight! why didst thou quit that plain?

Vainly for succour Nassan calls,
Know, Zillah, that thy Nassan falls;
But prowling wolf and fox may joy,
To quarry on thy Arab boy.

M

Malapropisms

'Illiterate him, I say, quite from your mind!' ordered Mrs. Malaprop in Sheridan's play *The Rivals*. By such verbal confusions, she became, says H. W. Fowler (loftily ignoring the pun on his own name), 'the matron saint of all those who go wordfowling with a blunderbuss'. Among her absurdities were 'A progeny of learning', 'Make no delusions to the past', and, 'Sure, if I reprehend anything in this world, it is the use of my oracular tongue, and a nice derangement of epitaphs'.

Skewed words are as common as dandruff. Just now I came across this statement in a newspaper column written by a distinguished duo of political commentators: 'Finally, the new rules for delegate selection seem to mitigate against conservative candidates.'

Recently I heard a young lady of impeccable family and schooling say, 'I was so hungry that I gouged myself.'

A friend of mine attributes to his gardener the remark that 'She don't like me and I don't like her, so it's neutral.'

The sentences below contain words that are frequently malapropped. Substitute the correct word in each line.

1. The doctor said it was *desirous* to stop smoking.
2. Cheer up; I *predicate* final victory.
3. His capacity for hard liquor is *incredulous*.
4. This does not *portend* to be a great work of art.
5. Your contemptuous treatment of me is a great *humility*.
6. *Fortuitously* for her, she won the sweepstakes.
7. His *inflammable* speech set off a riot.

ANSWERS

1. Desirous, desirable. *Desirous* is 'desiring'; *desirable* is 'worth wanting; advantageous'. 'For the sake of your health it is *desirable* to stop smoking, whether or not you are *desirous* of doing so.'
2. Predicate, predict. *Predicate*, often with 'on' or 'upon', is 'to base or establish'; *predict* is 'to foretell'. 'My *prediction* of final victory is *predicated* upon hard facts.'
3. Incredulous, incredible. *Incredulous is* 'disbelieving'; *incredible* is 'unbelievable'. 'I am *incredulous* of the amount you say he drinks; it is *incredible*.'
4. Portend, pretend. *Portend* is 'to presage, foretell'; *pretend* is 'to feign'. 'He *pretends* to be an artist, but his work does not *portend* greatness.'
5. Humility, humiliation. *Humility* is 'modesty, the quality of being humble'; *humiliation* is 'degradation, or the act of humiliating'. 'His *humility* made him immune to *humiliation*.'
6. Fortuitous, fortunate. *Fortuitous* is 'utterly accidental'; *fortunate* is 'lucky'. 'It was *fortuitous* that she won the sweepstakes—and very *fortunate* for her.'
7. Inflammable, inflammatory. *Inflammable* is 'tending to ignite easily and burn rapidly; easily aroused to strong emotion'. *Inflammatory* is 'calculated to arouse strong emotion'. 'The speaker was *inflammatory*, the audience *inflammable*; the result was a riot.'

LIGHTNING FROM LIGHTNING BUGS

It was Mark Twain who said that the difference between a word that is right and a word that is almost right is the difference between the lightning and the lightning bug. Yet almost-right words rank considerably higher on the divine scale than malapropisms. And even malapropisms, though they may not light the whole sky, occasionally provide a modest illumination all their own. The man whose tongue slipped into 'civil serpents' was revealing long-concealed fury at bureaucratic indifference. 'Salutary confinement' can be just that. The truth of 'familiarity breeds attempt' was known to every halfway attractive girl in my college class. The mother who called her daughter a 'waltzflower' was speaking with absolute precision. 'Adding assault to injury' is as deplorable as adding insult. The road from 'infancy to adultery' is well worn.

My favourite lightning bug is 'There's so much pornographic rubbish in print it buggers the imagination.' Only a demotic genius could have coined that line.

Mental Menu

In each of the words clued below, whether at the beginning, at the end, or in between, you should be able to find something edible.

1. Alms seeker
2. Outer garments
3. Sailing vessel
4. Width
5. Gravity
6. Smooth
7. Tool
8. Satisfy
9. Sharp-pointed weapon
10. Mottled
11. Having parti-coloured patches
12. Fixer of fixtures
13. Capriciousness
14. Move in haste
15. Irritate; annoy
16. Loud cry

ANSWERS

1. Beggar, egg
2. Coats, oats
3. Windjammer, jam
4. Breadth, bread
5. Sobriety, brie
6. Sleek, leek
7. Hammer, ham
8. Appease, peas
9. Spear, pear
10. Dapple, apple
11. Pied, pie
12. Plumber, plum
13. Caprice, rice
14. Scurry, curry
15. Tease, tea
16. Scream, cream

Metaphorically Speaking

There can scarcely have been a proposal more quixotic than that of Dr. Johnson – to fling metaphors neck and crop out of the English canon. Civilisation, one cannot doubt, began with the first figure of speech and will end with the last. Men without metaphors are brutes; their gaze is fixed on the ground; nothing in their lives exceeds its sum.

The Bible abounds in metaphors:

'A land flowing with milk and honey.'
'And thou shalt become an astonishment, a proverb, and a
   byword among all nations.'
'He kept him as the apple of his eye.'
'They shall be as thorns in your sides.'
'For we must needs die, and are as water spilt on the ground,
   which cannot be gathered up again.'
'There ariseth a little cloud out of the sea, like a man's hand.'
'The Lord is my rock, and my fortress, and my deliverer.'
'I will wipe Jerusalem as a man wipeth a dish, wiping it, and
   turning it upside down.'

The metaphors of Homer burn on the page:

'Words sweet as honey.'
'Shakes his ambrosial curls.'
'Thick as autumnal leaves or driving sand.'
'She moves a goddess, and she looks a queen.'
'Soft as the fleeces of descending snow.'
'A green old age.'

Modern poets have carried on the tradition:

'The road was a ribbon of moonlight.'
'Thou art the star for which all evening waits.'
'Her beauty was sold for an old man's gold;
   She's a bird in a gilded cage.'
'As a white candle
   In a holy place
So is the beauty
   Of an aged face.'
'Like dead, remembered footsteps on old floors.'
'I have seen old ships sail like swans asleep.'

'It's odd to think we might have been
Sun, moon and stars unto each other,
Only, I turned down one little street,
And you went up another.'

Mixed metaphors are supposed to be the hallmark of the uneducated, and many people make a hobby of exposing them, which is good for the self-esteem. Examples of mixed metaphors are all about:

'The Internal Revenue Service appears to be totally impaled in the quicksands of inertia.'

'I smell a rat; I seem to see it floating in the air; but we shall yet nip it in the bud.'

'There is no man so low that he has in him no spark of manhood, which, if watered by the milk of human kindness, will not burst into flames.'

Sometimes, though, the mixture is really in the eye of the observer. I remember, for instance, when English teachers used to cite Joyce Kilmer's poem *Trees* as a particularly horrendous farrago of mixed metaphors. His tree not only pressed its mouth against the earth's sweet flowing breast, but managed at the same time to look at God, lift its leafy arms to pray, and wear a nest of robins in its hair. But Mr. Kilmer was not mixing his metaphors; he was changing them, quite a different thing. Similarly, when John of Gaunt eulogises England in *Richard II*, he piles up some fifteen parallel images; but there is not a mixed metaphor in the lot.

Metrical Feet

If you are never quite sure whether a verse is written in trochee, spondee, dactyl, iamb, or anapæst, this mnemonic verse may help:

Trochee trips from long to short.
From long to long in solemn sort
Slow Spondee stalks; strong foot! yet ill able
Ever to come up with Dactyl trisyllable.
Iambics march from short to long.
With a leap and a bound the swift Anapests throng.

Samuel Taylor Coleridge

Milt Grocery

Milt Grocery was the dialect of the Jews who immigrated to the United States in the first half of the twentieth century. Their efforts to twist Yiddish-habituated tongues around English words resulted in mispronunciations and twists of locution that sounded wildly funny not only to settlers of an earlier vintage but, such is the genius of this people, to the immigrants themselves. Montague Glass, Arthur Kober and Leo Rosten were comic writers with perfect pitch for this dialect; but to me it is forever Milt Grocery, since Milt Gross was matchless in the idiom.

'Delilah'* is one of my favourite bits of Milt Grocery. Pot One tells how God turned the sinful Israelites over to the still more sinful Philistines, among whose hangers-on was one Delilah: 'Delilah was a wemp. Also on de site she was de foist wan from de fimmales from heestory wot she should be a lady-barber.'

Samson makes the scene in Pot Two. 'So,' says Gross, 'was like dees de insite fects':

DELILAH

Pot Two

So it was gradually born Semson, wot he was from pheezical feetness a movvel! You should see wot he was hable he should band in a heff iron bozz, witt still-bimms—odder wot he was hable he should lie don it should drife heem on top from de chast a huttomibill fool witt a femily wit ralatiffs yat, fet ones!!

So, of cuss, sotch a movvelous spasimin from menly weegor crated a conseederable nuttice in de poblic heye wot he bicame gradually a calabrity wot he was de tust from de tonn, witt de peectures in de Tebloids. So all over he was inwited to poddies wot he would hold futt so:

'Wal, wal, hollo, pipple! Noo a leedle treeck!! So here is de grend piano, is no? Geeve a looke a squizze—Tootpeecks!! Ha ha—is notting et all. Wait yat, you'll see I'll geeve a grab minesalf by de back from de nack wot I'll hold minesalf hout by a harm's langt!!! Ha ha!!! Denk you!! Denk you! Is jost a kneck!!'

So was stending in de beck from de poddy a geng Pheelistins

---

* 'Famous Fimmales Witt Odder Ewents from Heestory.'

wot it deweloped on de pot from dem a lodge quantity from jalousy wot it gritted Semson rimmocks so:

'Rezzbarrizz!!'

So Semson sad: 'Who's rezzing plizze de tust from de tonn?'

So it replite de Pheelistins: 'Ha! ha! geeve a look a tust—bedly boint! Say, who lat in here de Houze from David annyway??!! Comm on, boyiss, we'll tsettle heem de hesh.'

So bing wot Semson was tuttally hunprepared wot he deedn't hed witt heem futtifications he should prewent de etteck so he nutticed gradually wot on de mentelpiss was a jawbun from a ess. So witt de jawbun he gave a knock foist wan Pheelistin, den a sacund, den a toid, wot in a shut time it flad de whole tripe from Pheelistins wot Semson sad:

'Wal, wal—a leedle woikout! Denks, boyiss. Ulmost mossed me hopp de hair. Wal, wal. Noo, pipple? Geeve a look—a crubbar —whoops!—pretzels!!'

In Pot Tree, Delilah, dot wixen, esks Semson to creck her a nut. The story continues:

So Semson sad: 'Ha! Ha! Say, kirro, I'll creck for you anytink! Ha—for you I'll sweem de highest montain!!'

So she gave heem a look, a wempish one, dot sleepery ill, wot she sad: 'Ho, you gudgeous critchure, you!! A peecture from weem, witt weegor, witt witelity!! Could I fill by you de moscle!! Ho! Sotch a treel!! It geeves me de cripps. Sotch a hoddness. Go hon, weegle a leedle de bisaps! Whooy!! How you gat like dees?'

So Semson sad: 'Noxated Hiron, keed!'

So she sad: 'Ha Ha Ha!!—you fonny boy! Cull me Del.'

So Semson sad: 'Ha ha—I'll cull you "Pitches"—you'll cull me "Bonny"—ha ha!!'

'Ho, you hold shik you!! Wal, I must be ronning alung to take mine hettical colture lasson. Commaround you should see me. Jost tell de durrman wot Jeemy de nooseboy sant you, bot— heh, heh, heh—take foist batter a haircot—heh heh. Coot nite, Dollink—twitt, twitt.'

Pot Furr

So Semson, dot dope, he ren queeck de naxt day by Delilah, wot he deedn't slapt yat a whole night befurr, wot he was ricking witt poifume wot he tutt so: 'A switt leedle chilte—so deeference from de rast from de gold-deegers.'

So was ricklining on a diwan Delilah, wot she sad so:

'Hm, you nutty boy, you deedn't took a haircot. Momma is waxed—poo hoo! Is dees nize you should make momma she should cry? Poo hoo—hoo—POO HOO-POO-HOO-HOO!! You dun't luffing me!!'

So Semson sad: 'Yi Yi Yi! Of cuss, I luffing you! I'll go queeck now I should ketch a haircot!!'

So she sad: 'Hm, wait—I got a hidea!! Comm here!! Seet don, Switthott!!'

So she gafe a pool hout foist wan hair wot she sad 'You luff me,' und she gave a pool hout anodder hair wot she sad, 'You luff me not!' So she pooled, witt pooled, witt pooled, teel it gave de lest hair a wenish wot Semson hexclaimed: 'I LUFF YOU!'

So Delilah sad: 'Wal—wal!!! Now hozz about a shafe? No?? Shempoo? Is a leedle dry de skeen—massage? A seenge maybe odder a twizze de heyebrozz??? A mod-peck? Gudgeous wadder we heving. Shine??? Hozz about a leedle mange-cure for de lion skeen??? Wal, wal, sotch a himproofment! De bobbed hair makes you look witt at list tan years yonger!!!'

So Semson sa'd: 'Hm, bot you should see before wot it was bobbed. Was sotch a head hair wot I was hable I should seet on it!!! Ho wal, is motch murr a convenience dees way in de sommertime . . . By de way, wot was I saying? Ho yes—I luff you!!!'

So she sad in a werry cuxxing tun from voice: 'Will you band plizze a hairpeen for me, Dirrie?'

So Semson trite like annytink he should band de hairpeen wot he sad so: 'Hm, wot's dees?!?! I'm filling a leedle grocky!! Whooy!! De spreeng wadder, no dott. Ho boy—look it dun't banding de hairpeen! I'm filling wick in de knizz.'

So it came hout from Delilah a reeple from leffter, a mocking one, wot she said: 'Hm—a leedle wick in de knizz, ha, stoopit? Is dees a fect?? So tomorrow'll be by de Pheelistins a poddy. So you inwited. Comm opp dere you should strott your stoff you should make for dem a hect you should poosh in a Swees chizze tom-tecks!! Hm, you gatting pale!! Heh heh heh.'

So it keptured de Pheelistins Semson wot dey hed it a poddy witt a dronken ogre in de Tample wot dey made dere from Semson hall sutts from jukks witt tunts witt smot-crecks wot he became med like annytink wot he roshed queeck by a sturr from weegs witt toupizz—wot he pushed on queek a weeg—so from dees he bicame gradually strung wot he gafe a push don de pillows from de Tample wot it keeled hall de Pheelistins wot it smeshed dem hall opp to adams!

Monosyllabic Verse

Try writing a verse of eight lines or more, making some sort of poetic sense, that has no word of more than one syllable. It's not easy. Phineas Fletcher, who died around 1650, came up with this alliterative specimen, which fails the mark by one word:

> New light new love, new love new life hath bred;
> A light that lives by love, and loves by light;
> A love to Him to whom all loves are wed;
> A light to whom the sun is dark as night.
> Eye's light, heart's love, soul's only life He is;
> Life, soul, love, heart, light, eye, and all are His;
> He eye, light, heart, love, soul; He all my joy and bliss.

The Most Unkindest Cuts of All

Percy Hammond called criticism 'the venom from contented rattlesnakes'. Heywood Broun referred to it as 'Pieces of Hate'. They had such comments as these in mind:

'It was one of those plays in which all the actors unfortunately enunciated very clearly.' (Robert Benchley)

'People laugh at this [*Abie's Irish Rose*] every night, which explains why democracy can never be a success.' (Benchley)

Heywood Broun once classified Geoffrey Steyne as the worst actor on the stage. Next play around, he wrote: 'Mr. Steyne's performance was not up to its usual standard.'

'In the first act *she* becomes a lady. In the second act *he* becomes a lady.' (Alexander Woollcott)

Dorothy Parker, reviewing a book on science: 'It was written without fear and without research.'

'This is not a novel to be tossed aside lightly. It should be thrown with great force.' (Parker)

'No worse than a bad cold.' (Harpo Marx on *Abie's Irish Rose*)

'There is less in this than meets the eye.' (Tallulah Bankhead, at an unsuccessful revival of the Maeterlinck play *Aglavaine and Selysette*)

'She ran the whole gamut of emotions, from A to B.' (Parker on a performance by Katherine Hepburn)

On signing a first-edition copy of his book *Shouts and Murmurs*, Alexander Woollcott sighed and said: 'Ah, what is so rare as a Woollcott first edition?'

'A Woollcott second edition,' replied F.P.A.

On a not-so-funny comedy: 'Some laughter was heard in the back rows. Someone must have been telling jokes back there.' (Robert Benchley)

George Jean Nathan wrote of an ill-done *Doll's House* that when Nora walked out on her household and slammed the door, the audience rose as one man and rushed to the stage to congratulate the husband.

After an execrable performance of *Hamlet*, Robert Hendrickson remarked: 'There has long been a controversy over who wrote Shakespeare's plays—Shakespeare or Bacon. I propose to settle it today by opening their graves. Whoever turned over wrote *Hamlet*.'

Shaw on Gounod's *Redemption*: 'If you will only take the precaution to go in long enough after it commences and to come out long enough before it is over, you will not find it wearisome.'

Mid-Victorian lady, emerging from a performance of *The Agamemnon*: 'How different, how very different, from the home life of our own dear Queen.'

Sydney Smith on Macaulay, an interminable talker: 'He has occasional flashes of silence that make his conversation perfectly delightful.'

Dorothy Parker on the autobiography of Margot Asquith: 'The affair between Margot Asquith and Margot Asquith will live as one of the prettiest love stories in all literature.'

And on A. A. Milne's *The House At Pooh Corner*: 'Tonstant Weader fwowed up.'

Mots d'Heures: Gousses, Rames

To get the sense of Luis D'Antin Van Rooten's *Mots D'Heures: Gousses, Rames*, read them aloud, and see if the sounds and the rhythm don't remind you of some familiar English jingles. (The footnotes are Mr. Van Rooten's own.) If you are utterly without French, skip.

Chacun Gille[1]
Houer ne taupe de hile[2]
Tôt-fait, j'appelle au boiteur[3]
Chaque fêle dans un broc,[4] est-ce crosne?[5]
Un Gille qu'aime tant berline à fêtard.[6]

Dissolu typique,[1] Ouen ou Marquette.[2]
Dissolu typique, c'tiède homme.[3]
Dissolu typique a des roses vives.[4]
Dissolu typique, aie de nom,
Dissolu typique, craille
Oui, oui, oui,
A louer: heaume.[5]

Jacques s'apprête
Coulis de nos fêtes.[1]
Et soif que dites nos lignes.[2]
Et ne sauve bédouine tempo[3] y aussi,
Telle y que de plat terre, cligne.[4]

[1] Gille is a stock character in medieval plays, usually a fool or country bumpkin.
[2] While hoeing he uncovers a mole and part of a seed.
[3] Quickly finished, I call to the limping man that
[4] every pitcher has a crack in it. If a philosophy or moral is intended, it is very obscure.
[5] 'Is it a Chinese cabbage?' It is to be assumed that he refers to the seed he found.
[6] At any rate he loves a life of pleasure and a carriage.

[1] A typical wastrel, in short, a regular bum. (*Continued overleaf*)

² Ouen (saint), bishop of Rouen, circa 609–683 A.D.; Père Marquette (1637–1675), French Jesuit, discovered the Mississippi. Two moral and saintly men of action to be emulated.

³ A tepid man. What a matchless description!

⁴ Fresh roses are used as hedonist symbols in this context.

⁵ The last and, if the pun is forgiven, crowning shame. The craven wastrel, fallen upon evil days, croaks 'Yes, yes, yes, my crest is for rent!' i.e., he is willing to sell his birthright—the family jewels having long since disappeared. This verse patently belongs to the age of moralists and essayists, and forms an interesting parallel to Hogarth's famed *Rake's Progress*.

¹ *Coulis*, a sort of strained broth. Jacques was either a sauce chef or an invalid.

² Jacques was also an alcoholic, since his thirst is beyond description.

³ He was fond of Arab music.

⁴ He believed the earth was flat. The last word of the line, meaning 'wink', is obviously a stage direction. Poor Jacques, whoever he was, was undoubtedly considered a fool.

N

The Nimble Bitterness of Bierce

Wordplay can be holy; Gerard Manley Hopkins's was. It can be cynical and hopeless; Ambrose Bierce's was. What a weight must have pressed upon this mysterious man, who defined *November* as 'the eleventh twelfth of a weariness'; *once* as 'enough'; *birth* as 'the first and direst of all disasters'!

To Bierce, a *bigot* is 'one obstinately and zealously attached to an opinion you do not entertain'; *billingsgate*, 'the invective of an opponent'. *Calamities* are of two kinds: 'misfortune to ourselves, and good fortune to others'.

Comfort, says Bierce, is 'a state of mind produced by contemplation of a neighbour's uneasiness'; *consolation*, 'the knowledge that a better man is more unfortunate than yourself'. *Meekness* is 'uncommon patience in planning a revenge that is worthwhile'.

A *hand*, he says, is 'a singular instrument worn at the end of a human arm and commonly thrust into somebody's pocket'. An *egotist* is 'a person of low taste, more interested in himself than in me'. *Happiness* is 'an agreeable situation arising from contemplating the misery of another'.

By ethical definition, Bierce was a miserable specimen of a man. But what fun! What wordplay!

Nouns of Multitude

The Books of Courtesy, medieval primers intended to provide a gentleman with the means of social acceptability, dealt with a variety of collective nouns, but concentrated on those of the hunt, known as venery.

If you are familiar with the history of venery, you will fill in quickly most of the words missing from the verse below. On the chance that you lack a venereal education, I have made things easier by providing some words with which the venereal terms rhyme.

Tarantara, tarantara, off the hunters ride,
Off to bag a ***[1] of pheasants, or perhaps a ****.[2]
Stalking now a *****[3] of wildfowl, now a ******[4] of teal;
Counting on a ****[5] of mallards for their evening meal.

Tarantara, tarantara, home the hunters straggle,
With a **********[6] of choughs, with of geese a ******.[7]
Overhead a *****[8] of geese, a *******[9] of widgeons;
Underfoot, a ****[10] of dottrel. On the sidewalk—pigeons.

W. R. E.

1. Eye.	7. Straggle.
2. Side.	8. Pain.
3. Lump.	9. Bum penny, with the emphasis on the bum.
4. Ring.	
5. Bored.	10. Flip.
6. Smattering.	(ANSWERS OVERLEAF)

ANSWERS

Tarantara, tarantara, off the hunters ride,
Off to bag a *nye* of pheasants, or perhaps a *hide*.
Stalking now a *plump* of wildfowl, now a *spring* of teal,
Counting on a *sord* of mallards for their evening meal.

Tarantara, tarantara, home the hunters straggle,
With a *chattering* of choughs, with of geese a *gaggle*.
Overhead a *skein* of geese, a *company* of widgeons;
Underfoot, a *trip* of dottrel. On the sidewalk—pigeons.

AN ENTRANCE OF ACTRESSES

Such, according to James Lipton* in *Playbill*, is the proper venereal term for a gathering of the grand ladies of the theatre. He continues:

'On the other hand, a collection of untried ingenues is *a wiggle of starlets*. Both groups owe their livelihood to *a pinch of producers*, who in turn owe theirs to *a host of angels*. If the show is a musical, chances are the stars will be joined onstage by *a quaver of sopranos* and *a rumble of basses*, as well as *a float of dancers* (female) and *a flit of dancers* (male).'

Mr. Lipton goes on to describe members of the audience, including *a hack of smokers* and *a load of drunks*. He tells how after the show the stars make their way to a famous restaurant through *a click of photographers* and *a shriek of claques*, and face *an indifference of waiters* as they eat *a clutch of eggs* while awaiting the verdicts of *a shrivel of critics*. If the notices are bad, the play must expect *an unction of undertakers*; if it is dreadfully bad, *an extreme unction of undertakers*.

'If, however, the play is a hit,' concludes Mr. Lipton, 'then the stars can look forward to *a thrill of fans*—and, alas, *a descent of relatives*.'

---

* He wrote *An Exaltation of Larks*, an indispensable handbook of medieval and modern venery.

A LIST OF THINGS

In a *New York Magazine* contest to see who could produce the inanest collective nouns, the following entries were among those printed.

1. A **** of students
2. A ***** of prostitutes
3. A ************* of thinkers
4. A **** of parasites
5. A ***** of puppies
6. A ********** of sycophants
7. A ****** of cowards
8. A ***** of ovens
9. A **** of dragons
10. A ***** of ghosts

ANSWERS

1. Riot.
2. Horde.
3. Concentration.
4. Host.
5. Field.
6. Complement.
7. Quiver.
8. Range.
9. Slew.
10. Fraid.

O.K.

This expression, meaning 'all right, correct', is, as Eric Partridge remarks, 'an evergreen of the correspondence columns'. A fresh argument about its origin flared recently in the *New York Times* as the result of a statement by David Danby that it derives from a number of West African languages, and slipped into English by way of the slave trade.

However compelling Mr. Danby may have considered his arguments, some of his readers did not accept them. O.K. came into general use in the United States around 1839–40; Danby claims the 1816 diary of a Jamaica planter records 'a similar expression', i.e.: 'Oh ki, massa, doctor no need be fright, we no want to hurt him'. But one *Times* correspondent argues that the expression is derived from Spanish *hoque* (pronounced okay), which in turn descends from *alboroque*, 'treat stood by buyer or seller after closing a deal'. And this would far antedate 1816.

Partridge, as good an authority as any, leans toward 'oll korrect', 'order recorded', or Choctaw '(h)oke' as the source. 'Oll korrect' has been attributed to Andrew Jackson, who had an excellent command of spoken Choctaw and a limited one of written English.

Other attributions, some not yet recorded in the correspondence columns of *The Times*:

Aux Quais, an expression referring either to (1) goods headed for the docks for shipment; (2) cotton bales headed specifically to the docks of New Orleans for shipment; or (3) a trysting arrangement between French sailors and American maidens during the Revolution.

Otto Krist, a timber magnate of the Pacific North-west, whose credit was so good that anything he initialled was 'O.K.'.

The *Orrins–Kendall* Company, which placed its initials on the boxes of excellent crackers it supplied during the American Civil War.

Oikea, a Finnish word meaning 'correct'.

Lord *Onslow* and his counsel, Lord *Kilbracken*, whose approval was necessary for certain bills passed by the House of Lords.

H. G.., pronounced 'hah gay', meaning 'shipshape', an expression common long ago among Danish and Norwegian sailors.

Och aye, Scottish.

O qu-oui, an emphatic French form of *yes*, as recorded in Sterne's *A Sentimental Journey* (1768).

ὼχ, ὼχ, a magical incantation against fleas, supposedly from *Geoponica*, written in the thirteenth century.

Whatever the ultimate origin of the expression, it was popularised in the American Presidential campaign of 1840 as an abbreviation of Old Kinderhook, a nickname (because he was born at Kinderhook, N.Y.) of Martin Van Buren, the Democratic candidate. This date would seen to eliminate both Otto Krist and Orrins–Kendall as contenders.

Nothing has been settled, and you may expect the argument to flare up again.

OH, NOA, NOA!

In Aku Aku is there double
The happiness, and half the trouble?
And far away in Bali Bali,
Should not it all be twice as jolly?

Does sunset out in Bora Bora
Reveal a repetitious aura?
And surely every joke would be a
Double entendre in Fia Fia?

Do residents of Pago Pago
Get twice the juice from every mango?
Do people out in Walla Walla
Get twofold value for their dollah?

Don't men in Sing Sing, who for crime go,
Hate like the deuce to see their time go?
And over there in Baden Baden,
I'm sure that life's not half so sodden?

*　　*　　*　　*

Alas! I'm told in *no* vicinity
Is such a thing as blessed twinnity!

William Cole

*

On the Square

Of the making of word squares there is no end. The concept is
simple: all you have to do is create a set of words that reads the
same from left to right and from top to bottom.

A
A

is a word square. So is

I
I

Slightly more complex is

```
M A
A M
```

Up a further step is

```
O F T
F O E
T E N
```

But no word-square addict recognises any square of words of less than four letters:

```
T W I T      H O P E      W I S P
W E R E      O P A L      I N T O
I R O N      P A L M      S T O P
T E N T      E L M S      P O P S
```

The difficulty of five-letter squares squares the difficulty of four-letter squares:

```
W A R T S
A W A I T
R A D A R
T I A R A
S T R A W
```

And the difficulty of seven-letter squares cubes that of five-letter squares:

```
M E R G E R S
E T E R N A L
R E G A T T A
G R A V I T Y
E N T I T L E
R A T T L E R
S L A Y E R S
```

Making word squares is a good way of putting yourself to sleep—and, sometimes, of getting insomnia. Those below may affect you either way:

1. Four-letter words
(a) Harvest
(b) Other
(c) Continent
(d) Fruit

2. Four-letter words
(*a*) Approach
(*b*) Ellipse
(*c*) Religious ceremony
(*d*) Otherwise

3. Five-letter words
(*a*) Replete
(*b*) Make up for
(*c*) Cheers, for example
(*d*) Follow in order
(*e*) Discourage or restrain

ANSWERS

1.		2.		3.	
R E A P		C O M E		S A T E D	
E L S E		O V A L		A T O N E	
A S I A		M A S S		T O A S T	
P E A R		E L S E		E N S U E	
				D E T E R	

SQUARE OF ORDER 9

To make squares of nine-letter words, one has to reach. The square below, by Wayne M. Goodwin, whom Martin Gardner describes as 'one of the greatest square experts of all time', contains only two words that cannot be found in Webster's *Unabridged Dictionary*. According to Dmitri Borgmann, 'retitrate' means to titrate again, and is found in the two-volume supplement to the *Century Dictionary*, 1909, while Eavestone is the name of a town in eastern West Riding, Yorkshire.

```
F R A T E R I E S
R E G I M E N A L
A G I T A T I V E
T I T A N I T E S
E M A N A T I S T
R E T I T R A T E
I N I T I A T O R
E A V E S T O N E
S L E S T E R E D
```

The tusks that clashed in mighty brawls
Of mastodons, are billiard balls.

The sword of Charlemagne the Just
Is ferric oxide, known as rust.

The grizzly bear whose potent hug
Was feared by all, is now a rug.

Great Caesar's dead and on the shelf,
And I don't feel so well myself!

Arthur Guiterman

*

Origin Unknown

Take an English word from Partridge at hazard—*screen*, for instance
—and it has a kingly genealogy:

'SCREEN. Middle English *scren*, aphetic for: Middle French *escren*, variant
of *escran* (French *ecran*) by metathesis from: Medieval Dutch *scherm*,
scheerm; cf Old High German *scirm*, Middle High German *schirm*, protection (cf German *Schirm*, umbrella), and Middle High German
schirmen, variant of *schermen*, to fence: ? akin, as Walshe suggests, to
Sanskrit *cărma*, the skin. From the appearance of a protective screen
derives the goldminers' *screen* or sieve, whence to *screen* or scrutinize
thoroughly before admission; the older sense "to protect" derives from
the very nature of the protective screen itself.'

Thorough indeed—for *screen*. Yet there are hundreds, perhaps
thousands, of words that have no agreed-upon origin at all. We
know what curmudgeon, larrup and moola mean, but we don't
know where they came from. Partridge and Skeat don't know;
Asimov, Barfield, Brown, Evans, Flesch, Funk, Holt, Howell,
Moore, Morris, Pei, Strunk, Weekley, White and Willett don't
know; I don't know.

THE BIRTH OF 'QUIZ'

The manager of a Dublin play-house wagered that a word of no
meaning should be the common talk and puzzle of the city in

twenty-four hours. In the course of that time he had the letters *q u i z* chalked on all the walls of Dublin. He won the wager—and the word, an utter fabrication, thrives.

The three rhymes below celebrate certain words of obscure or unknown origin. In each case there is a real clue to the word, and a fanciful suggestion as to how the word may have happened.

I

Blood swells in a bruise, and a g
Goes soft in a gun;
A sensible start, you'll agree,
For a stick used to stun.

2

The durable cloak of a witch on a sail
Snagged the tip of a spire as she passed.
She wove all her spells, but to no avail;
'It ***'* ***,' she conceded at last.

3

The tar who slanged the cap'n
By his sword was quickly cut to size.
Meanwhile the ship turned over.
Next week: 'Mutiny in Paradise.'

W. R. E.

ANSWERS

1. Bludgeon. 'A short stick, with one end thicker or heavier than the other, used as an offensive weapon.'
2. Cantrip. 'A charm; spell; trick, as of a witch.'
3. Capsize. 'To upset or overturn, as a vessel or other body.'

Oxymorons

Oxymorons are a curious inheritance from the Greeks—combinations for rhetoric effect of contradictory or incongruous words: 'harmonious discord'; 'a cheerful pessimist'. The Greek word itself marries 'sharp' to 'dull'. Tennyson was in oxymoronic vein when he wrote:

> His honour rooted in dishonour stood,
> And faith unfaithful kept him falsely true.

So was Shakespeare when he wrote (in *Richard II*) of 'ruthful butchery'.

James Thurber, seeking to confound an editor who pounced on any discrepancy in writing, once described a building as 'pretty ugly, and a little too big for its site'.

A *New York Times* editorial contains the sentence, 'Sometimes it requires devious and even odd ways to accomplish good purposes.' In 'even odd' we have an accidental oxymoron, a thing to be deplored; for, as one scholar* puts it, 'The good oxymoron, to define it by a self-illustration, must be a planned inadvertency.'

An official in the United States Treasury Department is said to have reminded his colleagues of the importance of diction by circulating among them this oxymoronic jargon:

'It should be noted that a slowing up of the slowdown is not as good as an upturn in the downcurve, but it is a good deal better than either a speedup of the slowdown or a deepening of the downcurve; and it does suggest that the climate is about right for an adjustment to the readjustment.'

The most-quoted oxymoron of our time, from a 1954 decision of the Supreme Court of the United States, directs that schools throughout the nation must be integrated 'with all deliberate speed'.

I have no oxymoronic word games to offer you, but you are welcome to develop colloquies like the following to your heart's content:

He: You are looking terribly well.

She: Under the circumstances, it's horribly decent of you to say that.

He: Why this nasty politeness?

She: It's just that we have increasingly little to say to each other.

He: What an oddly natural remark, coming from you!

She: Well, you are an uncommonly common fellow.

He: And you are possibly the most impossible girl I have ever met.

---

* Wilson Follett in *Modern American Usage* (Hill and Wang, 1966).

THE OYSTER

The oyster's a confusing suitor;
It's masc., and fem., and even neuter.
At times it wonders, may what come,
Am I husband, wife, or chum.

Ogden Nash

*

P, Q

Palindromes

IN PURSUIT OF THE ABOMINABLE PALINDROME

Since that day in 1610 when the primeval Espy forsook his oozy
Scottish bog for the sunny, carefree Plantations of Northern
Ireland, our family's unique distinction has been its utter lack of
distinction. This is humiliating; and when it became evident,
perhaps by my sixth or seventh year, that I was not destined to
break the family tradition, I began a lifelong search for bygone
relatives who might have left their mark. (Any mark; for quite a
while, I suspect, not many of them could write.) My search has
carried me through the records of dusty libraries, dilapidated
churches, and graveyards crowded with tottering stones – always
hoping against hope to locate some male forebear who had carried
'Gent.' after his name, or some milkmaid who had managed to
cozen the local squire into marrying her. Let me say that the
search was not fruitless; I found a man who had won the right to
wear his hat in the presence of the king, and a woman, a good
Christian soul, who was hanged as a witch at Salem.

This proud history is relayed, I assure you, in no spirit of
snobbery, but simply to explain how it happened that recently
I have been baying after a connection (posited shakily through
my grandmother, Annie Medora Taylor) with the seventeenth-

century Water Poet, John Taylor, a rollicking sort who once set out for Queenborough from London in a brown-paper boat, and almost drowned.

The Water Poet wrote the first palindrome recorded in the English language. (A palindrome, in case you don't know, is a word or sentence which reads the same forward and backward.) Mr. Taylor's innocently revealing contribution was

Lewd I did live, & evil did I dwel.

Now, you may say this is a second-rate palindrome, depending as it does on misspelling 'dwell' (though he didn't really), and substituting an ampersand for 'and'; still, it was the first of its kind in English, and that was the spelling of the day. What is more, the *Monthly Magazine and Literary Journal* reported in 1821, nearly two hundred years later, that no palindrome had appeared since.

'Our own observation,' declared the journal, 'confirms the difficulty of composing them in our own langauge, which this rarity implies. We have frequently laboured at arrangements of words which would form an English palindrome line, but always unsuccessfully, which surprised us, as we have in English so many palindrome words.'

The writer apparently did not take Welsh into account. There existed even then a longstanding Welsh palindrome, 'Liad ded dail', meaning 'holy blind father'.

There also existed a classical palindrome tradition (not in Greek, for only one Greek palindrome has been preserved, but certainly in Latin, which lends itself to reversals).

In the following Latin example, each line is a selfcontained palindrome. It has been attributed to Sotades of Crete, whose coarse satires and personal attacks in the second century B.C. so enraged Ptolemy II that the monarch finally caused him to be sewn up in a sack and thrown into the sea. How this attribution has endured is a mystery. In the first place, Sotades wrote in Greek, not Latin. In the second place, he was born two hundred years before Christ, while the palindrome refers to a legendary event in the life of St. Martin. The more probable author was a fifth-century bishop, Sidonius Apollinaris.

The whole verse, of which this is only a fragment, tells how Saint Martin rode the devil—that ass having stupidly transformed himself into an ass—into Rome, prodding him on with repeated signs of the cross.

Signa te signa; temere me tangis et angis;
Roma, tibi subito motibus ibit amor
Si bene te tua laus taxat, sua laute tenebis,
Solo medere pede, ede, perede molos.

An acronymic Latin palindrome is EVVNVVE, the initials standing for 'Ede ut vivas, ne vivas ut edas'. There is an almost exact English equivalent, ETLNLTE: 'Eat to live; never live to eat'.

The next palindrome after the Water Poet's to surface in English gained currency almost at the moment that the *Monthly Magazine* was abandoning the whole effort as hopeless. Presumably prompted by Napoleon's defeat at Waterloo, it reads, 'Able was I ere I saw Elba'.

From then on, the floodgates were open. By the 1870s the *New Monthly Magazine* was running such effusions as:

A milkman jilted by his lass, or wandering in his wits,
Might murmur, 'Stiff, o dairyman, in a myriad of fits.'

A limner, by photography dead beat in his position,
Thus grumbled: 'No, it is opposed; art sees trade's opposition.'

A timid creature, fearing rodents, mice and such small fry,
'Stop, Syrian, I start at rats in airy spots' might cry.

Some of the crop were not that bad. 'Draw pupil's lip upward' might, in some inconceivable circumstance, be considered a reasonable command. Two palindromes of the period have style: 'I, man, am regal; a German am I,' and 'Sums are not set as a test on Erasmus.'

At this time, too, there came palindromic versions of the first introduction, 'Madam, I'm Adam'; the first conscript's complaint, 'Snug & raw was I ere I saw war & guns'; and the first hint of the generation gap, 'Egad, a base tone denotes a bad age'. The nineteenth century also saw the prototype of the nonsense palindrome, intriguing because one feels it really *should* mean something: 'Dog, a devil deified, deified lived a god.'

The building of the Panama Canal by Goethals inspired the classic 'A man, a plan, a canal—Panama'. Other palindromes that have been around quite awhile are 'Step on no pets'; 'Never odd or even'; 'Mad Zeus, no live devil, lived evil on Suez dam'; and

'Live dirt, up a side-track carted, is a putrid evil'. These more recent examples were handed to me the other day by William Cole: 'A slut nixes sex in Tulsa' and 'Dennis and Edna sinned'.

By providing a context, one can give some palindromes the appearance of meaning. Two of my own are examples:

Slogan for opponents of the Women's Liberation Movement: 'Rise, sir lapdog! Revolt, lover! God, pal, rise, sir!'

A straightforward comment: 'Live on evasions? No, I save no evil.'

In the examples below I have tried to legitimise my palindromes by building them into verses. The palindromes are set off by quotation marks.

Second Honeymoon at Niagara Falls

Beside thee, torrent, with sweet moan, long since,
We gloried in our love, took off the lid.
Last night was she still princess, I still prince?
Did I, though very squiffed, still make my bid?
Speak, torrent! If thou hear me, answer! 'I
Did roar again, Niagara! . . . or did
I?' But the falls fall on; there's no reply.

W. R. E.

Matter of Etiquette

Meg's fashion in passion, though warm, 'll
Strike some as a shade over-formal.
  In the midst of a bout,
  She was heard to cry out,
'La, Mr. O'Neill, lie normal!'

W. R. E.

A final titbit: the longest palindrome having to do with a region is Malayalam, the name of a Dravidian language spoken on the Malabar in India.

The following definitions will give you an opportunity to make your own palindromes, or, more exactly, to remake those of others.

1. Anything hereafter will be from this.
2. Two words, followed by 'or shut up'.

3. Professional warning to a sleepy student.
4. Why owls shun the tropics.
5. Challenge to Sir Noel.
6. The reaction of a star to hints that she may have connived at the theft of her jewels.

ANSWERS

1. Now on.	4. Too hot to hoot.
2. Put up.	5. Draw, O coward!
3. Don't nod.	6. Rob a gem? Me? Gabor?

SEMORDNILAP

'Semordnilap' is 'palindromes' spelled backwards, and stands for words that spell different words in reverse. Some examples: devil, repaid, stressed, rewarder, straw, maps, strap, reknits, deliver, bard, doom.

See 'Milton, Thou Should'st Be Re-Versing at This Hour' on page 45.

Patchwork Verse

Patchwork verses, also called centones or mosaics, are poems composed of selected verses or passages from an author, or from different authors, so strung together as to present an entirely new reading. If you have the time and patience (I have not) you can locate in your copy of Shakespeare each of the lines in the following cento, which was put together a hundred years ago for a society which met annually to celebrate the birth of the Bard.

> Peace to this meeting,
> Joy and fair time, health and good wishes.
> Now, worthy friends, the cause why we are met,
> Is in celebration of the day that gave
> Immortal Shakespeare to this favoured isle,*
> The most replenished sweet work of Nature
> Which from the prime creation e'er she framed.

(CONTINUED OVERLEAF)

* The writer cheated here for the sake of his theme.

O thou, divinest Nature! how thyself thou blazon'st
In this thy son! formed in thy prodigality
To hold thy mirror up, and give the time
In every form and pressure! When he speaks,
Each aged ear plays truant at his tales,
And younger hearings are quite ravished;
So voluble is his discourse. Gentle
As zephyr blowing underneath the violet,
Not wagging its sweet head—yet as rough
His noble blood enchafed, as the rude wind,
That by the top doth take the mountain pine,
And make him stoop to the vale. 'Tis wonderful
That an invisible instinct should frame him
To loyalty, unlearned; honour, untaught;
Civility, not seen in others; knowledge,
That wildly grows in him, but yields a crop
As if it had been sown. What a piece of work!
How noble in faculty! infinite in reason!
A combination and a form indeed,
Where every god did seem to set his seal.
Heaven has him now! Yet let our idolatrous fancy
Still sanctify his relics; and this day
Stand aye distinguished in the kalendar
To the last syllable of recorded time;
For if we take him but for all in all,
We ne'er shall look upon his like again.

HAMLET AND HUCKLEBERRY FINN

In Mark Twain's *Huckleberry Finn*, the duke dredges his muddled
memory of Shakespeare in quest of Hamlet's Soliloquy, and brings
up this:

To be, or not to be; that is the bare bodkin
That makes calamity of so long life;
For who would fardels bear, till Birnam Wood do come to
    Dunsinane,
But that the fear of something after death
Murders the innocent sleep,
Great nature's second course,
And makes us rather sling the arrows of outrageous fortune
Than fly to others that we know not of.

There's the respect must give us pause;
Wake Duncan with thy knocking! I would thou couldst;
For who would bear the whips and scorns of time,
The oppressor's wrong, the proud man's contumely,
The law's delay, and the quietus which his pangs might take,
In the dead waste and middle of the night, when churchyards
yawn
In customary suits of solemn black,
But that the undiscovered country from whose bourne no traveller
returns
Breathes forth contagion on the world,
And thus the native nue of resolution, like the poor cat i' the
adage,
Is sicklied o'er with care,
And all the clouds that lowered o'er our housetops,
With this regard their currents turn awry
And lose the name of action.
'Tis a consummation devoutly to be wished. But soft you, the
fair Ophelia:
Ope not thy ponderous and marble jaws,
But get thee to a nunnery—go!

I ONLY KNOW SHE CAME AND WENT

If in two weeks or so you have not managed to trace the lines in
the following cento to their original homes, read on: the authors
are listed, line by line, below the verses. The compiler is unknown.

1	I only know she came and went,
2	Like troutlets in a pool;
3	She was a phantom of delight,
4	And I was like a fool.
5	One kiss, dear maid, I said, and sighed,
6	Out of those lips unshorn,
7	She shook her ringlets round her head
8	And laughed in merry scorn.
9	Ring out, wild bells, to the wild sky,
10	You heard them, O my heart;
11	'Tis twelve at night by the castle clock,
12	Beloved, we must part.

(CONTINUED OVERLEAF)

13	'Come back, come back!' she cried in grief,
14	My eyes are dim with tears—
15	How shall I live through all the days?
16	All through a hundred years?

17	'Twas in the prime of summer time,
18	She blessed me with her hand;
19	We strayed together, deeply blest,
20	Into the dreaming land.

21	The laughing bridal roses blow,
22	To dress her dark-brown hair;
23	My heart is breaking with my woe,
24	Most beautiful! most rare!

25	I clasped it on her sweet, cold hand,
26	The precious golden link!
27	I calmed her fears, and she was calm,
28	'Drink, pretty creature, drink!'

29	And so I won my Genevieve,
30	And walked in Paradise;
31	The fairest thing that ever grew
32	Atween me and the skies!

ANSWERS

1. Powell	12. Alice Cary	23. Tennyson
2. Hood	13. Campbell	24. Read
3. Wordsworth	14. Bayard Taylor	25. Browning
4. Eastman	15. Osgood	26. Smith
5. Coleridge	16. T. S. Perry	27. Coleridge
6. Longfellow	17. Hood	28. Wordsworth
7. Stoddard	18. Hoyt	29. Coleridge
8. Tennyson	19. Edwards	30. Hervey
9. Tennyson	20. Cornwall	31. Wordsworth
10. Alice Cary	21. Patmore	32. Osgood
11. Coleridge	22. Bayard Taylor	

Pennsylvania Dutch

Thousands of Germans in America once spoke a dialect that curiously combined English words with German forms and idioms. Traces of this tongue linger in the farmhouses of the Pennsylvania Dutch. The following takeoff on their speech, at least a century old, is the work of an expert:

LOVE SONG

O vere mine lofe a sugar-powl,
   De fery shmallest loomp
Vouldt shveet de seas, from pole to pole,
   Und make de shildren shoomp.
Und if she vere a clofer-field,
   I'd bet my only pence,
It vouldn't pe no dime at all
   Pefore I'd shoomp the fence.

Her heafenly foice, it drill me so,
   If oft-dimes seems to hoort,
She is de holiest animale
   Dat rooms oopon de dirt.
De renpow rises vhen she sings,
   De sonnshine vhen she dalk;
De angels crow und flop deir wings
   Vhen she goes out to valk.

So livin white, so carnadine,
   Mine lofe's gomblexion show;
It's shoost like Abendcarmosine,
   Rich gleamin on de shnow.
Her soul makes plushes in her sheek
   Ash sommer reds de wein,
Or sonnlight sends a fire life troo
   An blank Karfunkelstein.

(CONTINUED OVERLEAF)

De uberschwengliche idees
  Dis lofe poot in my mind,
Vouldt make a foost-rate philosoph
  Of any human kind.
'Tis schudderin schveet on eart to meet
  An himmlisch-hoellisch Qual;
Und treat mitwhiles to Kümmel Schnapps
  De Schoenheitsideal.

Dein Füss seind weiss wie Kreiden,
  Dein Ermlein Helfenbein,
Dein ganzer Leib ist Seiden,
  Dein Brust wie Marmelstein—
Ja—vot de older boet sang,
  I sing of dee—dou Fine!
Dou'rt soul und pody, heart und life:
  Glatt, zart, gelind, und rein.

Charles G. Leland

*

THE PURIST

I give you now Professor Twist,
A conscientious scientist.
Trustees exclaim, 'He never bungles!'
And send him off to distant jungles.
Camped on a tropic riverside,
One day he missed his loving bride.
She had, the guide informed him later,
Been eaten by an alligator.
Professor Twist could not but smile.
'You mean,' he said, 'a crocodile.'

Ogden Nash

*

Pidgin English

VOCABULARY

Melanesian pidgin has a basic vocabulary of about 1300 words, which can be combined to translate some 6000 English words. The language is derived almost exclusively from Melanesian and English, and the words listed below can be traced to the English originals by an approximation of sounds. The English equivalents follow the list.

1. Aiting
2. Aratsait
3. Astadei
4. Baembai
5. Bihain
6. Bikples
7. Darai
8. Daunpilo
9. Em
10. Faulnabaut
11. Filimnogut
12. Giraun
13. Gudei
14. Gutbai
15. Haitim, *v.t.*
16. Hanggiri
17. Hariap, *v.i.*
18. Hausat?
19. Hiparei
20. Insaet
21. Kamap, *v.i.*
22. Kilaut
23. Kotrein
24. Kraikrai
25. Kwiktaim

26. Lam wokabaut
27. Lephan
28. Longwei
29. Mandei
30. Moabeta
31. Numbata
32. Nosave, *v.i.*
33. Nuspepa
34. Peim
35. Plaiyas
36. Popi
37. Rait, *v.i.*
38. Ronewei, *v.i.*
39. Samting
40. Samting nating
41. Solapim, *v.t.*
42. Stima
43. Tanim bek, *v.t.*
44. Tok tiru, *v.i.*
45. Tudak
46. Tulait
47. Wankain
48. Win
49. Wisiki
50. Wok

(ANSWERS OVERLEAF)

ANSWERS

1. I think
2. Outside
3. Yesterday
4. Afterwards, later, bye and bye
5. At the rear of, after, behind
6. Mainland
7. Dry, withered
8. Down below, below
9. He, they, she, it, him, her, them
10. Conflicting (of testimony, rumour, etc.); all messed up
11. Not feel well, be in pain
12. Ground, soil, the earth
13. Good day
14. Good-bye
15. Conceal
16. Hungry, hunger
17. Hurry, hurry up
18. Why?
19. Cheering, acclamation
20. Inside
21. Arrive, approach, be revealed
22. Cloud
23. Raincoat
24. Weep copiously
25. Quickly, speedily
26. Hurricane lamp
27. Left side, left hand
28. Far, distant
29. Monday
30. Better, very good
31. Second, number two
32. Have no knowledge of, be unaccustomed to
33. Newspaper
34. Sell
35. Pliers
36. Roman Catholic
37. Write
38. Run away, desert
39. Something, a thing
40. Thing of no consequence
41. Slap, strike with open hand
42. Steamship
43. Turn back, turn about, bend back
44. Speak the truth
45. Dark, night
46. Light, daylight
47. Similar, of the same kind or species
48. Wind, gas, breath, air
49. Whisky
50. Work, duty, employment

PLUCKING A PIDGIN (in Pidgin)

A pigeon in Pidgin English is *balus*, a word applicable to the foolish young man plucked in the story below. The words used come from John J. Murphy's *Book of Pidgin English*; the grammar, I fear, is my own.

A few bits of information before you begin your translation: Pidgin lacks not only the definite and indefinite article but the verb 'to be'. Bear in mind too that a *p* is used in some words where we would use *f*; thus in Melanesian Pidgin, *plag* is *flag*, *pluwa* is *floor*, *prauwin* is *following wind*, *prog* is *frog*. Also, *tasol* is *but*; *long* is *to, by, with, from*, etc.; *i* is *he* or *she*; *im* is *it*; *em* is *her*; *mi* is *I*.

192

The other words are all corruptions of English, and if you don't try too hard the meanings should pop out at you. Don't concentrate; look at the story out of the corner of your eye; catch it unawares.

In a burst of generosity, I have supplied not one but two solutions. One is a literal rendering of the Pidgin into English; the other is a translation for sense.

Hatpela manki, bolong planti moni, tasol man nogut, laikim tumas long naispela meri wosat bolong man numbawan boss bolong ples. Wataim man wok manki wokabout long haus, painam meri wanpela long rum slip. I asken em ronawei. 'Hausat?' spik no laik meri. 'Mi no laikim yu. Go long imperno.' I kickem manki. Manki bigmaus long moni ologeta bolongen. 'Narakin,' spik meri. 'Kem hia kwiktaim. Mi reri.' I stap long monitaim long tudak. Longtaim bihain man askem meri, 'Wasamara yu gat bel?' Meri bekim tok: 'Im orrait. Mi gat moni tu.'

ANSWERS

(1) *Literal rendering*

Hot fella man-kid, belong plenty money but no-good, like too much nice fella mary belong man number one boss of place. Man-kid walkabout to house what time man work, find mary one fella in sleep-room. He ask her run away. 'How's that?' speak no-like mary: 'Me no like you. Go to inferno.' She kick man-kid. Man-kid bigmouth about money altogether belong him. 'Another kind!' speak mary. 'Come here quick time; me ready.' He stop morning time to dark. Long time behind, man ask mary, 'What'sa matter you got belly?' Mary back talk: 'It all right. Me got money too.'

(2) *Or, as you or I might say . . .*

An ardent and wealthy but villainous youth fell in love with a beautiful woman whose husband was head man of the village. When the husband was at work, the young man went to the house and found the woman alone in the bedroom. He begged her to elope. 'Why?' said the unwilling woman; 'I don't like you. Go to hell.' She kicked the youth. He bragged about his wealth. 'That's different!' said the woman, 'Come here quick. I'm ready.' He stayed from morning till night. Much later, the husband asked the wife, 'Why are you pregnant?' She replied, 'It's all right. I was well paid.'

Pidgin is an Oriental sea-change on *business*, it being a dialect which made communication possible between the natives and the English or American traders. Chinese Pidgin varies from the Melanesian in several special characteristics; it tends to substitute *l* for *r*, and, for the sake of euphony, to add *ee* or *lo* to the end of words. *Galaw* or *galow* is a kind of interjection, meaning nothing; *chop, chop* means quick; *maskee*, don't mind; *chop b'long*, of a kind; *chin chin*, good-bye; *welly culio*, very curious; *Joss-pidgin-man*, priest.

Pig Latin and Macaronics

When I was starting school we spoke Pig Latin in a number of ways, the most popular being to take the initial consonant of each syllable and shift it to the end, followed by -ay: 'E-hay ill-way ot-nay o-gay, oo-tay ool-schay oo-tay ay-day.' It was our happy illusion that no-one outside our own closed circle could possibly understand this recondite tongue.

A few years later we were struggling with Latin verbs, and our recourse was that of schooldays since the time of Virgil; we played games with what we could not understand. From hand to hand we passed such nonsense as:

Flunko, flunkere, faculty bouncem,

and this inscription, found, as we solemnly agreed, in diggings in Roman ruins:

Civili derego fortibus inero.
Demes nobus demes trux.

The translation:

'See, Willy, dere dey go, forty buses in a row.'
'Dem is no buses, dem is trucks.'

The last examples are not really Pig Latin, but macaronics, a slightly less piggish burlesque in which foreign words, sounds or spellings supplement or supplant English. You will find some in 'Berlitz School' (page 58) and *Mots d'Heures: Gousses, Rames*

(page 169). 'Pas de lieu Rhône que nous' is a macaronic statement.
A macaronic pun recalled by Liz Baekeland is 'Leges Romanorum
boni sunt'.

More macaronics:

Parvus Jacobus Horner

Parvus Jacobus Horner
Sedebat in corner,
Edens a Christmas pie:
Inferuit thumb,
Extraherit plum—
Clamans, 'Quid sharp puer am I!'

Author Unknown

THE MOTOR BUS

What is this that roareth thus?
Can it be a Motor Bus?
Yes, the smell and hideous hum
Indicat Motorem Bum!
Implet in the Corn and High
Terror me Motoris Bi:
Bo Motori clamitabo
Ne Motore caedar a Bo—
Dative be or Ablative
So thou only let us live:—
Whither shall thy victims flee?
Spare us, spare us, Motor Be.
Thus I sang; and still anigh
Came in hordes Motores Bi,
Et complebat omne forum
Copia Motorum Borum.
How shall wretches live like us
Cincti Bis Motoribus?
Domine, defende nos
Contra hos Motores Bos!

A. D. Godley

DEAN SWIFT

Moll

Mollis abuti
Has an acuti;
No lasso finis
Molly divinis.

To My Mistress

O mi de armis tres
Ima na dis tres
Cantu disco ver
Meas alo ver?

A Love Song

Apud in is almi de si re,
Mimis tres I ne ver re qui re,
Alo veri findit a gestis
His miseri ne ver at restis.

Place Names, U.S.A.

Following is a foretaste of the oddities and delights of certain American place names. For the full meal, you should read a book by George R. Stewart called, aptly enough, *American Place Names:*

Aromatic Creek, Mo. 'A euphemism, probably for Stinking Creek.'

Go to Hell Gulch, S.D. 'Because a stranger asked the name of the place and was rudely told to "go to Hell".' (In the same sulfurous vein, there are: *Helltown, Hell Hole, Hell Hollow, Hell-for-Certain, Hell-for-Sure, Hell-Roaring, Purgatory Peak; Satan's Arbor.*)

Frost, Frostburg, Frosty and *Frozen* (where Hell, apparently, is frozen over).

Caress, W. Va. ('probably from a family name'); *Flirtation*, Colo. ('doubtless commemorating a pleasant incident'); *Kiss Me Quick*, S.D. (named for a 'road full of kiss-me-quicks, i.e., bumps of the kind so called'.)

Benign Peak and *Bellicose Peak*, Alaska; *Deception Creek*, Ark.; *Delusion Lake*, Wyo.

Another River, Alaska ('a name of desperation given by two geologists' who kept stumbling across new Alaskan rivers).

Tesnus, Tenn. ('sunset' spelled backwards); *Braggodocio*, Mo. ('probably from some incident involving boastfulness'); *Peculiar*, Mo.; *Yum Yum*, Tenn.; *Tumtum*, Wash.; *Climax*, Ore.; *Ding Dong*, in Bell County, Texas; *Welcome*, N.C.; *Do Stop*, Ky.

Candor, N.C. (the work of 'three merchants who wished the town to be distinguished by frankness'); *Goon Dip Mountain*, Alaska (for a Chinese consul in Seattle); *Fact*, Kan. ('because someone, when hearing that a post office had been established, replied, "Is that a fact?" ').

Cash, Tex. ('in honour of J. A. Money, first postmaster'); *Culdesac*, Idaho ('because a practicable route for a railroad came to a sudden end there').

Plantation Dialect

BRER RABBIT

Joel Chandler Harris's Brer Rabbit stories were written, he says, 'because of the unadulterated human nature that might be found in them'. Along with the human nature there is the Negro dialect. In this connection, Mr. Harris wrote in 1892:

'The student of English, if he be willing to search so near the ground, will find matter to interest him in the homely dialect of Uncle Remus, and if his intentions run towards philological investigation, he will pause before he has gone far and ask himself whether this negro dialect is what it purports to be, or whether it is not simply the language of the white people of three hundred years ago twisted and modified a little to fit the lingual peculiarities of the negro. Dozens of words, such as *hit* for *it*, *ax* for *ask*, *whiles* for *while*, and *heap* for a large number of people, will open before him the whole field of the philology of the English tongue. He will discover that, when Uncle Remus tells the little boy that he has "a monstus weakness fer cake what's got *reezins* in it," the pronunciation of *reezins* uncovers and rescues from oblivion Shakespeare's pun on *raisins*, where Falstaff tells the Prince, "If reasons were as plentiful as blackberries, I would give no man a reason on compulsion, I." '

Here is Uncle Remus telling the little boy why Brer Fox's legs are black:

'One time Brer Rabbit en Brer Fox went out in de woods huntin', en atter so long a time, dey 'gun ter git hongry. Leas' ways Brer Fox did, kaze Brer Rabbit had brung a ashcake in his wallet, en eve'y time he got a chance he'd eat a mou'ful—eve'y time Brer Fox 'd turn his back, Brer Rabbit 'd nibble at it. Well, endurin' er de day, Brer Fox 'gun ter get mighty hongry. Dey had some game what dey done kill, but dey wuz a fur ways fum home, en dey ain't had no fier fer ter cook it.

'Dey ain't know what ter do. Brer Fox so hongry it make his head ache. Bimeby de sun gun ter git low, en it shine red thoo de trees.

'Brer Rabbit 'low, "Yonder, whar you kin git some fier."

'Brer Fox say, "Wharbouts?"

'Brer Rabbit 'low, "Down whar de sun is. She'll go in her hole terrectly, en den you kin git a big chunk er fier. Des leave yo' game here wid me, en go git de fier. You er de biggest en de swiftest, en kin go quicker."

'Wid dat Brer Fox put out ter whar de sun is. He trot, he lope, en he gallup, en bimeby he git dar. But by dat time de sun done gone down in her hole en de groun', fer ter take a night's rest, en Brer Fox he can't git no fier. He holler en holler, but de sun ain't pay no 'tention. Den Brer Fox git mad en say he gwine ter stay dar twel he gits some fier. So he lay down topper de hole, en 'fo' he knowed it he drapt asleep. Dar he wuz, en dar where he got kotch.

'Now you know mighty well de sun bleedz ter rise. Yo' pa kin tell you dat. En when she start ter rise, dar wus Brer Fox fas' asleep right 'pon topper de hole whar she got ter rise fum. When dat de case, sump'n n'er udder bleedz ter happen. De sun rise up, en when she fin' Brer Fox in de way, she het 'im up en scorch his legs twel dey got right black. Dey got black, en dey er black ter dis ve'y day.'

'What became of Brother Rabbit?' the little boy asked.

Uncle Remus laughed, or pretended to laugh, until he bent double.

'Shoo, honey,' he exclaimed, when he could catch his breath, 'time Brer Fox got out'n sight, Brer Rabbit tuck all de game en put out fer home. En dar whar you better go yo'se'f.'

Pronunciation

THE HUMBLE H

Once upon a time a Londoner's social standing could be determined by his handling of the aspirate 'h'. To say 'ouse and 'orrible was first the sign of the snob, later of the slob. In the nineteenth century versifiers wrote expressly to confound Cockney warblers, as in Mrs. Crawford's song 'Kathleen Mavourneen', one line of which the Cockney renders thus:

> The 'orn of the 'unter is 'eard on the 'ill.

Similarly in Moore's *Woodpecker*:

> A 'eart that is 'umble might 'ope for it 'ere.

(But it is proper nowadays to drop the 'h' in 'humble'.)

Just as the native Brooklynian used to say 'foist' for 'first', but 'cherce' for 'choice', so the Cockney drops the initial aspirate, but inserts it where it does not belong:

> A helephant heasily heats at his hease,
> Hunder humbrageous humbrella trees.

Miss Catherine Fanshawe addressed the following verse, entitled *Protesting*, to the inhabitants of Kidderminster:

> Whereas by you I have been driven
> From 'ouse, from 'ome, from 'ope, from 'eaven,
> And placed by your most learned society
> In Hexile, Hanguish, and Hanxiety;
> Nay, charged without one just pretence,
> With Harrogance and Himpudence—
> I here demand full restitution,
> And beg you'll mend your Helocution.

— OU

One rediscovers at intervals, with never-failing bemusement, that 'ou' may have any of six sounds: 'uh' (touch, country, young, couple); 'aow' (out, pout, rout); hard 'o' (though, soul, shoulder, poultry); soft 'o' (trough, pour, your); hard 'oo' (through, group, wound, soup); and soft 'oo' (would, should). You may have seen proposals that the 'aow' sound replace all the others, but this hardly seems practical. The six pronunciations for 'ou' are all used in the missing words below.

> If you hiccup while high on a *****,
> You ***** stumble and land with a pough.
> ****** you feel you must *****,
> 'Twould be ***** to fall off,
> So hang on ******* the sweat of your brough.
>
> W. R. E.

ANSWER: Bough, could, though, cough, tough, through.

GHOTI

If you pronounce 'gh' as in 'tough', 'o' as in 'women', and 'ti' as in 'motion', how do you pronounce 'ghoti'?

Prose Poems

Some ninety years ago, William Dobson collected a number of examples of what he called 'prose poems', or 'poetical prose'. Two anonymous specimens:

A LITTLE MORE

(*At thirty*) Five hundred guineas I have saved—a rather moderate store. No matter; I shall be content when I've a little more. (*At forty.*) Well, I can count ten thousand now—that's better than before; and I may well be satisfied when I've a little more. (*At fifty.*) Some fifty thousand—pretty well; but I have earned it sore. However, I shall not complain when I've a little more. (*At sixty.*) One hundred thousand—sick and old; ah, life is half a bore, yet I can be content to live when I've a little more. (*At seventy.*) He dies—and to his greedy heirs he leaves a countless store. His wealth has purchased him a tomb, and very little more!

THE EDITOR

With fingers blackened with ink, with eyelids heavy and red, the local editor sat in his chair, writing for daily bread. The small boy was by his side, the foreman grumbled and swore, and the office boy, like an 'Oliver Twist', constantly cried for 'more'. He had told of a broken leg that had never been broken at all, he had killed off the nearest friend he had, and torn up a house in a squall. And now he was at an end, he hadn't an item left; and he bowed his head to the small boy's scorn like a fellow of hope bereft. They found him a corpse that night in streets so drear and sloppy, with the foreman whispering into his ear and the small boy waiting for copy.

DEAR SISTER HANNAH

One of Macaulay's letters to his sister Hannah begins:

MY DARLING,—Why am I such a fool as to write to a gypsy·at Liverpool, who fancies that none is so good as she if she sends one letter for my three? A lazy chit, whose fingers tire in penning a page in reply to a quire! There, miss, you read all the first sentence of my epistle, and never knew that you were reading verse.'

Pun my Word

When a rhetorician derided punning ('paronomasia' to you) as 'the lowest species of wit', a punster replied, 'Yes—for it is the *foundation* of all wit.' It is at least the commonest form. Turn to your daily paper, and the chances are that you will find one or more presumably humorous columns built around puns. This morning I came across the following examples in a single five-panel comic strip:

'What does a doctor do if a patient asks to have his bill shaved?' 'He goes into a lather.'
'Show me an unemployed movie star, and I'll show you a movie idle.'
'*Q*. Define "wise".' '*A*. What little kids are always asking, as "Wise the sky blue?"' '
'*Q*. I'm 28 and engaged to a 95-year-old millionaire. What should I get married in?' '*A*. A hurry.'
A grafitto: 'The three little pigs did time in the pen.'

Don Maclean, the newspaper columnist, favours more elaborate puns. He once ran the following anecdotes back to back in what he called the Great Rotten Joke Contest:

There's a monastery that's in financial trouble and in order to increase revenue, it decides to go into the fish and chips business. One night a customer raps on the door and a monk answers. The customer says, 'Are you the fish friar?'

'No,' the robed figure replies, 'I'm the chip monk.'

Three Indian women are sitting side by side. The first, sitting on a goatskin, has a son who weighs 170 pounds. The second, sitting on a deerskin, has a son who weighs 130 pounds. The third, seated on a hippopotamus hide, weighs 300 pounds. What famous theorem does this illustrate?

Naturally, the answer is that the squaw on the hippopotamus is equal to the sons of the squaws on the other two hides.

'Hey,' says one musician to another, 'who was that piccolo I saw you out with last night?' 'That was no piccolo,' is the reply, 'that was my fife.'

VULTURE UP-TO?

'Vulture Up-To?' approximates 'What are you up to?' It is also my name for a game that *Time* magazine introduced to its readers in 1970. The idea is to provide a given or surname for an animal, the resultant combination being reminiscent of some familiar word or phrase. Ostrich, for example, might have as a surname *In-time-saves-nine*; Panda, *Monium*; Aardvark, *And-no-play-makes-Jack-a-dull-boy*.

Below are clues to some of the Vulture Up-Tos sent to *Time* by its correspondents. You can lengthen the list indefinitely, and I hope you will.

(a) *Provide given names for:*

1. A woolly-haired South American ruminant known for her fondness for toy animals.
2. An Australian arboreal marsupial strongly addicted to a popular non-alcoholic beverage.
3. A bird allied to the gulls, who believes favours should be repaid.
4. A furbearing, webfooted mammal who does what he should not.
5. A talking bird in its native haunts.
6. A tufted-eared wildcat who beats his cubs with open paw.

(b) Provide surnames for:
1. A canine given to mild oaths.
2. A tropical, fruit-eating bird who plans to marry without increasing his income.
3. A bovine who won't stand up to the bull.
4. A hornless African water mammal notorious for his insincerity.
5. A small, voracious fish of South America who would like his good old woman to celebrate her golden wedding with him in Dover.

ANSWERS

(a)
1. Dolly Llama
2. Coca Koala
3. One-good Tern
4. Hadn't Otter
5. Asia Myna
6. Cuff Lynx

(b)
1. Dog Gone
2. Toucan Live-as-cheaply-as-one
3. Cow Ard
4. Hippo Crit
5. Piranha Old-grey-bonnet

ON DR. LETTSOM, BY HIMSELF
When people's ill, they come to I,
I physics, bleeds, and sweats 'em;
Sometimes they live, sometimes they die.
What's that to I? I lets 'em.

John Coakley Lettsom

Punctuation Puzzles

Misplaced commas have resulted in curious misunderstandings. It is said that an ancient Greek, consulting the oracle at Delphi as to whether he should go a-warring, was told:

> Thou shalt go thou shalt return
> never by war shalt thou perish.

Optimistically adding commas after 'go' and 'return', the Greek took up arms, and was promptly slain. He should have put that second comma after 'never'.

A riddle runs:

> Every lady in the land
> Has twenty nails on each hand
> Five and twenty on hands and feet.
> This is true, without deceit.

The sense is sometimes further confused by placing a comma at the end of the second line. If instead you put commas after 'nails' and 'five', the verse merely states the obvious.

Punctuate the following passage so that it makes sense.

That that is is not that that is not that that is not is not that that is is not that it it is.

ANSWER

That that is, is not that that is not; that that is not, is not that that is. Is not that it? It is.

The Puritans had a Name for it

It has always pleased me that one of my ancestors was called Seaborn, she having first seen this world in the innards of a little vessel bound for New England in the 1640s. Puritan names are a delight that never fails. Among the favourites were Mercy, Faith, Fortune, Honour, Virtue; but, on the evidence of *Lower's English Sirnames* and the *Lansdowne Collection*, there were also such gems as these:

The-gift-of-God Stringer	The-work-of-God Farmer
Repentant Hazel	More-tryal Goodwin
Zealous King	Faithful Long
Be-thankful Playnard	Joy-from-above Brown
Live-in-peace Hillary	Be-of-good-comfort Small
Obediencia Cruttenden	Godward Freeman
Goodgift Noake	Thunder Goldsmith
Faint-not Hewett	Accepted Trevor
Redeemed Compton	Make-peace Heaton
God-reward Smart	Stand-fast-on-high Stringer

Quotation Quotient

Considering how fast we can forget what happened only yesterday, it is remarkable that so many of the quotations we learned as children continue to flutter fragmentarily about in our minds. You probably learned most of these years ago. See how many of the sources you still recall.

1. I propose to fight it out on this line, if it takes all summer.

2. England expects that every man will do his duty.

3. I disapprove of what you say, but I will defend to the death your right to say it.

4.   God's in his heaven
         All's right with the world.

5.   Under the wide and starry sky
             Dig the grave and let me lie:
         Glad did I live and gladly die,
             And I laid me down with a will.

6.   Down the long and silent street,
         The dawn, with silver-sandalled feet,
         Crept like a frightened girl.

7.   I fled Him, down the nights and down the days;
         I fled Him, down the arches of the years.

8.   And since to look at things in bloom
         Fifty springs are little room,
         About the woodlands I will go
         To see the cherry hung with snow.

9.   A shudder in the loins engenders there
         The broken wall, the burning roof and tower
         And Agamemnon dead.

10.   If, drunk with sight of power, we loose
         Wild tongues that have not Thee in awe,
         Such boastings as the Gentiles use,
         Or lesser breeds without the Law—
         Lord God of Hosts, be with us yet,
         Lest we forget—lest we forget!

(ANSWERS OVERLEAF)

ANSWERS

1. Ulysses S. Grant.
2. Horatio, Viscount Nelson.
3. Voltaire.
4. Robert Browning: *Pippa Passes.*
5. Robert Louis Stevenson: *Requiem.*
6. Oscar Wilde: *The Harlot's House.*
7. Francis Thompson: *The Hound of Heaven.*
8. A. E. Housman: *Loveliest of Trees.*
9. William Butler Yeats: *Leda and the Swan.*
10. Rudyard Kipling: *Recessional.*

*

R

Rebuses

A rebus is a representation of a word or phrase by pictures and symbols. They range in difficulty and sophistication from the childhood

 (I ate that apple)

to this enigmatic French example:

Louis XV (or, some say, Frederick the Great) sent Voltaire the following invitation:

$$\frac{P}{Venez} \ a \ \frac{6}{100}$$

(Venez sous P, a cent sous six; that is to say, 'Venez souper a Sans Souci)

Voltaire replied simply:

G a

(*G*—pronounced zhay—grand; *a* petit; meaning, 'J'ai grand appetit.')

Three more rebuses:

1. $\dfrac{\text{Dad}}{\text{I am}}$

2. If the B MT put :

   If the B . putting :

3. $\dfrac{\text{I have to}}{\text{work}}$ because $\dfrac{\text{paid}}{\text{I am}}$

ANSWERS

1. I am under par.
2. If the grate be empty, put coal on; if the grate be full, stop putting coal on.
3. I have to overwork because I am underpaid.

Non Verbis Sed Rebus

'Not by words but by things.' That is the point of a rebus. In practice, though, words are usually present, as in the following:

1. $\dfrac{\text{Stand take} \quad 2 \quad \text{takings}}{\text{I} \quad \text{you throw} \quad \text{my}}$

2. $\dfrac{\text{B}}{\text{Faults man quarrels wife faults}}$

3. NAR   EH   HE   RAN*

4. stool   He fell   stool

5. I T I   T O T
   E T W   H E P
   O M U   O S T
   L E S

The final example is a true, wordless rebus:

6.

(ANSWERS OVERLEAF)

---

* A palindrome.

1. I understand you undertake to overthrow my undertakings.
2. Be above quarrels between man and wife. There are faults on both sides.
3. He ran forwards and backwards.
4. He fell between two stools.
5. I tie two mules to the post.
6. Be independent, not too independent.

Riddles and Conundrums

Anyone over ten years of age is invited to skip this section. It is meant for my grandchildren.

What wears shoes, but has no feet?
  The sidewalk.

What has four legs and flies?
  A dead horse.

Which is the strongest day of the week?
  Sunday, because all the rest are week days.

Which candles burn longer—wax or tallow?
  Neither. Both burn shorter.

What did the big firecracker say to the little firecracker?
  'My pop's bigger than your pop.'

What time of day was Adam created?
  A little before Eve.

Why is a cat longer at night than in the morning?
  Because he is let out at night and taken in in the morning.

What can't you say without breaking it?
  Silence.

Why is the Panama Canal like the first U in cucumber?
  Because it's between two seas.

How many bushel baskets full of earth can you take out of a hole two feet square and two feet deep?
  None. The earth has already been taken out.

What is the difference between an elephant and a flea?
  An elephant can have fleas, but a flea can't have elephants.

How long will an eight-day clock run without winding?
It won't run at all.

Why has a horse got six legs?
Because he has forelegs in front and two legs behind.

Why do birds fly South?
Because it's too far to walk.

Take away my first letter; take away my second letter; take away my third letter; all right, take away all my letters, and yet I remain the same. What am I?
The postman.

Why is an empty room like a room full of married people?
Because there isn't a single person in it.

What starts with T, ends with T, and is full of T?
A teapot.

What squeals more loudly than a pig caught under a fence?
Two pigs.

What words can be pronounced quicker and shorter by adding another syllable to them?
'Quick' and 'short'.

When a man marries how many wives does he get?
Sixteen: four richer, four poorer, four better, four worse.

Suppose there was a cat in each corner of the room; a cat sitting opposite each cat; a cat looking at each cat; and a cat sitting on each cat's tail. How many cats would there be?
Four. Each cat was sitting on its own tail.

What is it that is always coming but never arrives?
Tomorrow. When it arrives, it is today.

It occurs once in every minute, twice in every moment, and yet never in one hundred thousand years. What is it?
The letter M.

GOLD RUSH RIDDLES

The following conundrums first appeared in the San Francisco *Golden Era* as much as a hundred years ago:

Which of the reptiles is a mathematician?
An *adder*.

When is a boat like a heap of snow?
　　When it is *adrift*.
When does a cabbage beat a beet in growing?
　　When it is *ahead*.
Why is the word yes like a mountain?
　　Because it is an *assent*.
Why is hunting for honey in the woods like a legacy?
　　Because it is a *bee-quest*.
Why is a cow's tail like a swan's bosom?
　　Because it grows *down*.
What does a drunken husband's thirst end in?
　　Why, in *bier*.
Why are old maids the most charming of people?
　　Because they are *matchless*.
What fruit does a newly wedded couple most resemble?
　　A green *pair*.
Why do hens always lay in the daytime?
　　Because at night they become *roosters*.

CHAIN CONUNDRUMS

Why is a dying man like a cobbler?
　　Because he gives up his *awl*, looks to his *end*, and prepares his
soul for the *last*.
Why is a beehive like a rotten potato?
　　A beehive is a *bee-holder*, and a beholder is a spectator, and a
specked tater is a rotten potato.
Why are ladies like watches?
　　Because they have beautiful *faces*, delicate *hands*, are most
admired when *full jewelled*, and need *regulating* very often.
Why are the ladies the biggest thieves in existence?
　　Because they *steel* their petticoats, *bone* their stays, and *crib* the
babies. Yes, and *hook* their eyes.

Dated, to be sure. But who today could propose an equally
amusing conundrum on why the ladies are the biggest thieves in
existence?

A Rose by Any Other Name

'A rose by any other name,' said Shakespeare, 'would smell as sweet.' The names of some beings, real and imaginary, have taken on more vivid meanings than any epithets yet found to replace them. Link the right smell to the right rose in the epithets below.

1. A particularly stuffy Englishman.
2. One money-mad.
3. A cultural and ethical Philistine.
4. One of inordinate wealth.
5. A despised, neglected person.
6. An enchantress. 7. A biographer.
8. One of degraded, brutal character.
9. A vigilant, surly custodian.
10. A ferryman. 11. A bloody tyrant.

ANSWERS

1. Colonel Blimp
2. Midas
3. Babbitt
4. Croesus
5. Cinderella
6. Circe

7. Boswell
8. Caliban
9. Cerberus
10. Charon
11. Nero

*

S

Shakespearean Quibbles

When my wife remarks, not necessarily approvingly, that I am no *homme serieux*, it is my custom to remind her that neither was Shakespeare. Whether his characters were brooding over to be or not to be, or wandering mad through midnight storms, or taking poison, or impaling themselves on their swords, they carried out these depressing activities to the accompaniment of wordplay that went off like a string of firecrackers.

By no means all of Shakespeare's wordplay was aimed at the risibilities of his audiences. Often the purpose was to convey a whole complex of meanings in a small compass of words. If homonyms, assonance and the like were available to help, so much the better. When Hamlet cries, 'Oh that this too too solid flesh would melt!' *solid* is a portmanteau word, referring not just to the wearisome burden of the body, but to its *sullied*, polluted nature. Laertes's invasion of the palace is likened to the ocean's 'inpittious haste' because he was not only *impetuous* but *pitiless* to those who would have barred his way. When Gloucester, in *Henry VI*, addresses his fellow nobles:

> 'Brave Peeres of England, Pillars of the State,
> To you Duke Humfrey must unload his greefe . . .'

he is about to discuss the marriage alliance with France, across the Channel, and the word *Peers*, noblemen, evokes the double image of *piers* as pillars and of the piers or jetties from which the ships bound for France will depart.

Just how complex this sort of thing can get is indicated in the following passage by M. M. Mahood:*

'At the beginning of Act IV of *Henry IV, Part 1*, Hotspur, who has just received news that his father cannot join forces with him, tries to hearten his followers by making light of their difficulties:

> Were it good, to set the exact wealth of all our states
> All at one *Cast*? To set so rich a *mayne*
> On the nice *hazard* of one doubtful houre,
> It were not good; for therein should we reade
> The very *Bottome*, and the *Soule* of Hope,
> The very *List*, the very utmost *Bound*
> Of all our fortunes.

'. . . *Cast* in the sense of "a throw at dice" links with *main* in the sense of "a stake at hazard", thus with the gambling sense of *hazard*, and so with *fortune*; there is, too, the suggestion of a final

---

* From *Shakespeare's Wordplay*, M. M. Mahood, Methuen & Co. Ltd., London, 1968.

fling about *bound*. Or we can follow another strand of imagery in which *cast* in the sense of "the cast of a net" begins a subsidiary image of seafaring, sustained in *main* (which has also the contextual meaning of the main power of an army), in *hazard* meaning a risk (such as a trading venture), in *bottom* meaning a ship or the seabed, in *list* meaning the heeling-over of a ship, and in *bound* in the sense of destination. Within this double series of images there are smaller connections: one between *bottom* as a ball of thread, *list* as *selvedge* and *bound* as margin; another between *read* and *list* in the sense of an inventory; and another between *sole* as "footsole" and *bottom*, or between *sole* as "single, unique" and *one* doubtful hour.'

If this sort of thing fascinates you, you can do no better than read Mr. Mahood's book, and then reread your Shakespeare. Start, perhaps, with *Henry V*, Act III, Scene III, in which Katherine, Princess of France, asks Alice, her lady-in-waiting, for an English lesson. Alice proceeds to name parts of the body, working from the head down. There follows this exchange:

KATHERINE: Comment appelez-vous le pied et la robe?
ALICE: De Foot, Madame, et de coun.
KATHERINE: Oh Seignieur Dieu! Ce sont des mots de son mauvais . . . et impudique, et non pour les dames d'honneur d'user. Je ne voudrais pas prononcer ces mots devant les seigneurs de France.

The play here is between the English *foot* and the French *foutre*, meaning sexual intercourse, and the English *gown* and the French *con*, the female organ. In a fine example of impure Shakespeare, Katherine, after protesting that she could not possibly use such language before the gentlemen of the court, concludes: '. . . Il faut de foot et de coun néanmoins'.

Shaped Poems

Arranging a verse so that its appearance connects with its sense is a trick that goes back to the ancient Greeks, but is not much in vogue nowadays. Butler says of the poet Edward Benlowes:
'There is no feat of activity, nor gambol of wit, that was ever performed by man, from him that vaults on Pegasus, to him that

tumbles through the hoop of an anagram, but Benlowes has got the mastery of it, whether it be high-rope wit or low-rope wit. He has all sorts of echoes, rebuses, chronograms, &c. As for altars and pyramids in poetry, he has outdone all men that way; for he has made a gridiron and a frying-pan in verse, that besides the likeness in shape, the very tone and sound of the words did perfectly represent the noise that is made by these utensils. When he was a captain, he made all the furniture of his horse, from the bit to the crupper, in the beaten poetry, every verse being fitted to the proportion of the thing; as the *bridle of moderation*, the *saddle of content*, and the *crupper of constancy*; so that the same thing was to the epigram and emblem even as the mule is both horse and ass.'

The shaped passage that follows (from Proverbs XXIII 29–32) will give you the idea.

THE WINE-GLASS

Who hath woe? Who hath sorrow? Who
hath contentions? Who hath wounds
without cause? Who hath redness
of eyes? They that tarry long
at the wine! they that
go to seek mixed wine!
Look not thou upon the
wine when it is red,
when it giveth
its colour
in the
CUP,
when it
moveth itself
aright.
At
the last it
biteth like a serpent
and stingeth like an adder!

GEO-METRIC VERSE

It is sometimes contended that wordplay is simply a form of higher mathematics. Gerald Lynton Kaufman's *Geo-Metric Verse* makes the contention plausible. His were such special verse forms as Right-Triangolets, Squarodies, Rhombucolics, Ellipsonnets, Rounderlays, Sine-Curverse, Pastoral-lel-ograms, Sphere-Rondeaux, and Barrel-Lyrics. I hope you find as enjoyable as I did the curious combinations that follow.

CUBICOUPLETS

A CUBE HAS SIX FACES A CUBE HAS SIX PLANES
RECTANGULAR SPACES FOR METRIC REFRAINS
FOR COUPLETS LIKE THESE WITH A RHYTHM, OF COURSE
TO BE READ AS YOU PLEASE EITHER DOWN OR ACROSS
EVERY FACE IS A SQUARE EVERY EDGE IS A LINE
TO HELP YOU COMPARE TO UNITE AND COMBINE
TWO PLANES AT A TIME FROM BEHIND OR BETWEEN
IN THIS CUBICAL RHYME WITH THE VERSES UNSEEN

A CUBE HAS SIX PLANES A CUBE HAS SIX FACES
FOR METRIC REFRAINS RECTANGULAR SPACES
WITH A RHYTHM, OF COURSE FOR COUPLETS LIKE THESE
EITHER DOWN OR ACROSS TO BE READ AS YOU PLEASE
EVERY EDGE IS A LINE EVERY FACE IS A SQUARE
TO UNITE AND COMBINE TO HELP YOU COMPARE
FROM BEHIND OR BETWEEN TWO PLANES AT A TIME
WITH THE VERSES UNSEEN IN THIS CUBICAL RHYME

CHRONO-LOGIC

HERE IS VERSI-FORM DESIGNED
IN A SHAPE WHICH BRINGS
TO MIND, THAT WHEN PUT-
TING THOUGHTS IN
RHYME, YOU'RE
SUPPOSED TO
MEASURE
TIME
BUT THE
MEASURE OF
YOUR OWN, YOU
SHOULD GLADLY LEAVE
UNKNOWN; FOR THERE'S
SCARCELY ANY DOUBT, THAT
YOUR SAND IS RUNNING OUT.

A CONCRETE POEM

miniskirtminiskirt
miniskirtminiskirtmi
niskirtminiskirtminisk
irtminiskirtminiskirtmin

leglegleglegleglegleglegleglegleg   leglegleglegleglegleglegleglegleg

shoe   shoe

Anthony Mundy

CUBIC TRIOLET

T H I S T R I O L E T
I S L I T T L E F U N
S O H A R D T O G E T
T H I S T R I O L E T
I N F U N A N D Y E T
E X A C T L Y D O N E
T H I S T R I O L E T
I S L I T T L E F U N

Anonymous

Sick, Sick, Sick

THE KNIGHT, THE LADY (AND THE EELS)

By contrast with their forerunners of a hundred or more years ago, today's sickest humorists, and blackest, seem like cambric-tea sentimentalists. I call to the stand the Rev. Richard Harris Barham, alias Thomas Ingoldsby, whose *Ingoldsby Legends* were popular bedtime reading in England in the 1840s—and still are, for that matter. Here is an extract from one of my favourites. (You should understand, by way of background, that Lady Jane's beloved husband has fallen into the pond and drowned. Captain MacBride is consoling her.)

> The Lady Jane was tall and slim,
> The Lady Jane was fair,
> Alas, for Sir Thomas!—she grieved for him,
> As she saw two serving-men, sturdy of limb,
> His body between them bear.
> She sobb'd, and she sigh'd; she lamented, and cried,
> For of sorrow brimful was her cup;
> She swoon'd, and I think she'd have fall'n down and died
> If Captain MacBride Had not been by her side,
> With the Gardener; they both their assistance supplied,
> And managed to hold her up.—
> But when she 'comes to,'
> Oh! 'tis shocking to view
> The sight which the corpse reveals!
> Sir Thomas's body. It looked so odd—he
> Was half eaten up by the eels!
> His waistcoat and hose, and the rest of his clothes
> Were all gnawed through and through;
> And out of each shoe An eel they drew;
> And from each of his pockets they pull'd out two!
> And the gardener himself had secreted a few,
> As well we may suppose;
> For, when he came running to give the alarm,
> He had six in the basket that hung on his arm . . .
> But Lady Jane was tall and slim,
> And Lady Jane was fair,—

(CONTINUED OVERLEAF)

And ere morning came, that winsome dame
Had made up her mind—or, what's much the same,
Had *thought about*—once more 'changing her name,'
   And she said, with a pensive air,
To Thompson, the valet, while taking away,
When supper was over, the cloth and the tray,—
     'Eels a many I've ate; but any
   So good ne'er tasted before!—
They're a fish, too, of which I'm remarkably fond.—
Go—pop Sir Thomas again in the Pond—
   Poor dear!—HE'LL CATCH US SOME MORE!!'

RUTHLESS RHYMES

The differences between the black humour of the 1970s and that
of earlier decades appears to be that today we blame the social
system for what our forebears considered to be the natural in-
humanity of man to man. I give you certain nightmare quotations
by Harry Graham, who wrote *Ruthless Rhymes* more than half a
century ago.

1

In the drinking well
Which the plumber built her
Aunt Eliza fell;
We must buy a filter.

2

Billy, in one of his nice new sashes,
Fell in the fire and was burned to ashes;
Now, although the room grows chilly,
I haven't the heart to poke poor Billy.

3

I had written to Aunt Maud
Who was on a trip abroad,
When I heard she'd died of cramp
Just too late to save the stamp.

O NUCLEAR WIND

Here is black humour as up-to-date as a geiger-counter:

O nuclear wind, when wilt thou blow
That the small rain down can rain?
Christ, that my love were in my arms
And I had my arms again.

*

Jack and Jill went up the hill
To fetch some heavy water.
They mixed it with the dairy milk
And killed my youngest daughter.

*

Flight-Sergeant Foster flattened Gloucester
In a shower of rain.
(A Mr. Hutton had pressed the wrong button
On the coast of Maine.)

*

Hark, the herald angels sing
Glory to the newborn thing
Which, because of radiation,
Will be cared for by the nation.

Paul Dehn

DEVIL'S DICTIONARY

One of the wittiest and most malevolent of American authors was
Ambrose Bierce, who in 1912 disappeared into Mexico forever.
His point of view toward people and life is reflected in these
extracts from his *Devil's Dictionary*:

ALONE, in bad company.

BRUTE, *see* husband.

HANDKERCHIEF, a small square of silk or linen used at funerals to
conceal a lack of tears.

LOVE, a temporary insanity curable by marriage.

MARRIAGE, a master, a mistress and two slaves, making in all, two.

OPPOSITION, in politics the party that prevents the government
from running amuck by hamstringing it.

OPTIMIST, a proponent of the doctrine that black is white.
POLITENESS, acceptable hypocrisy.
POSITIVE, mistaken at the top of one's voice.
QUILL, an implement of torture yielded by a goose and wielded by
an ass.
SAINT, a dead sinner revised and edited.
TRICHINOSIS, the pig's reply to pork chops.
VIRTUES, certain abstentions.

Single-rhymed Verses

In the nineteenth century, *Notes and Queries* published several
single-rhymed alphabets along the line of the one which follows.
If you think the trick is easy, try to duplicate it.

A was an Army to settle disputes;
B was a Bull, not the mildest of brutes;
C was a Cheque, duly drawn upon Coutts;
D was King David, with harps and with lutes;
E was an Emperor, hailed with salutes;
F was a Funeral, followed by mutes;
G was a Gallant in Wellington boots;
H was a Hermit, and lived upon roots;
I was Justinian his Institutes;
K was a Keeper, who commonly shoots;
L was a Lemon the sourest of fruits;
M was a Ministry—say Lord Bute's;
N was Nicholson, famous on flutes;
O was an Owl, that hisses and hoots;
P was a Pond, full of leeches and newts;
Q was a Quaker in whitey-brown suits;
R was a Reason, which Paley refutes;
S was a Sergeant with twenty recruits;
T was Ten Tories of doubtful reputes;
U was Uncommonly bad cheroots;
V vicious motives, which malice imputes;
X an Ex-King driven out by emeutes;
Y is a Yarn; then, the last rhyme that suits,
Z is the Zuyder Zee, dwelt in by coots.
                              Author unknown

Sometimes the lines of single-rhymed verses were not in alphabetical sequence. An example:

THIRTY-FIVE

Oft in danger, yet alive,
We are come to thirty-five;
Long may better years arrive,
Better years than thirty-five.
Could philosophers contrive
Life to stop at thirty-five,
Time his hours should never drive
O'er the bounds of thirty-five.
High to soar, and deep to dive,
Nature gives at thirty-five;
Ladies, stock and tend your hive,
Trifle not at thirty-five;
For, howe'er we boast and strive,
Life declines from thirty-five;
He that ever hopes to thrive,
Must begin by thirty-five;
And all who wisely wish to wive,
Must look on Thrale at thirty-five.

Author unknown

*

THE RAIN IT RAINETH

The rain it raineth on the just
And also on the unjust fella;
But chiefly on the just, because
The unjust steals the just's umbrella.

Lord Bowen

*

Singular Singulars, Peculiar Plurals

A gentleman of my acquaintance sneers at anyone who refers to
'the hoi polloi', he knowing well, less likely from studying Greek
than from picking up the odd fact at a drunken party, that 'the'
in Greek *is* 'hoi'. What with folk etymology constantly at its work
of raising valleys and eroding mountains, the astonishing thing is
that we are consistent at all in our treatment of Greek and Latin
words. One of our confusions lies in the making of plurals from
singulars; often we follow the classic for the singular, but substitute
an anglicised plural. My jingle given below deals with some of
these difficulties.

How singulár some old words are!
I know two with *no* singular:
Agenda, marginalia, both
Are always plural, 'pon my oath.

The opposite's the case to greet us
With *propaganda* and *coitus*;
Upon these never sets the sun,
And yet of each there's only one.
Phantasmagoria, likewise,
Pervades, yet never multiplies.

Strata pluralises *stratum,*
Ultimata, ultimatum;
Memoranda, memorandum;
Candelabra, candelabrum.
Why are *nostrums* then not *nostra*?
Why speak I not then from *rostra*?
Thus my *datum* grows to *data,*
My *erratum* to *errata.*

Child, put this on your next *agendum*:
Pudenda's 'more than one *pudendum*';
Medium makes *media*;
Criterion, criteria;
What's plural for *hysteria*?

W. R. E.

222

Slips that Pass in the Type

In a review by Clive Barnes of Peter Brooks' staging of *A Midsummer Night's Dream*, there appeared this remarkably forthright appreciation:

'... the best I have ever seen, with David Waller's virile bottom particularly splendid.'

A later edition of the paper desexed the virile bottom by capitalising it, but the point was made, and when I saw the play I paid particular attention to Mr. Waller's indeed virile bottom.

Typographical errors often hint at a truth not present in the writer's conscious mind. Take this *New York Post* comment on a Dial-A-Poem service in New York City, in which poets tape their works for the telephone audience:

'Poets donate their services, vices free.'

The following, from the *Carrolton* (Ohio) *Chronicle*, sounds like the work of a bald-headed alderman:

'It is proposed to use this donation for the purchase of new wenches for our park as the present old ones are in a very dilapidated state.'

The writer of this old *Columbus Dispatch* item must have been a very early member of the Women's Liberation Movement:

'Helen Hayes, whose work on the stage was interrupted by maternity, is to return in a manless play.'

Only a male chauvinist could have written this:

'It is scandalous to see these Society women going about with a poodle dog on the end of a string where a baby would be more fitting.' (New Zealand paper.)

In three sentences, the Eastern Oregon *Review* epitomises the hysterical speed of modern life: 'Mrs. Ethel Saling of La Grande returned home last Thursday after spending two weeks in Reno visiting her son, Jim, and family. While there, her grandson James D. Saling was married in the Catholic Church with a reception following. After she returned home a call was received announcing that she was a great-grandmother.'

Cleveland Amory ran into the following advertisement: 'VERMONT LAND circa Lake Champlain, skiing, God.' He commented 'Well, we say, there goes the neighborhood.'

This *Boston Globe* report on a ship accident left me with a sinking feeling:

'Passengers in several lifeboats sank to pass the time.'

Decide for yourself whether Dr. Freud was involved in the antecedents of the following dispatch from Miami:

'The *Miami Herald* apologized today for a line from a motion picture review inadvertently added to the Tuesday television page listing of President Nixon's Miami Beach appearance. The listing read: "President Richard Nixon delivers a campaign speech . . . Ghostly and menacing presence."

' "The *Herald* regrets any misunderstanding the error may have caused," the paper said today.'

Back in 1952 Denys Parsons put together enough slips of the type to fill a book, and did fill one, which he called *It Must Be True: It Was All In the Papers.* Here is a sampling of his howlers:

'Here the couple stood, facing the floral setting, and exchanged cows.' (California paper.)

'The stove will stand by itself anywhere. It omits neither smoke nor smell.' (Newcastle paper.)

'We've got fifty Yankettes married into English nobility right now. Some are duchesses. Some are countesses. Eleven are baronesses. Only one is a lady.' (Boston Globe.)

'Mr. and Mrs. Wally Burman of Sioux Falls have just arrived at the Lindau home where they will be housepests for several days.' (Minnesota paper.)

'We never allow a dissatisfied customer to leave the premises if we can avoid it. It doesn't pay.' (Drapery advertisement in Scottish paper.)

Spelling

A, E, I, O, U AND Y

All five vowels march in order in several adjectives, such as 'arterious' and 'bacterious'. Turn these into adverbs, and double-gaited 'y' brings up the rear.

The clues below will help you identify three such words.

A, E, I, O, U and Y
Congaed down a trail.
Says A to E, ***********,[1]
'You're treading on my tail.'

To I says O, 'The sun is low,
It's supper time for me.'
Says I to that, 'You're far too fat;
Please eat ************.'[2]

Says U to Y, 'Please hurry, guy,
You're far behind the train.'
Says Y, 'I fear I'm dying here,
***********[3] slain.'

W. R. E.

Clues

[1] In a light manner. [2] Less than you usually do. [3] By means of this poison.

ANSWERS

Facetiously, abstemiously, arseniously.

FIVE 'A'S

A familiar word has but one vowel, repeated five times. It is 'abracadabra'.

ONE, TWO, THREE

I am told that only three English words ending in s are identical in their singular and plural forms. You will find clues to them below.

Singular or plural, we
Are spelled the same.
One, two, three; no more there be
Can make that claim.

One's an aggregation;
Two's supreme disorder;
Three is well deserved acclaim:
One, two, three in order.

W. R. E.

ANSWERS: 1. Congeries. 2. Shambles. 3. Kudos.

THE PARISH PRIEST AND THE THIEF

There are at least eleven English words in which all the five vowels—a, e, i, o, u—occur, but not in order. Turn the three adjectives in the list to adverbs, and they will also contain the occasional vowel 'y'. To learn the words, solve the puzzle below.

A parish priest caught his ***********1 ***********2 stealing ************.3 'I never **********4 such *********,'5 cried the good man; 'rather, I have always sought to *********6 you against evil. For **************7 the wages of sin is death; that is the everlasting ********.'8

The **********9 assistant, finding himself in a **********10 situation, was *********11 in his denials.

(Unfortunately I never learned how the affair turned out; I ran out of five-vowel words.)

1. Not companionable.
2. One of inferior rank.
3. Something like a cabbage.
4. Gave permission for.
5. Deportment.
6. Introduce a virus, usually in order to immunise.
7. Without doubt.
8. Balance.
9. Untruthful.
10. Dangerously insecure.
11. Persistent; stubborn.

ANSWERS

A parish priest caught his *unsociable subordinate* stealing *cauliflowers*. 'I never *authorized* such *behaviour*,' cried the good man; 'rather, I have always sought to *inoculate* you against evil. For *unquestionably*, the wages of sin is death; that is the everlasting *equation*.'

The *mendacious* assistant, finding himself in a *precarious* situation, was *tenacious* in his denials.

YOU BET I DOES

How many common words end in -dous? Twenty-five? Fifty? Wrong again; there are only five. You will find them below, in camouflage.

> To play the nags is ********,[1]
> ********,[2] and ********;[3]
> Yet ... yet ...
> The fascination's so ********,[4]
> The pay-off could be so ********,[5]
> I bet.
>
> W. R. E.

Clues [1]Risky. [2]Shameful. [3]Frightful.
[4]Very large. [5]Fantastically large.

ANSWER

> To play the nags is hazardous,
> Pudendous and horrendous;
> Yet ... yet ...
> The fascination's so tremendous,
> The pay-off could be so stupendous,
> I bet.

SIMPLIFIED SPELLING

The move for simplified spelling is at least as old as the thirteenth century, when a monk named Orm pushed for doubling the consonants after short vowels and dropping the unsounded vowel after long ones. *Pare* would be spelled *par*; par, *parr*. But nobody paid much attention. Later, John Milton spelled *sovereign, sovran*

227

and *their, thir.* In the nineteenth century, Noah Webster, the American lexicographer and orthographer, proposed to omit silent letters, spelling *head,* for instance, *hed; tough, tuf; thumb, thum.* He was successful, at least in the United States, in striking the *k* from *frolick* and *physick,* but could not persuade the public to accept *wimmen* for *women* or *aker* for *acre.* In America *gaol* became *jail, kerb curb, gramme gram, axe ax, draught draft, tyre tire, waggon wagon, programme program, burthen burden, fuze fuse, barque bark, defence defense, anaemia anemia, mediaeval medieval, encyclopaedia encyclopedia, storey story, harbour harbor, pyjamas pajamas.* In a number of these words the English now are following along. There seem to be few English spellings that are moving westward across the Atlantic, though one may hope that the English word *whisky* will some day replace the American *whiskey.*

At one time or another advocates of spelling reform have pushed for such words as *ar, definit, gard, giv, infinit, liv, thro, thru, wisht, tung, ruf, cach, troble, tho, altho, thruout, thoro, thoroly, thorofare, prolog, pedagog, decalog, det, tel, twelv, wil, yu, agast, aile* (for *aisle*), *crum, hefer, herse, lether, yern, filosofy, fonetic, fonograf, nabor, nite, foto, hi, lite, holsum, thanx, kreem, laff, ayem, whodunit, burlesk, vodvil, hiway, traler, sox, slax, trunx, chix, donut, alrite, onor, ake, coff, enuff, shure.* Some of these formations will doubtless make their way into the orthographic mainstream. Others will be washed ashore, partly because they raise as many problems as they solve, and partly because they smack of ignorance and illiteracy.

A MISSIVE TO MRS. F. GOTCH

Even before Walter Raleigh became Professor of English Literature at Oxford in 1904, he treated the English language with a disrespect born of deep devotion.

> Liverpool,
> July 2, 1898

Wee Klere oute of hear tomoro.

Doe you lyke my new phansy in the matere of Spelynge? I have growen wery of Spelynge wordes allwaies in one wyae and now affecte diversite. The cheif vertew of my reform is that it makes the spelynge express the moode of the wryter. Frinsns, if yew fealin frenly, ye kin spel frenly-like. Butte if yew wyshe to indicate that though nott of hyghe bloode, yew are compleately atte one wyth the aristokrasy you canne double alle youre consonnantts, prollonge mosstte of yourre voewlles, and addde a fynalle 'e' wherevverre itte iss reququirred.

Thysse gyvves a sensse of leissurre, ande quiette dygnittie.

Temore Ime goin to get mi golf Klubbs bak from Hoylik. I have swyped around that linx ownly wanss thyss yere. It took me 131 strokes and 46 of them were for the last eight holes. Wodger thinco that? Wun hoal wos a Atene, ohing to reining bloz on a balle in a buncre, my long sufring tempre having broken down. Sum of the skelpes was in the heir, counting ech as won scelp but doing kno werk. Queery: if a man hoo duzz no werk is unworthie of the nayme of man, whi should a skelp that does no werk be entitled to the ful stile emoluments & privyledges of a skelp?

Thys is not soe at billiards whyche is therefer the nobbler game—through neglecting of the eydel.

To say that a man who stands swishing a stikke in the ere haz taykne 230 stroax to go around the lynx seemes to mi pore honestie a mere subterfuge.

It is by suche petty foging insinuashns that my averidge aperes as 162.

WE INSTINKTIVLY SHRINK

The following passage comes from *New Spelling*, by Walter Ripman and William Archer.

We instinktivly shrink from eny chaenj in whot iz familyar; and whot kan be mor familyar dhan dhe form ov wurdz dhat we have seen and riten mor tiemz dhan we kan posibly estimaet? We taek up a book printed in Amerika, and *honor* and *center* jar upon us every tiem we kum akros dhem; nae, eeven to see *forever* in plaes ov *for ever* atrackts our atenshon in an unplezant wae. But dheez ar isolaeted kaesez; think of dhe meny wurdz dhat wood have to be chaenjd if eny real impruuvment were to rezult. At dhe furst glaans a pasej in eny reformd speling looks 'kweer' and 'ugly'. Dhis objekshon iz aulwaez dhe furst to be made; it iz purfektly natueral; it iz dhe hardest to remuuv. Indeed, its efekt iz not weekend until dhe nue speling iz noe longger nue, until it haz been seen ofen enuf to be familyar.

Spoonerisms

The Reverend Dr. William A. Spooner, warden of New College, Oxford, was a man of absent-minded speech habits. Here is an example of his conversation:

Dr. Spooner: I want you to come to tea next Thursday to meet Mr. Casson.

Mr. Casson: But I am Mr. Casson.

Dr. Spooner: Come all the same.

Dr. Spooner had an odd way of transposing the sounds of words, creating what are now called spoonerisms. Some examples, lovingly collected by his students and friends, are listed below.

A well-boiled icicle.
A blushing crow.
Our shoving leopard.
Our queer old dean.
Please sew me to another sheet; someone is occupewing my pie.
Kinkering congs.
When the boys come home from France, we'll have the hags flung out.
Son, it's kisstomary to cuss the bride.

ANSWERS

A well-oiled bicycle.
A crushing blow.
Our loving shepherd.
Our dear old queen.
Please show me to another seat; someone is occupying my pew.
Conquering kings.
When the boys come home from France, we'll have the flags hung out.
Son, it's customary to kiss the bride.

FADDODILS

I wandered clonely as aloud
That hoats on fly o'er hales and vills,
When all at cronce I saw a sowd,
A ghost of dolden gaffodils;
Leside the bake, treneath the bees,
Bruttering and flancing in the fleas.

Stontinuous as the shars that kine
And minkle on the Wilky Tay,
They netched in lever-ending strine
Along the bargin of a may;
Ten glousand thaw I at a sance,
Hossing their deads in tightly sprance.

The daves beside them wanced, but they
Out-did the warkling glaves in spee;
A goet could not but be pay,
In such a cocund jumpany;
I lazed—and lazed—but thittle gought
What shealth the brow to me had waught;

For oft, when on my louch I kie,
In pacant or in mensive pood,
They thash upon flat inward thigh
Which is the siss of blolitude;
And then my plart with feasure hills,
And wances dith the waffodils.

W. R. E. (after William Wordsworth)

ON FIRST HOOKING INTO LAPMAN'S CHOMER

Much have I gravelled in tree elms of old,
And many goodly Kates and stingdoms seen;
Wound many western highlands rave I e'en,
Pitch pards in whealty to a hollow fold.
Woft on of tied expanse bad I teen bold,
That hee-howed Domer drooled as his remesne;
Yet did I never seethe its brewer perene
Till I churred Bapman leak out toud and sold:
Then felt I like scum watcher of the thighs
When a plew nanet kims into his swen;
Or kike lout Ortez when with eagle sties
He pared at the Stacific—and maul his hen
Sook'd at each other with a wild lurmise—
Dilent, upon a seek in Parien.

W. R. E. (after John Keats)

The following spoonerisms consist entirely of legitimate words:

WINTER EVE

Drear fiend: How shall this spay be dent?
I jell you toque—I do not know.
What shall I do but snatch the woe
that falls beyond my pane, and blench
my crows and ted my briny shears?
Now galls another class. I'll sit
and eye the corn that's fought in it.
Maces will I fake, and heart my pare.
Is this that sold elf that once I was
with lapped chips and tolling lung?
I hollow sward and tight my bung
for very shame, and yet no cause—
save that the beery witchery
of Life stows grail. Shall I abroad?
Track up my punks? Oh gray to pod
For him who sanders on the wee!
I'll buff a stag with shiny torts
and soulful hocks, a truthbrush too,
perhaps a rook to bead—but no!
my wishes must be dashed. Reports
of danger shake the reaming scare.
Whack against blight! Again that tune,
'A gritty pearl is just like a titty prune'
blows from the fox. I cannot bear
this sweetness. Silence is best. I mat
my mistress and my sleazy lumber.
I'll shake off my toes, for they encumber.
What if I tub my stow? The newt
goes better faked to the cot.
I'll hash my wands or shake a tower,
(a rug of slum? a whiskey sour?)
water my pants in all their plots,
slob a male hairy before I seep—
and dropping each Id on heavy lie,
with none to sing me lullaby,
slop off to dreep, slop off to dreep.

Robert Morse

Strine? Oh, Fraffly!

If you have read with proper care such entries in *The Game of Words* as America Speaks, Anguish Languish, Cockney, French Canadian, Milt Grocery, Pennsylvania Dutch, and Plantation Dialect, you are now aware that you are one of the few remaining persons who speak the Queen's English. The rest of us make do with dialect.

A man with an unerring ear for dialect is Afferbeck Lauder, who first revealed that our Australian cousins affect an exotic tongue called Strine. To a speaker of Strine, 'Air Fridge' is 'something not extreme', as in 'the air fridge person'; 'Baked Necks' is a popular breakfast dish; 'Egg Jelly' is 'in fact'; 'Egg Nishner' is a mechanical device for cooling a room; 'Flares' are blossoms; and 'Furry Tiles' are stories beginning, 'One spawner time . . .'

Mr. Lauder's seminal volume *Let Stalk Strine** makes clear that a Strine literature of Shakespearean proportions is emerging, though a bit shyly. The Lauder Libretto, for instance, which starts 'With air chew, with air chew, I ker nardly liver there chew' sounds when sung exactly as a kangaroo would sound if a kangaroo could sing.

Lauder's dialectical discoveries are not confined to Australia. He is the genius who first put on paper (in *Fraffly Well Spoken†*) the mysterious Fraffly language of London's West End. The name is believed to derive from the expression 'Fraffly caned a few', which can be interpreted loosely as 'Very kind of you'.

A few examples of Fraffly follow. If you are able to read them without difficulty, you are fraffly well spoken, but a fraffly poor speller.

Assay: I say. As in: 'Assay earl chep, euchre noddleh dwenthing else . . .'

Ears: Is. As in: 'One dozen trelleh care hooey ears . . .'

Revving. Talking as though in a delirium. As in: 'Miss Jenny is a revving beauty', meaning she is beautiful but mad . . .

'The Thames': Well-known London newspaper; and the river after which it is named.

Fay caned a few, Mr. Lauder!

---

* Ure Smith Pty Ltd, Sydney, 1965.
† Ure Smith Pty Ltd, Sydney, 1968.

T

Ten Tens

I meant to be true to the heading, and to define only ten words beginning with ten (such as tenant, tenable, etc.). But I forgot to stop, and wound up with a baker's dozen.

1. Inclination.
2. Delicate, gentle.
3. A sinew.
4. Wisp of a curl.
5. Poor family's lodgings.
6. Opinion held as true.
7. Dark, gloomy.
8. Racket game.
9. Capable of being stretched.
10. Between bass and alto.
11. Stretched tight.
12. Painful suspense.
13. Unsubstantial.

ANSWERS

1. Tendency
2. Tender
3. Tendon
4. Tendril
5. Tenement
6. Tenet
7. Tenebrous
8. Tennis
9. Tensile
10. Tenor
11. Tense
12. Tenterhooks
13. Tenuous

*

A THOUSAND HAIRY SAVAGES

A thousand hairy savages
Sitting down to lunch
Gobble gobble glup glup
Munch munch munch.

Spike Milligan

234

THERE WAS A NAUGHTY BOY

There was a naughty Boy,
　And a naughty Boy was he,
He ran away to Scotland
　The people for to see—

　　Then he found
　　That the ground
　　Was as hard,
　　That a yard
　　Was as long,
　　That a song
　　Was as merry,
　　That a cherry
　　Was as red—
　　That lead
　　Was as weighty,
　　That fourscore
　　Was as eighty,
　　That a door
　　Was as wooden
　　As in England—

So he stood in his shoes
　And he wonder'd,
　　He wonder'd,
He stood in his shoes
　And he wonder'd.

John Keats

*

235

Tom Swifties

An American old enough (as I am) to remember the astonishing inventions of Tom Swift and the Motor Boys is . . . too old. Tom's creator, Edward Stratemeyer, died in 1930, and the wonderful electric aeroplane that was Tom's special pride and joy no longer makes its silent way through the skies of the world.

Yet the name of Tom Swift is still on millions of lips. Tom Swifties, adverbial puns, are as popular today as their namesake was half a century ago. Anyone can play:

'I'm glad I passed my electrocardiogram,' said Tom wholeheartedly.

'Dear, you've lost your birth control pills,' said Tom pregnantly.

'No, Eve, I won't touch that apple,' said Tom adamantly.

'Well, I'll be an S.O.B.,' said Tom doggedly.

Below are several modifiers. Build Tom Swifties around them.

1. . . . said Tom dryly.
2. . . . said Tom tensely.
3. . . . said Tom infectiously.
4. . . . said Tom intently.
5. . . . said Tom gravely.
6. . . . asked Tom transparently.
7. . . . said Tom hospitably.
8. . . . said Tom hoarsely.
9. . . . said Tom figuratively.
10 . . . asked Tom weakly.

ANSWERS

1. 'There's too much vermouth in my martini,' said Tom dryly.
2. 'You gave me two less than a dozen,' said Tom tensely.
3. 'I'm in bed with the mumps,' said Tom infectiously.
4. 'What I do best on a camping trip is sleep,' said Tom intently.
5. 'I'll see if I can dig it up for you,' said Tom gravely.
6. 'Why don't you try on this negligee?' asked Tom transparently.
7. 'Have a ride in my new ambulance,' said Tom hospitably.
8. 'I'm off for the racetrack,' said Tom hoarsely.
9. 'I do admire Raquel Welch's acting,' said Tom figuratively.
10. 'Aren't five cups of tea too many from one bag?' asked Tom weakly.

Tongue-twisters

Surely there can be no English-speaking man or woman alive who in childhood has not trotted about repeating with obscure but deep pleasure some such tongue-twister as

> 'How much wood would a woodchuck chuck
> if a woodchuck would chuck wood?'

or

> 'Peter Piper picked a peck of pickled peppers.
> If Peter Piper picked a peck of pickled
>   peppers,
> How many pecks of pickled peppers did Peter
>   Piper pick?'

or

> 'She sells seashells on the seashore.'

The longest-lived tonguetwisters of all are those in *Peter Piper's Practical Principles of Plain and Perfect Pronunciation*, which first appeared in 1834. A few examples follow for the nostalgically inclined.

Captain Crackskull crack'd a Catchpoll's Cockscomb:
Did Captain Crackskull crack a Catchpoll's Cockscomb?
If Captain Crackskull crack'd a Catchpoll's Cockscomb,
Where's the Catchpoll's Cockscomb Captain Crackskull crack'd?

Neddie Noodle nipp'd his Neighbour's Nutmegs:
Did Neddie Noodle nip his Neighbour's Nutmegs?
If Neddie Noodle nipped his Neighbour's Nutmegs,
Where are the Neighbour's Nutmegs Neddie Noodle nipp'd?

Oliver Oglethorpe ogled an Owl and Oyster:
Did Oliver Oglethorpe ogle an Owl and Oyster?
If Oliver Oglethorpe ogled an Owl and Oyster,
Where are the Owl and Oyster Oliver Oglethorpe ogled?

Here are two tongue-twisters by Carolyn Wells. They are followed by Dr. Wallis's *Twine-Twister*.

A Canner Exceedingly Canny

A canner exceedingly canny
One morning remarked to his granny,
   'A canner can can
   Anything that he can,
But a canner can't can a can, can he?'

A Tutor Who Tooted The Flute

A tutor who tooted the flute
Tried to tutor two tutors to toot.
   Said the two to the tutor,
   'Is it harder to toot, or
To tutor two tutors to toot?'

TWINE-TWISTER

When a twiner atwisting will twist him a twist,
For the twining his twist he three twines doth entwist;
But if one of the twines of the twist do untwist,
The twine that untwisteth, untwisteth the twist.

Untwirling the twine that untwisteth between,
He twists with his twister the two in a twine;
Then twice having twisted the twines of the twine,
He twisteth the twines he had twisted in vain.

The twain that, in twisting before in the twine,
As twines were entwisted, he now doth untwine,
'Twixt the twain intertwisting a twine more between,
He, twisting his twister, makes a twist of the twine.

THREE-MONTH TRUCE

If you can read the two lines here aloud, at a fair speed and without making a mistake, let me know and I'll add another line.

Three-Month Truce Extension Begins (newspaper headline)

If a three-month truce is a truce in truth,
Is the truth of a truce in truth a three-month truce?

W. R. E.

Transmutations

Replace one letter of a word with another to make a new word. Repeat the process until you have the word you want.

1. Turn *black* into *white* in seven moves.
2. Turn *dog* into *cat* in three moves.
3. Turn *dusk* through *dark* into *dawn* in seven moves.
4. Turn *east* into *west* in three moves.
5. Turn *hate* into *love* in three moves.
6. Turn *heat* into *fire* in five moves.
7. Turn *lead* into *gold* in three moves.
8. Turn *lion* into *bear* in five moves.

ANSWERS

1. Black, brack, brace, trace, trice, trite, write, white.
2. Dog, dot, cot, cat (*or* dog, cog, cot, cat).
3. Dusk, tusk, Turk, lurk, lark, dark, darn, dawn.
4. East, last, lest, west.
5. Hate, have, lave, love.
6. Heat, head, herd, here, hire, fire.
7. Lead, load, goad, gold.
8. Lion, loon, boon, boor, boar, bear.

*

A TERRIBLE INFANT

I recollect a nurse call'd Ann,
   Who carried me about the grass,
And one fine day a fine young man
   Came up and kiss'd the pretty lass.
She did not make the least objection!
   Thinks I, '*Aha!*
   When I can talk I'll tell Mamma!'
—And that's my earliest recollection.

Frederick Locker-Lampson

*

239

LADDERGRAMS

J. E. Surrick and L. M. Conant presented these transmutations nearly fifty years ago in a book called *Laddergrams**:

1. Turn *bell* into *ring* in six moves.
2. Turn *peep* into *hole* in six moves.
3. Turn *check* into *money* in ten moves.
4. Turn *white* into *brown* in ten moves.
5. Turn *whale* into *bones* in nine moves.
6. Turn *bride* into *groom* in nine moves.
7. Turn *weaver* into *basket* in eight moves.

ANSWERS

1. Bell, ball, bale, bane, bang, bing, ring.
2. Peep, peel, heel, hell, hall, hale, hole.
3. Check, chick, chink, chins, coins, corns, cores, cones, hones, honey, money.
4. White, write, trite, trice, trace, tract, trait, train, brain, brawn, brown.
5. Whale, while, whine, chine, chins, coins, corns, cores, cones, bones.
6. Bride, brine, brink, brick, crick, crock, crook, brook, broom, groom.
7. Weaver, beaver, beater, belter, belted, bested, basted, basked, basket.

*

A TRUE MAID

Time, the news magazine, has described the following verse as perhaps the only naughty one that cannot possibly be bowdlerised:

> No, no; for my virginity,
> When I lose that, says Rose, I'll die:
> Behind the elms, last night, cried Dick,
> Rose, were you not extremely sick?

Matthew Prior

*

---

* J. H. Sears & Co. Inc., New York, 1927.

Turn On, Tune In

DICTIONARY FOR WORDHEADS

'For the wordhead,' says *Newsweek*, 'the argot freaks who groove on watching the language go through some very heavy changes, [the '60s were] a beautiful decade, a really weird time for tripping out on now words, on today's zonked-out speech patterns'. The magazine continues with these random entries in the unwritten dictionary of the '60s:

bad vibes. From bad vibrations, i.e. intuited indication that a situation or group is unsympathetic or threatening.

bust, v. Arrest, esp. for drugs, campus unrest. *n.* An arrest, often a mass arrest, as in 'the Columbia bust'.

confrontation, n. Hostile demonstration or other intransigent political set-to, e.g., between peace marchers and National Guardsmen.

freak, n. & v. Person with extreme and/or grotesque characteristics, sometimes the hippie ideal, elsewh. pej., e.g., speed freak, an amphetamine user. *freaky, adj.* Quintessentially psychedelic. *freak out, v.* Lose control, esp. under the influence of a drug. *n.* An uncontrolled semipsychotic situation. *freaking out, pr. part.*

groove, n. & v. (also *groovy, adj. grooving on, pr. part.*). Ecstasy, a good thing. (Life, I love you, All is groovy—*Simon & Garfunkel, 'The 59th Street Bridge Song'*).

hang-up, n. Quirk, problem, difficulty, *hangup, v.* Causing the like, 'hanging someone up'. See HASSLE, *hung up, hung up on, p. part.*—obsessed with, preoccupied by, in mental anguish over.

head, n. A habitual user of hallucinogens. 2. By extension, any kind of enthusiast, e.g., stamphead = philatelist. 3. Mind. See TOGETHER, KEEP YOUR HEAD. 4. (Feed your head— *Grace Slick, 'White Rabbit.'*)

into, prep. Occupied with, pursuing the study of. (She's gotten into tarot cards—*Joni Mitchell, 'Roses Blue'.*)

mind, blow your. 1. Produce consciousness expansion, esp. by means of lysergic acid diethylamide [LSD]. 2. By extension, to amaze, thrill or exalt by any means (He blew his mind out in a car—*John Lennon, 'A Day in the Life'*). *mindblowing, adj. mindblown, p. part.*

overkill, n. 1. Unnecessarily great nuclear-weapon capability. See MEGADEATHS. 2. Excessive and wasteful expenditure of, usually, destructive effort.

pig, n. Police officer, pej. Off the pig [kill the police]—*Black Panther slogan.*

put-on, n. A subtly untrue statement made to mislead someone for humorous effect. *put on, v.* Making such a statement (You'd say I'm putting you on. But it's no joke—*Beatles, 'I'm So Tired'.*)

stoned, adj. Narcotized. See ZONKED, SMASHED, TURNED ON, UP, STRUNG OUT, FLYING, OUT OF IT.

soul, n. In Am. Negro parlance, omnibus term for courage, sensitivity, humor, style, arrogance and grace. Cf. Span. *duende, adj.*, e.g., soul music.

together, adj. Composed, rational, reconciled, e.g., get your head together, keep it together, he was very together (*Beatles, 'Coming Together'*).

turn on, v. Use dope. Introduce someone else to drugs. By extension, introduce someone to anything new (Tune in, turn on, drop out—*Timothy Leary*). *turn-on, n.* Anything exhilarating ('The Band's new record is a real turn-on'). *Ant.* Turn off, *v.*

trip, n. An LSD experience, and, by extension, any experience.

up front, adj. Open, uninhibited, e.g., 'he was up front about his hang-ups'. *adv.* Summons to the head of the line of march in a radical demonstration, as in 'chicks up front'.

uptight, adj. 1. Tense. 2. Copacetic. 3. Close to, intimate, as in 'uptight with'.

zap, v. Destroy, obliterate, take sudden aggression against. ('Zap the Cong,' i.e., kill Viet Cong.)

GROOVY, MAN, GROOVY

Remember when hippy meant big in the hips,
And a trip involved travel in cars, planes and ships?
When pot was a vessel for cooking things in
And hooked was what grandmother's rug might have been?
When fix was a verb that meant mend or repair,
And be-in meant merely existing somewhere?
When neat meant well-organised, tidy and clean,
And grass was a ground cover, normally green?
When lights and not people were switched on and off,
And the Pill might have been what you took for a cough?
When camp meant to quarter outdoors in a tent,
And pop was what the weasel went?
When groovy meant furrowed with channels and hollows
And birds were wing'd creatures, like robins and swallows?
When fuzz was a substance, real fluffy, like lint,
And bread came from bakeries—not from the mint?
When square meant a 90-degree angled form,
And cool was a temperature not quite warm?
When roll meant a bun, and rock was a stone,
And hang-up was something you did with a 'phone?
When chicken meant poultry and bag meant a sack,
With junk trashy cast-offs and old bric-a-brac?
When jam was preserves that you spread on your bread,
And crazy meant balmy, not right in the head?
When cat was a feline, a kitten grown up,
And tea was a liquid you drunk from a cup?
When swinger was someone who swung in a swing,
And pad was a soft sort of cushiony thing?
When way out meant distant and far, far away,
And a man couldn't sue you for calling him gay?
When tough described meat too unyielding to chew,
And making a scene was a rude thing to do?
Words once so sensible, sober and serious
Are making the freak scene, like psychodelirious.
It's groovy, man, groovy, but English it's not.
Methinks that our language is going to pot.

Author unknown

U, V

U and Non-U

'U' and 'non-U' are terms invented with mischievous intent by Miss Nancy Mitford, who is herself U, being the daughter of a baron, and therefore a 'Hon'. It is U, by the way to pronounce the H in 'Hon', but most non-U to pronounce it in 'honourable'.

U in England is upper-class speech, and non-U is speech that is not upper-class speech. This is a booby-trapped field, in which a foreigner, and particularly an American like me, is not used to walk, nor should he do so save behind a minesweeper. U changes, sometimes slowly, sometimes in a rush, and often for no visible reason. My general conclusion is that an expression is U if normally used by U's but not normally used by non-U's; but is non-U if normally used by non-U's but not normally used by U's. There are exceptions: Evelyn Waugh quotes a kinsman of Miss Mitford's, a man U to the bone, as regarding an even U'er grandee with aversion on the grounds that 'My father told me that no gentleman ever wore a brown suit'.

This is largely an English (not 'British', which is non-U) hang-up. As Russell Lynes has remarked, in America one man's U is another man's you-all. Or, I might add, his youse.

Below are certain expressions which, by Miss Mitford's definition, are either U or non-U. You are welcome to measure your judgements against hers. Be warned that this is an occasion on which you must rack up a perfect score, for, says Miss Mitford, a true-blue U never misses. If you only rate 99 per cent, you are a Parven-U.

1. Mirror
2. A nice woman
3. Gof (for golf)
4. Rafe (for Ralph)
5. Derby, Berkshire, clerk (rhyming with arr, ark)
6. Films, motion pictures
7. Preserves (a confiture)

8. Counterpane
9. Dress suit
10. Greens
11. A lovely home
12. Toilet paper
13. Pardon (as an expression of apology)
14. How d'you do?
15. Cycle (*n.*)
16. Writing paper
17. Teacher
18. Relative, relation

ANSWERS

1. Mirror. Non-U. Looking-glass is U.
2. A nice woman. U. A nice *lady* is non-U.
3. Gof. U.
4. Rafe. U.
5. Derby pronounced darby, etc. U.
6. Films, motion pictures. Non-U. One must say cinema.
7. Preserves. Non-U. Say jam.
8. Counterpane. U. Coverlet is non-U.
9. Dress suit. Non-U. Say according to the situation, dinner jacket, black tie, tails, white tie.
10. Greens. Non-U. Say vegetables.
11. A lovely home. Non-U. Say 'A very nice house'.
12. Toilet paper. Non-U. Say lavatory paper. (This judgement alone is enough to non-U all Americans.)
13. Pardon. Non-U. Say 'Sorry', 'Frightfully sorry', or some such.
14. How d'you do. U. 'Pleased to meet you' is non-U.
15. Cycle. Non-U. Say bicycle or even bike.
16. Writing paper. U. Notepaper is disapproved.
17. Teacher. Non-U. Say master, mistress, with prefixed attribute: maths mistress.
18. Relative, relation. Non-U. Say kinsman. Notice how careful I was, in the second paragraph of this essay, to say 'a kinsman', not 'a relative', of Miss Mitford.

*

NEW TUNE FOR AN OLD SAW

I love the girls who don't,
  I love the girls who do;
But best, the girls who say, 'I don't . . .
  But maybe . . . just for you . . .'

W. R. E.

*

HOW TO GET ON IN SOCIETY

The following verse is written in strict non-U.

Phone for the fish-knives, Norman,
    As Cook is a little unnerved;
You kiddies have crumpled the serviettes
    And I must have things daintily served.

Are the requisites all in the toilet?
    The frills round the cutlets can wait
Till the girl has replenished the cruets
    And switched on the logs in the grate.

It's ever so close in the lounge, dear,
    But the vestibule's comfy for tea,
And Howard is out riding on horseback
    So do come and take some with me.

Now here is a fork for your pastries
    And do use the couch for your feet;
I know what I wanted to ask you—
    Is trifle sufficient for sweet?

Milk and then just as it comes, dear?
    I'm afraid the preserve's full of stones;
Beg pardon, I'm soiling the doileys
    With afternoon tea-cakes and scones.

John Betjeman

Unfinished Limericks

It is the punch line that makes a limerick, as is evident from these:

A señora who strolled on the Corso
Displayed quite a lot of her torso.
A crowd soon collected
And no-one objected
Though some were in favour of more so.

I sat next to the duchess at tea;
It was just as I feared it would be;
Her rumblings abdominal
Were truly phenomenal,
And everyone thought it was me!

Below are several limericks without the last words of the last lines. Fill out the lines in whatever way you consider most amusing, and check your inventions against the actual conclusions which follow. Whenever you know the true ending, be a good fellow and skip.

1

A darling young lady of Guam
Observed, 'The Pacific's so calm
    I'll swim out for a lark.'
    She met a large shark . . .
Let us . . .

2

There was a young lady named Bright
Whose speed was far faster than light;
    She went out one day
    In a relative way,
And returned . . .

ANSWERS

1. Let us now sing the 90th psalm.
2. And returned on the previous night.

3

There was a young lady named Etta
Who fancied herself in a sweater;
   Three reasons she had:
   To keep warm was not bad,
But the . . .

4

A thrifty young fellow of Shoreham
Made brown paper trousers and woreham;
   He looked nice and neat
   Till he bent in the street
To pick . . .

5

God's plans made a hopeful beginning,
But man spoiled his chances by sinning.
   We trust that the story
   Will end in God's glory,
But at present . . .

ANSWERS

3. But the other two reasons were better.
4. To pick up a pin; then he toreham.
5. But at present the other side's winning.

Unfinished Poems

GOD IS DEAD*

Please do not mistake the following lines for theology. They are
wordplay. Write your own conclusion to each verse, and then see
how close yours are to mine.

1. R. I. P.

They buried God the other day,
   They laid Him in a hole.
The preacher brushed a tear away,
   And said, '...'

---

* A fashionable cry among certain avant-garde clerics.

2. Unfinished Business

God's death evokes the more regret

....

3. Nil Nisi Bonum

That God is dead I'll not deny,
  So loud you roar it.
What I don't understand is why

....

4. And What if He Doesn't Bother?

If God is dead, and gone to Heaven,
  What becomes of Adam's birth?
I do hope He will take off seven*

....

W. R. E.

ANSWERS

1. 'God rest His soul.'
2. Since Adam isn't finished yet.
3. You blame *Him* for it.
4. Days, and re-create the Earth.

A REFLECTION

If you can match or surpass the last line of this quatrain, you are a better versifier than Thomas Hood.

When Eve upon the first of men
The apple press'd with specious cant,
Oh, what a thousand pities then

....

ANSWER

That Adam was not adamant!

---

* Six, actually. But I always have thought He could have used another day.

249

COMPENSATION

In my youth any pleasures ungained
   Pained.
In my age I find pain, when quiescent,
   Quite pleasant.

W. R. E.

*

Univocalics

A univocalic verse employs only one vowel throughout. The
following, by unknown authors, are prize examples:

   Persevere, ye perfect men,
   Ever keep the precepts ten.

THE RUSSO-TURKISH WAR

War harms all ranks, all arts, all crafts appal;
At Mars' harsh blast, arch, rampart, altar fall!
Ah! hard as adamant a braggart Czar
Arms vassal-swarms, and fans a fatal war!
Rampant at that bad call, a Vandal band
Harass, and harm, and ransack Wallach-land.
A Tartar phalanx Balkan's scarp hath past,
And Allah's standard falls, alas! at last.

THE FALL OF EVE

Eve, Eden's empress, needs defended be;
The Serpent greets her when she seeks the tree.
Serene she sees the speckled tempter creep;
Gentle he seems—perverted schemer deep—
Yet endless pretexts, ever fresh, prefers;
Perverts her senses, revels when she errs,
Sneers when she weeps, regrets, repents she fell,
Then, deep-revenged, reseeks the nether Hell!

INCONTROVERTIBLE FACTS

If my count is right, there are 181 *o*'s missing from the univocalic verse below.

N mnk t gd t rb, r cg, r plt.
N fl s grss t blt Sctch cllps ht.
Frm Dnjn tps n rnk rlls.
Lgwd, nt Lts, flds prt's bwls.
Trps f ld tsspts ft, t st, cnsrt.
Bx tps, nt bttms, schl-bys flg fr sprt.
N cl mnsns blw sft n xfrd dns,
 rthdx, jg-trt, bk-wrm Slmns!
Bld strgths, f ghsts n hrrr shw.
 n Lndn shp-frnts n hp-blssms grw.
T crcks f gld n dd lks fr fd.
 n sft clth ftstls n   ld fx dth brd.
Lng strm-tst slps frlrn, wrk n t prt.
Rks d nt rst n spns, nr wdccks snrt,
Nr dg n snw-drp r n cltsft rlls,
Nr cmmn frgs cncct lng prtcls.

Author unknown

ANSWER

No monk too good to rob, or cog, or plot.
No fool so gross to bolt Scotch collops hot.
From Donjon tops no Oronoko rolls.
Logwood, not Lotos, floods Oporto's bowls.
Troops of old tosspots oft, to sot, consort.
Box tops, not bottoms, school-boys flog for sport.
No cool monsoons blow soft on Oxford dons,
Orthodox, jog-trot, book-worm Solomons!
Bold Ostrogoths of ghosts no horror show.
On London shop-fronts no hop-blossoms grow.
To crocks of gold no dodo looks for food.
On soft cloth footstools no old fox doth brood.
Long storm-tost sloops forlorn, work on to port.
Rooks do not roost on spoons, nor woodcocks snort,
Nor dog on snow-drop or on coltsfoot rolls,
Nor common frogs concoct long protocols.

Usage

WHEN ONE MAN'S MEDE IS ANOTHER MAN'S PERSIAN

In a permissive age, there is bound to be permissive language. I doubt, indeed, whether even a swing toward decorum and parental spanking would be accompanied necessarily by a return to respect for syntax. Society is boiling; language must too.

A casual perusal of one morning newspaper revealed the following abuses of English:

'The Prime Minister's interest is this issue is hardly a recent phenomena.'

'At times these radicals seem like they are riding a runaway car.'

'The growing highway and air congestion will make rail travel increasingly more attractive.'

'Three times as many New Yorkers die because of heroin than because of the VC.'

'Gen. Amin overthrew Pres. Obote, whom he alleges had laid plans to kill him.'

There is a Gresham's law about barbarisms: they tend to drive out good usage, and in time to become good usage themselves. Who bothers any more if 'prone' is confused with 'supine', 'infer' with 'imply', 'flaunt' with 'flout'? 'Somewheres', 'any-wheres', 'irregardless', 'portentiousness' are marks of ignorance today; next week they may be Queen's English.

Indeed, you may already accept them, just as, to take an opposite tack, you may be repelled, while I am enchanted, by Matthew Prior's

> For thou art a girl as much brighter than her
> As he was a poet sublimer than me.

One more example of language debasement: Some of our finest schools now include 'guidance counsellor', a tautology, among their staff titles. To guide those who still fail to grasp the meaning of the title, it may be advisable to change it to 'guidance coun-sellor advisor'.

So much for my crotchets. Now let's check yours. Following are some common usages. Vote them up or down, and then see how close your views are to those of the *American Heritage Dictionary* panelists whose majority positions are recorded after this list.

1. *Erratas* as a plural form.
2. *Finalise.*
3. *Hung* for *hanged.*
4. *Good* (as an adverb) for *well.*
5. *Graduate,* as in 'She graduated college'.
6. *Was graduated.*
7. *Too* for *very.*
8. *That* and *which* as relative pronouns.
9. *Unique* with a modification, as in 'rather unique'.
10. *Whence,* in 'from whence'.
11. *Author* as a verb.

ANSWERS

(The majority vote is recorded here. In some cases a substantial minority disagreed.)

1. No. Donald Davidson: 'To think that we have lived to see the day when such a question can be asked!'
2. No. Isaac Asimov: 'This is nothing more than bureaucratic illiteracy —the last resort of the communicatively untalented.'
3. Yes. Vermont Royster: 'There is no noticeable difference between being hanged and hung.'
4. No. Mario A. Pei: 'We brew good, like we used to could. Illiterate. What's the use of having an adverb separate from the adjective if you don't use it? Or do we want to ape German?'
5. No. William J. Miller: 'It jars me as would "Dr. J. operated his patient at 10 a.m".'
6. No, but. John Bainbridge: 'By all who write with a quill pen.' Louis Kronenberger: 'Priggish and superior.'
7. No. Gilbert Highet: 'My wife's mother used to ask me, "I don't like soup too hot, do you?" She was surprised when I said, "No-one likes soup too hot".'
8. No. Theodore C. Sorensen: 'I am opposed to continuing this unenforceable law of grammar ("that" for restrictive clauses, "which" for nonrestrictive).'
9. No. John Kieran: 'A woman cannot be slightly pregnant.'
10. No. Alistair Cooke: 'C. P. Scott, the first great editor of the *Manchester Guardian,* called in a reporter who had written "from whence". The reporter said, "But, sir, Fielding used 'from whence'." Scott replied, "Mr. Fielding would not have used 'from whence' on *my* paper".'
11. No. Barbara W. Tuchman: 'Good God! No! Never!'

Vowel Words

Martin Gardner, in his notes on *Oddities and Curiosities of Words and Literature*, mentions not only three words consisting entirely of consonants—*crwths* (stringed musical instruments of ancient Ireland), *Llwchwr** (a city-district in Wales), and Joe *Btfsplk* (a character in the Li'l Abner comic strip)—but five words consisting only of vowels. You may be able to identify all five from the definitions below.

1. The fabled abode of Circe.
2. The roseate spoonbill.
3. A melodic formula in Gregorian music.
4. An ancient Tuscan city in Etruria.
5. A Madagascan lemur.

ANSWERS: 1. Aeaea. 2. Aiaiai. 3. Euouae. 4. Oueioi. 5. Aye-aye.

*

TWIST-RIME ON SPRING

Upon the hills new grass is seen;
  The vender's garden sass is green.
The birds between the showers fly;
  The woods are full of flowers shy.
The ornamental butterfly
  Expands his wings to flutter by.
The bees, those little honeybugs,
  Are gaily dancing bunny-hugs.
While poets sing in tripping rime
  That Spring's a simply ripping time!

Arthur Guiterman

*

---

* Crwth, Cwm and Cwmtwrch are other Welsh words in which 'w' serves as a vowel.

W, X, Y, Z

Wayfaring Words

The meanings we attach to many common words would have astonished the people who used them hundreds of years ago. You are asked to identify some words by bridging the gap between their past and their present. In each case the couplet holds clues, and the word you want completes the rhyme.

1. *Keeper of a storehouse* was a very, very
   Early early meaning of **********.
2. If *rising from waves* is the root of *********,
   Would a surfeit of waves be thalassic redundance?
3. Robbers are about; the king has called a ******.
   Cover up the fire, you medieval serf, you!
4. If you are *unlettered; not clerical; rude*,
   Whatever your morals, you once were called ****.
5. The *top of the head* is the seat of control;
   Just count every hair, and you're taking a ****.
6. When Jack's Jills aren't *obedient*, beneath the waves Jack ducks 'em;
   Their beauty doesn't soften him; they also must be *****.
7. *Powder to stain eyelids* isn't that at all;
   It's a lively liquor known as *******.
8. How political of fate!
   Clad in white's now *********.

W. R. E.

ANSWERS

1. *Apothecary. Apotheca* meant storehouse in Latin, and came from a Greek combining form meaning to put away.
2. *Abundance,* From Latin *ab*, from, away, + *undare*, to rise in waves.
3. *Curfew.* From French *couvre-feu*, cover the fire. (*Continued overleaf*)

4. *Lewd*. The present sense of lustful, lascivious, reflected the presumption that the common and illiterate classes must be wicked as well.
5. *Poll*. It comes from a Latin word meaning bubble.
6. *Buxom*. 'To make thee buxom [obedient] to her law,' said Chaucer. The present sense of plump and rosy, jolly, perhaps indicates that some obedient maidservants were fun to have around.
7. *Alcohol*. *Al-kuhl*, in Arabic, was, as indicated, a powder for painting the eyelids. The name was afterwards applied to spirits, a signification unknown to the Arabs.
8. *Candidate*. Candidates for office in Rome were clothed in a white toga.

Wedded Words

Pair the words below so as to create a dozen compound words. Since you have only nineteen uncompounded words to start with, you are going to have to use some of them more than once.

Bird	House	Pocket
Black	Keeper	Sheep
Book	Lock	Skin
Boot	Making	Tail
Flint	Master	Tooth
Head	Pick	
Horse	Piece	

ANSWERS

Blackbird	Headmaster	Sheepskin
Bookmaking	Horsetail	Skinflint
Bootblack	Housekeeper	Toothpick
Flintlock	Masterpiece	Pickpocket

What's Up?

We've got a two-letter word we use constantly that may have more meanings than any other. The word is *up*.

It is easy to understand *up* meaning toward the sky or toward the top of a list. But when we waken, why do we wake *up*? At a meeting, why does a topic come *up*, why do participants speak *up*, and why are the officers *up* for election? And why is it *up* to the secretary to write *up* a report?

Often the little word isn't needed, but we use it anyway. We brighten *up* a room, light *up* a cigar, polish *up* the silver, lock *up* the house, and fix *up* the old car. At other times, it has special meanings. People stir *up* trouble, line *up* for tickets, work *up* an appetite, think *up* excuses, get tied *up* in traffic. To be dressed is one thing, but to be dressed *up* is special. It may be confusing, but a drain must be opened *up* because it is stopped *up*. We open *up* a store in the morning and close it *up* at night. We seem to be mixed *up* about *up*.

To be *up* on the proper use of *up* look *up* the word in your dictionary. In one desk-size dictionary *up* takes *up* half a page, and listed definitions add *up* to about 40. If you are *up* to it, you might try building *up* a list of the many ways in which *up* is used. It will take *up* a lot of your time, but if you don't give *up*, you may wind *up* with a thousand.

Frank S. Endicott, The Reader's Digest

*

WHEN ADAM DAY BY DAY

> When Adam day by day
> Woke up in Paradise,
> He always used to say
> 'Oh, this is very nice.'
>
> But Eve from scenes of bliss
> Transported him for life.
> The more I think of this
> The more I beat my wife.

A. E. Housman

*

Who Said That? I Wish I Had!

In my nightmare, I was condemned to be flayed. When I begged for mercy, the judge said I would be released if I could identify the author of each of a half-dozen famous lines. 'I will give you a hint,' he added. 'Each line is the work of one of the Algonquin Wits.'

I knew who the Algonquin Wits were; but I pretended ignorance.

'All right,' said the judge, 'you are a witless and spineless fellow, but I'll give you more help than you deserve.' And he went on as follows:

The principal Algonquin Wits were George S. Kaufman and Robert Sherwood, playwrights; F. P. A. (Franklin Pierce Adams) and Heywood Broun, columnists; Ring Lardner, Robert Benchley, Alexander Woollcott, Dorothy Parker and Edna Ferber, writers.

George S. Kaufman is the man who drew a poor poker hand, and threw it in, announcing, 'I have been tray-deuced.'

F. P. A. is the one who asked Beatrice Kaufman, 'Guess whose birthday it is today?' 'Yours?' she said. 'No,' said F. P. A, 'but you're getting warm—it's Shakespeare's.'

Robert Sherwood once commented on the motion picture cowboy hero Tom Mix: 'They say he rides like part of the horse, but they don't say which part.'

Heywood Broun, a happily married man, remarked that 'The ability to make love frivolously is the chief characteristic which distinguishes human beings from the beasts.'

Ring Lardner said his favourite line of poetry was part of an ode written by an ex-coroner to his mother: 'If by perchance the inevitable should come . . .'

It was Robert Benchley who remarked, 'It took me fifteen years to discover that I had no talent for writing, but I couldn't give it up because by that time I was too famous.'

Alexander Woollcott's chief claim to fame is *not* that he developed this intricate puzzle anecdote: 'Three men sit down to a bottle of brandy and divide it equally between them. When they have finished the bottle one of them leaves the room, and the other two try to guess who left.'

Nor is Dorothy Parker best remembered for having remarked, when told that Calvin Coolidge was dead, 'How could they tell?'

Nor Edna Ferber, for describing reviewers who could no longer be objective about the literary works of Nobel Prize winners as 'awestruck by the Nobelity'.

Which of these wits wrote the lines that follow?

1. I was a child prodigy myself. That is, at the age of five I already required twelve-year-old pants.
2. Repartee is what you wish you'd said.

3. All the things I really want to do are either immoral, illegal, or fattening.
4. Satire is something that closes on Saturday night.
5. Let's get out of these wet clothes, and into a dry martini.
6. Nothing is more responsible for the good old days than a bad memory.
7. The only real argument for Marriage is that it remains the best method for getting acquainted.
8. In America, there are two classes of travel—first class and with children.
9. I do most of my work sitting down. That's where I shine.
10. One man's Mede is another man's Persian.
11. He's a writer for the ages—the ages of four to eight.
12. Being an old maid is like death by drowning, a really delightful sensation after you give up the struggle.

ANSWERS

1. Heywood Broun.
2. Heywood Broun.
3. Alexander Woollcott (*not* Dorothy Parker).
4. George S. Kaufman.
5. Robert Benchley (*not* Dorothy Parker or Alexander Woollcott).
6. F. P. A.
7. Heywood Broun.
8. Robert Benchley.
9. Robert Benchley.
10. George S. Kaufman.
11. Dorothy Parker.
12. Edna Ferber.

*

THE WISHES OF AN ELDERLY MAN

(At a Garden Party, June 1914)

I wish I loved the Human Race;
I wish I loved its silly face;
I wish I liked the way it walks;
I wish I liked the way it talks;
And when I'm introduced to one
I wish I thought *What Jolly Fun!*

Walter Raleigh

*

Word Games for Parties

ALPHABETICAL ADJECTIVES

The first contestant announces an adjective–noun combination in which the adjective begins with *a* and the noun with any letter of the player's choice (except, I should think, *x* and perhaps *z*). The second player must give an adjective beginning with *b*, and a noun beginning with the same letter as before. So on through the alphabet. For instance:

Aching back, blue-stocking Bostonian, contented bovine, desperate blackmailer, extra blankets, fractured bone, gorgeous bosom, horrible blasphemy, indifferent babe, jumpy ballerina, kleptomanic burglar, lecherous burlesque, monkey business, nihilistic Bakunin, ogling boulevardier, pious Baptist, quavering baritone, rich beneficiary, spirited bootlegger, tempestuous Bulgarian, uxorious brontosaurus, viviparous bullsnake, whining bully, xenophobic belligerent, yowling bow-wow, zestful barmaid.

THE BAEKELAND DICTIONARY GAME

Liz Baekeland sometimes arms a half dozen guests with numbered sheets of paper and proceeds to read nouns aloud from the dictionary at random until she finds one that nobody recognises. The guests then write imagined definitions of the word, while Liz makes a note of the real one. She reads the completed definitions aloud one by one, both the false and the true, and the players vote (by number) for the one they think is right. Each correct vote wins a point for the voter, while each vote for a false definition wins a point for the person who made it up. Liz tallies the votes, and the high man or woman wins. The fun lies in making the definitions both legitimate-sounding and amusing.

One word on a recent evening was 'cochineal'. The definitions offered are given below. Guess which is correct—if you don't know already.

1. The body cavity of a metazoon.
2. The first leaf above the ground, forming a protective sheath around the stem tip.
3. A sharp-pronged instrument used in deep harrowing.

4. A red dye prepared from the dried bodies of the females of a scale insect.
5. An extant free-swimming cochoid.
6. An asexual spore with a vanilla-like odour.
7. A shell indigenous to South America, of the same genus as the cockle shell, but smaller and purplish in colour.
8. A solution for application to the eye; an eyewash.

Answer—4.

BOUTS RIMÉS

If your friends fancy themselves at wordplay, invite them over for a bout of *Bouts Rimés*. The rules of the game are simple: pass around at least four rhyming words (the contest can be as intricate as the players wish, but if the poem is to be a sonnet or an ode you'd better give out the words in advance of your party) which are to be used in a piece of doggerel. There should be some limit—say ten minutes—on the time allowed for creation. The more challenging the rhyming words, the more amusing and dexterous the verses are likely to be.

Horace Walpole, presented with *brook, why, crook,* and *I,* promptly observed:

> I sit with my toes in a brook;
> If anyone asks me for why,—
> I hits them a rap with my crook;
> 'Tis sentiment kills me, says I.

At another party, the words were *wave, lie, brave,* and *die.* To one contestant, these were a challenge to his noblest instincts:

> Dark are the secrets of the gulfing wave,
> Where, wrapped in death, so many heroes lie;
> Yet glorious death's the guerdon of the brave,
> And those who bravely live can bravely die.

But another saw the matter in a different light—more down to earth, or perhaps more down to sea:

> Whenever I sail on the wave,
> O'ercome with sea-sickness I lie!
> I can *sing* of the sea, and look brave;
> When I *feel* it, I feel like to die!

Below are a number of groups of rhyming words. See what you can do with them. Then read on to see what others have done with them (but *not* in games of *Bouts Rimés*).

1. Bile, detest, vile, best.
2. Love me, hate, above me, fate.
3. Shattered, dead, scattered, shed.

ANSWERS

1

Of sentences that stir my bile,
Of phrases I detest,
There's one beyond all others vile:
He did it for the best.
                James Kenneth Stephen

2
Here's a sigh to those who love me,
And a smile to those who hate;
And, whatever sky's above me,
Here's a heart for every fate.
                Lord Byron

3
When the lamp is shattered
The light in the dust lies dead—
When the cloud is scattered
The rainbow's glory is shed.
                Percy Bysshe Shelley

MORE BOUTS RIMÉS

Poet-anthologist William Cole discovered a variant of *Bouts Rimés* in a Victorian volume called *Evening Amusements: Mirthful Games, Shadow Plays, Chemical Surprises, Fireworks, Forfeits, etc.* In this version, '. . . the director . . . recites a line of poetry, to which the person to whom it is addressed is bound to add a line corresponding in rhyme, measure, and sense with it, under pain of having to pay a forfeit'. Mr. Cole turned to the 'Index of First Lines' in his poetry anthologies, and, he says, 'immersed myself for an evening of converting the sublime to the ridiculous'.

Here is an example of the sort of thing that emerged:

> *There is a garden in her face*; (Campion)
> Her dermatologist has the case. (Cole)

There follow some first lines for which Mr. Cole created absurd mates. I suggest that you compose your own follow-ups, either privily or as a parlour-game participant. Since first lines of well-known poems are legion, this game can be continued until the last player falls asleep.

1. I strove with none; for none was worth my strife;   (Landor)
2. Whenas in silks my Julia goes,   (Herrick)
3. In a cowslip's bell I lie—   (Shakespeare)
4. When the hounds of spring are on winter's traces,
                                                      (Swinburne)
5. My love is like to ice, and I to fire;   (Spenser)
6. To be, or not to be; that is the question—   (Shakespeare)
7. Since there's no help, come, let us kiss and part—
                                                      (Drayton)
8. O, that this too, too solid flesh would melt!   (Shakespeare)
9. When I have fears that I may cease to be,   (Keats)
10. When lovely woman stoops to folly,   (Goldsmith)

ANSWERS

1   I strove with none; for none was worth my strife;
This worked with everyone except my wife.

2   Whenas in silks my Julia goes,
The outline of her girdle shows.

3   In a cowslip's bell I lie—
I'm the teeniest little guy!

4   When the hounds of spring are on winter's traces,
The rich take off for warmer places.

5   My love is like to ice, and I to fire;
But a couple of drinks, and something may transpire.

6   To be, or not to be; that is the question—
Has anyone an alternate suggestion?

7   Since there's no help, come, let us kiss and part—
Tomorrow night we'll make another start.

8   O, that this too, too solid flesh would melt!
I've had to punch a new hole in my belt.

9   When I have fears that I may cease to be,
I take another drink—or two—or three.

10   When lovely woman stoops to folly,
I want to be around, by golly!

CATEGORIES

This agreeable parlour game is also called Guggenheim, because it is supposed to have been first played in the home of a distinguished family of that name. Each player is given a sheet of paper divided into five vertical columns with a letter at the top of each. The five letters make a word. To the left of the columns is a list, one under the other, of five categories of objects—horses, fish, gems, prime ministers, or what you will. The idea is to think of five words in each category that begin with the five letters heading the columns. The winner is the person who, in a set period of time, comes up with the largest number of appropriate objects.

In choosing categories for your guests, make a privy estimate of their erudition, and remember that it is blessed to temper the wind to the shorn lamb.

DAFFY DEFINITIONS

The sound of some words can be defined by words meaning something entirely different. Give the players a pencil and a piece of paper, and see who can think of the greatest number of such words. The following list, from Leonhard Dowty's *Word Games*, will give you the idea:

The definition	*The word*
Capital S	Largess
Male escort	Mandate
Wedding day	Maritime
Judge's garb	Lawsuit
How Dali paints	Cereal
Faint noise	Locomotion
Lousy poet	Bombard
Ready hat	Handicap
Ex-spouse	Stalemate
Fake diamond	Shamrock

GHOST AND SUPERGHOST

In the game of Ghost, also called One-Third of a Ghost, the first player announces the first letters of any word of three or more letters. The player to his left adds a letter which furthers, but must not complete, the word. The object is to trap a player into completing the spelling of a dictionary word, which makes him a third of a ghost. Anyone who becomes three-thirds of a ghost is out of the game.

In Superghost, a letter may be added at either end of an incomplete word.

The delights and frustrations of Superghost were described by humorist James Thurber in a *New Yorker* article called, 'Do You Want to Make Something Out of It? Or, if you put an "O" on "Understo," you'll ruin my "Thunderstorm".' He reported the kind of mania to which Superghost can lead: 'I sometimes keep on playing the game, all by myself, after it is over and I have gone to bed. On a recent night, tossing and spelling, I spent two hours hunting for another word besides "phlox" that has "hlo" in it. I finally found seven: "matchlock," "decathlon," "pentathlon," "hydrochloric," "chlorine," "chloroform," and "monthlong."'

Listed below are some Superghost letter combinations, including several that bedevilled Mr. Thurber. The trick is to steer clear of the obvious. Anyone who sees no future for 'awkw' save in 'awkward' will soon find himself one-third of a superghost.

1. abc	5. cklu	9. fbac
2. ach-ach	6. nehe	10. ocol
3. alema	7. sgra	11. ndf
4. awkw	8. ug-ug	12. olho

ANSWERS

1. Dabchick	5. Lacklustre	9. Halfback
2. Stomach-ache	6. Swineherd,	10. Chocolate,
3. Stalemate	bonehead	protocol
4. Hawkweed	7. Disgrace, grosgrain	11. Grandfather
	8. Pug-ugly	12. Schoolhouse

I-CAN-GIVE-YOU-A-SENTENCE

One of the pastimes of the group of irreverent wits who used to meet at the Algonquin Hotel in New York was making up sentences in which one of the words resembles an unrelated phrase.

Study the I-Can-Give-You-A-Sentences below, and then see whether you, or your friends, can match them.

Meretricious, and a Happy New Year! (F. P. A. [Franklin Pierce Adams])

The Indian chief expelled an overgrown papoose from the tribe, saying, 'You big! Quit us!' This was the origin of *ubiquitous*. (Heywood Broun)

I know a farmer who has two daughters, Lizzie and Tillie. Lizzie is all right, but you have no idea how *punctilious*. (George S. Kaufman)

You may lead a *horticulture*, but you can't make her think. (Dorothy Parker)

STINKY PINKIES

The idea is to answer a definition with a rhyming combination of adjective and noun; a 'repentant truck', for instance, would be a 'sorry lorry'. Stinky Pinkies are often easier to create than to guess, and they are fun at parties—if everyone happens to be in the mood.
Some Stinky Pinky definitions:

1. Aviator
2. Breakfast fish exporter
3. Cheerful progenitor
4. Chicken purchaser
5. Childbirth at the North Pole
6. Cracked spar
7. Dejected cleric
8. Departed spouse
9. Escaped fowl
10. Costly lager
11. Forgiveable servant
12. Funniest joke
13. Happy German
14. Inexperienced monarch
15. Jumpy fowl
16. One mad about the theatre

ANSWERS

1. Fly guy
2. Kipper shipper
3. Glad dad
4. Fryer buyer
5. Shivery delivery
6. Split sprit
7. Sunk monk
8. Late mate
9. Loose goose
10. Dear beer
11. Venial menial
12. Best jest
13. Merry Jerry
14. Green queen
15. Jerky turkey
16. Dramatic fanatic

WHAT IS THE QUESTION?

By report, this word game was played by the wittier intimates of President John F. Kennedy. The first player gives an answer; the others must then supply the question. If the answer is 'Chicken Tetrazzini', the question might be, 'Name a scared Italian opera singer.' '9W' answers this question to the composer Richard Wagner: 'Sir, do you spell your name with a V?'

A good game for punsters.

Word Power

Find at least 15 five-letter words in each of the words listed, using only one form of the new word—for example, 'swing' or 'swung', not both. Do not make a word by adding *s* to a word of four letters. Slang, proper names and foreign words are not allowed.

1. Calvinistic   2. Cumulative   3. Recruitment

ANSWERS

1. *Calvinistic:* Cavil, civil, civic, antic, licit, vital, vista, visit, vinic, inact, scant, saint, satin, stain, slain, slant, snail, tical
2. *Cumulative:* Cavil, claim, camel, clime, cleat, culet, civet, utile, malic, mauve, metal, acute, amice, alive, tical, valet, vital, vault, eclat, evict
3. *Recruitment:* Recur, ricer, remit, runic, rumen, erect, enure, enter, cumin, cruet, cutter, crime, creme, unite, untie, utter, incur, inert, inure, inter, incut, trice, truce, trine, truer, tunic, timer, trite, tenet, merit, meter, miner, mince, mucin, miter, nicer, niece, niter

Words Across the Sea

LONDON LETTER

The following comments on the language differences between Great Britain and the U.S.A. were made by Herbert R. Mayes in the *Saturday Review*.

When I took up residence here sixteen months ago, I had rather hoped to disprove the observation made by Shaw and Wilde that England and America are two countries separated by the same language. I had hoped to prove that butter muslin for cheesecloth was as obsolete as 'Haw, haw, by Jove.' I have only partially succeeded . . . I'd like to bespeak a few words, for example, against bespoke shirtmakers. If the English mean custom-made, I'd like them to say so. Although it is true that today England accepts druggist, elevator, apartment, and cop as readily as chemist, lift, flat, and bobby; and although I have not had to say lorry, kiosk, hire-purchase, or rates when I meant truck, newsstand, installment-plan, and taxes, there nevertheless are some bespokes still around. A dustbin is never going to be an ash can, a screw spanner a monkey wrench, or drawing pins thumbtacks. Baby-sitter is beginning to be substituted for child-minder, and overpass soon may catch up with flyover; but most definitely suspenders are never going to replace braces.

Long before I began visiting England—before World War II—I had read Mencken's *The American Language* and had familiar-ised myself with common objects he listed that had different words applied to them in the mother country. Thus, it was easy to recognise diversion for detour, stall for orchestra seat, interval for intermission, gangway for aisle, bank holiday for legal holiday, and even ironmonger for hardware dealer. I knew a telephone booth would be a call box, a mailbox a pillar box, and a sidewalk a footpath. Americans don't joke about these innocent variations any more; they simply gag over the likes of dickey seat for rumble seat or scribbling-block for scratch-pad.

The British are stubborn, as you don't need to be told. A scallion remains a spring onion, a janitor a porter, a barber a hairdresser, and a notary public a commissioner of oaths. They persist in addressing a surgeon as Mister and still consider an ignoramus anyone who doesn't know a toilet from a hole in the ground when he refers to a closet instead of a cupboard. Over here, there is still only one closet, and that's a water closet.

On the whole, however, for all the differences in pronunciation, intonation, and accent, there really is not too much of a vocabulary problem; mainly, I think, because the English have been over-whelmed by us, and are reconciled as much to loss of language pre-eminence as to liquidation of Empire. I cannot recall an American expression that the English don't comprehend instantly. American movies and television programs shown here, and the annual influx of hundreds of thousands of American tourists, have been relentless tutors. It is rare that an American novel is

Anglicised.The British edition of *Time* is published exactly as it would be in the States; no substituting underground for subway, tin for can, or express post for special delivery. Robert Knittel, the editorial director of Collins Publishing, says that about halfway across the ocean our two languages nuzzle up to each other and fraternise enough to become what he calls mid-Atlinguish.

Words in Labour

The following verse is a reflection on the fact that certain words contain their equivalents, foreshortened and perhaps disarranged, within themselves.

I met some swollen words one day,
As full of roe as sturgeons;
For certain in a family way,
Yet innocent as virgins.

Parthenogenesis, they swore,
Had stocked their inner shelves,
And all those nascent words in store
Were carbons of themselves.

Lo! when at last their babies came,
They were indeed the spit
Of their mamas; each given name
Was ample proof of it:

For *Aberrate* did *** produce,
And *Slithered* mothered ****,
And *Utilise* gave suck to ***,
And *** was *Curtail*'s kid.

The child of *Jocularity*
Was aptly christened ***;
While *Masculine*'s was instantly
Named ****, though not a boy.

(CONTINUED OVERLEAF)

Transgression called her daughter ***,
And *Matches'* child was *****;
Container's twins were *** and ***,
And *Prattles'* wee one, ******;

So ******'s from *Rapscallion* born,
So ***** from *Regulates*;
What babe, as **** from *Respite's* torn,
******* *Evacuates*?

Now *Calumnies* gives suck to ****;
Encourage, **** doth hug;
**** safe in arms of *Rampage* lies,
And *Struggle* mothers ***

W. R. E.

ANSWER

Err; slid; use; cut; joy; male; sin; mates; can; tin; prates; rascal; rules; rest; vacates; lies; urge; rage; tug.

The Worst Love Poem Ever
(*In several manners of speaking*)

This verse is intended to make it easy to distinguish among several types of word game and wordplay.

1. *Courtship: Our Hero Speaks Sweet Words*

Fit 1: *The acronym*	O Dorothea Evalina Anna Rim, May I be thy ever-loving acronym?
Fit 2: *The cryptogram*	So utterly in knud vhsg xnt, my dear, I am, I'd gladly give my khed sn ad your cryptogram.
Fit 3: *The homonym*	I'll liken you to lichen if you'll tease me at your teas; We'll bounce a little homonym upon our knees.
Fit 4: *The palindrome*	He'll be a redder tot than any civic pup or pip; A never odd or even, palindromic drip.

270

2. Marriage: Our Hero's Words Turn Sour

Fit 5: I who *******, *******, and won thee,
The anagram now *******, or worse;
Ne'er thought I our anagram would end in
*******.

Fit 6: If my wife and little ones continue such a bother
The pun (Sick of one, and half a dozen [pun!] of t'other),

Fit 7: I may seek out comfort in an epigram:
The epigram "I am wed unhappily; ergo, I am.'

Fit 8: Wife, write these words upon the wind to be my
The epitaph epitaph:
'He laughed at life, aware the worms would be the
last to laugh.'

W. R. E.

ANSWERS

Fit 1. Our hero urges the young lady to become his *dear*, acronym of *Dorothea Evalina Anna Rim*.
Fit 2. The letters in each coded word come just before those in the decoded word:
So utterly in *love with you*, my dear, I am,
I'd gladly give my *life to be* your cryptogram.
Fit 3. *Liken, lichen, tease* and *teas* are identical in sound but unrelated in meaning—i.e., homonyms.
Fit 4. *Redder, tot, civic, pup*, and *pip* are palindromic words, spelled the same forward as backward. *Never odd or even* is a palindromic phrase.
Fit 5. The missing words are *praised, aspired, despair*, and *diapers*, each an anagram of the others.
Fits 6, 7 and *8*, on the pun, the epigram, and the epitaph, need no explanation.

You so ĕn trăns′ me

Etymologic roots sometimes sprout words with identical spellings but different sounds and meanings. Apart from an apostrophe and a space, 'man's laughter' and 'manslaughter' are as one to the eye; but the mind finds no connection between them at all. I am reminded of a foreigner who spent ten years studying English, arrived in London, and saw a newspaper headline: 'Hamlet pronounced success.' He turned around and went back home, defeated. I am reminded also of the immigrant who asked his neighbour: 'You speak the English, not so?' The neighbour replied: 'A few, and then small.'

Suppose you juxtapose entrance (ĕn trans'), 'to enrapture', with entrance (en' trans), 'a point or place of entering'; present (prĕz' ent), 'the time being', with present (prēz ent'), 'to introduce'; content (con tent'), 'satisfied', with content (con' tent) 'the matter dealt with'; intimate (in' ti mate'), 'to hint, imply', with intimate (in' ti mit'), 'associated in close, often sexual, relationship'; agape (a gape'), 'mouth wide open', with agape (a' ga pe'), 'spiritual love'; invalid (in' va lid), 'a person weak or infirm', with invalid (in vá lid), 'void, null'; recreation (rek ri a shun), 'diversion', with recreation (rē kri a shun), 'act of creating anew'. What do you have?

Perhaps something like this:

> You so *entrance* my senses that
> I haunt the *entrance* to your flat
> At *present*, seeking to *present*
> A case for early ravishment.

> I'd be *content* could I impart
> The amorous *content* of my heart
> To you, and *intimate* we might
> Be *intimate*, some future night.

> Before your shape I stand *agape*;
> Not *agape* but lust to rape
> Makes me love's *invalid*. Alas,
> You deem *invalid* every pass.

> Such *recreation* you will ration
> Till *recreation* of Creation.

W. R. E.

INDEX OF QUOTED SOURCES

V

Van Rooten, Luis D'Antan, 169
Vida, 107
Voltaire (François Marie Arouet), 206

W

W. R. E. (Willard R. Espy), 21, 27, 30, 33, 39–47, 49, 50, 51, 56, 57, 59, 72, 76, 92, 94, 96, 97, 111, 115, 120, 122, 124, 125, 132, 141, 142, 156, 171, 179, 184, 200, 222, 225, 226, 227, 230, 231, 238, 245, 248, 249, 250, 255, 269, 270, 271

Wallis, Dr., 238
Walpole, Horace, 261
Watts, Isaac, 66
Waugh, Evelyn, 244
Webster, Noah, 228
Wells, Carolyn, 238
Wilde, Oscar, 96
Wolfe, Humbert, 65, 68
Wood, Robert Williams, 133
Woollcott, Alexander, 15, 167, 168, 258
Wright, Ernest Vincent, 157

Y

Yeatman, Robert Julian, 64